MURDER OUT YONDER

TRUE CRIME STORIES FROM AMERICA'S FRONTIER

STEWART H. HOLBROOK

DOVER PUBLICATIONS, INC.
MINEOLA, NEW YORK

Bibliographical Note

This Dover edition, first published in 2016, is an unabridged republication of the work originally published by The Macmillan Company, New York, in 1941 under the title and subtitle *Murder Out Yonder: An Informal Study of Certain Classic Crimes in Back-Country America.*

Library of Congress Cataloging-in-Publication Data

Names: Holbrook, Stewart H., 1893–1964, author.
    Title: Murder out yonder : true crime stories from America's frontier /
    Stewart H. Holbrook.
    Description: Mineola, New York : Dover Publications, 2016. | "This Dover edition, first published in 2016, is an unabridged republication of the work originally published by The Macmillan Company, New York, in 1941 under the title and subtitle Murder Out Yonder: An Informal Study of Certain Classic Crimes in Back-Country America." | Includes index.
    Includes bibliographical references and index.
    Identifiers: LCCN 2015041057
    ISBN-13: 978-0-486-80387-6
    ISBN-10: 0-486-80387-2
    Subjects: LCSH: Murder—United States—Case studies. | Rural crimes—United States—Case studies.

Classification: LCC HV6524 .H8 2016
DDC 364.152/30973091734—dc23 LC record available at
http://lccn.loc.gov/2015041057

Manufactured in the United States by RR Donnelley
80387201   2016
www.doverpublications.com

For Kathie

CONTENTS

MURDER
OUT YONDER

CHAPTER ONE

DEATH AND TIMES OF A PROPHET

ON WHAT DATE a shaft of divine light transformed Franz Edmund Creffield from an obscure rural evangelist into Prophet Joshua the Second in all his glory is not known. Neither is the exact spot where the visitation took place. But the time is certain. It was 1903, and the neighborhood of the miracle was Corvallis, Oregon.

Troubles follow in the wake of a prophet as naturally as water runs downhill. If the prophet has a set of Old Testament whiskers and a chronic case of satyriasis, then the troubles are sure to be multiplied and likewise interesting.

This particular backwoods Joshua had both the whiskers and the affliction. And when he raised his voice in holy anger, as he did on one remembered occasion, the vast city of San Francisco shook horribly in the grip of an Act of God, then went down, writhing and smoking, in one of the greatest disasters within the memory of living men.

Driving up the lush green Willamette Valley from Portland to Corvallis, one scarcely wonders that this land once produced a veritable prophet. It is amazing there have not been more of them. Here was the Promised Land where the creaking covered

1

wagons came to rest at the far end of the Oregon Trail; where the immigrants shouted "Glory to God!" and drove their stakes, naming their settlements Amity, Sweet Home, Salem, Aurora, and Corvallis—which last is said to mean "heart of the valley." Here along the many creeks is beaver-dam soil, richer than the delta of the Nile. Vegetables grow as large as the pictures on the seed packages. Enormous prunes and the finest walnuts on earth hang heavy on the trees. Vetch and clover grow thick and big enough to stop the wheels of powered farm machinery. The climate is damp and mild. Seldom is there more than a trace of snow.

Here and there along the ninety miles the highway plunges into groves of Douglas fir, tall and mighty before Lewis and Clark and the Hudson's Bay Company came. To the east rises the backbone of Oregon, the majestic peaks of the Cascades and on the west are the Coast Range mountains, faintly hung with mist and with haze in season—brooding, black, faraway hills to make a prophet out of almost any man.

In the heart of this valley is Corvallis, seat of Oregon State College, a spick-and-span town in 1941 that holds court for Benton County; sells things to farmers; makes considerable lumber; has a daily paper, a radio station, and a library of 130,000 volumes including "a 15th century antiphony composed of Gregorian chants in Flemish, hand-printed and illuminated on parchment, and bound in calf over the original board covers."

Corvallis is sedate enough today, as serene as any campus town in the land. It has, in fact, been sedate throughout most of its three-quarters of a century. Only during the days of Joshua the Second, when signs and portents were on every hand, did Corvallian blood run hot and fast.

2

Unheralded, Franz Edmund Creffield made his first appearance in the Corvallis of 1902 in the form and style of a Salvation Army worker. He was thirty-five years old, smooth-shaven, short of stature, and had large brown eyes. He retained a slight but noticeable accent from his native Germany.

A few months later, or early in 1903, he either left or was discharged from the religious group, and seems to have disappeared for a time. It was likely during this obscure period that the great light beat upon him and he talked with God somewhere in the tall forests that edged close to the town. In any case, he was soon back in Corvallis.

In 1903 no man could be a true prophet who did not have a beard, and when Creffield emerged from the timber he was wearing an astonishing growth. It was of the veritable Moses type, flowing down over his chest and spreading to left and right, unruly, wild, burgeoning like everything in the Willamette Valley, while over his shoulders tumbled falls of unkempt hair. Both beard and hair were of a reddish, golden brown.

He was Edmund Creffield no longer, but Joshua the Second —sole prophet and for a short period sole communicant of the Church of the Bride of Christ. Even the tone of his voice had changed. It no longer had the supplication, the winning humbleness, of street and field evangels. It now boomed like muffled thunder and in it, many came to think, was the authority of Jehovah.

It must have been that the Corvallis of the time, in spite of its several churches, was lacking somewhat in spiritual life, at least so far as the women were concerned. In those days, of course, there were no movies, no serial radio dramas, no bridge clubs to entertain and thus protect the dim minds of vapid females; so it is conceivable that time in Corvallis, as in any other American town, often seemed interminable to those who live chiefly to kill time.

And it is conceivable, too, in view of the record, that this brand-new Joshua possessed a magnetic if not a downright hypnotic personality. Within a month he had a sizable cult of converts. It was all done so quietly that even the town fathers, who fancied they knew almost everything that went on locally, were wholly unaware of the great harvest of souls that was going forward.

The first meetings were held openly in the homes of converts, of whom at least six were men. At this period the prophet seems to have had no particular message other than that the ways of the world were all wrong and should be changed. One by one the male converts dropped away, leaving Joshua and a stooge known as Brother Brooks to carry on with the increasing flock of girls and women.

If you think that the apostasy of the few men was discouraging to the prophet, then you don't know how an Oregon Joshua works when he gets going Full Gospel style. The meetings in the homes of converts were continued; but they now were held in the afternoons, when menfolk were away.

There must have been a female Judas in the flock, for it was presently whispered around town that never before had there been seen such manifest workings of the Spirit as Joshua Creffield brought about. Pulling down all the blinds of the meeting place—so this she-Judas reported—Joshua began a chant, swaying to its rhythm, waving his arms, and calling upon what he addressed rather familiarly as the Full Spirit to descend upon the meeting.

The girls and women soon began to sway. They chanted; they moaned; they "spoke in tongues" and cried aloud while the prophet seemed to gain in stature and his normally calm eyes sank deep into his head, where they glowed like two pits of fire. The swaying and the chanting went on.

Suddenly, like a thunderbolt, the prophet's voice boomed out: "Vile clothes, begone!" The whiskered fellow then disrobed and, without urging on his part, many of the women present did likewise. There was nothing coy about it, no sense of shame. They threw off their peekaboo waists, their skirts, and their multitude of petticoats; they tore wildly at their whalebone corsets, meanwhile moaning like all get-out.

"Roll, ye sinners, roll!" thundered Joshua; and roll they did, some in chemises, some without, all over the bare floor, with Joshua and Brother Brooks rolling happily among them.

Either at this or at a subsequent meeting Joshua began to expound the canons of his sect. He had already announced that he and his followers were members of the Church of the Bride of Christ. Now he let it be known that the Lord had commanded him to select from among his followers she who was to become the Mother of a Second Christ.

It soon became apparent to the faithful that Joshua was going about his quest for a second Mother in a thorough and searching manner, which manner was obviously of the empirical school. Several married women left the sect at this point, taking their daughters with them. But many remained, and new females appeared at every meeting. So many came, in fact, that Joshua and Brother Brooks felt the need for more room.

On Kiger Island, in the near-by river, the prophet and his stooge, with girls and women helping, built a large wigwam of poles covered with boughs. The boughs were interwoven cleverly and tightly, and the entrance was closed with a door curtain. It is recalled that one of the most willing workers was a beautiful and young ash-blonde girl, Esther Mitchell.

Their hands torn and covered with the pitch of Douglas fir (*Pseudotsuga taxifolia*) but with their eyes shining with the light of Gospel, girls of fourteen and women of fifty-five toiled on the pretty wooded island. Some brought small tents that were set up, and small wigwams also were built.[1] Throughout the summer of 1903 meetings were held on the island almost every afternoon, and the vast workings of the Spirit could be heard on either shore of the mainland.[2]

---

[1] Years afterward an ex-member recalled that one of the small tents or wigwams of the island retreat was the "whipping place," where Joshua switched this or that girl or woman to "drive out the devils." But this ex-member was unacquainted with the name of the late Marquis de Sade.

[2] Even the Oregon State Agricultural College at Corvallis was affected by the workings of Joshua. Miss Ellen Chamberlain, who was a teacher there in

With cooler weather and heavy rains, the island retreat was not a happy place to roll in the altogether. A new and suitable spot was soon found in the residence of O. P. Hunt, in Corvallis. Mr. Hunt was a respected citizen, member of a pioneer family, and Corvallians were shocked one day in early fall to see a large sign over the door of his house.

"Positively No Admittance, Except on God's Business," said the sign, and a smaller one attached to the gate repeated the warning. Now things began to happen in quiet Corvallis. A reporter of the local *Times* viewed the premises and wrote:

Certain caprices of religious fanaticism have been manifested at the house that are so unusual as to suggest a condition bordering insanity. Walks about the house have been torn away. Much of the furniture of the house has been reduced to ashes in a bonfire held last night in the yard, on the theory that God wills it. The shrubbery and fruit trees and all the flowers have been digged up and destroyed. Kitchen utensils have been beaten to pieces and buried. . . . It is reported that house cats and dogs have been cremated.

Joshua and Brother Brooks were taken to the courthouse for a sanity hearing. Joshua sneered at the proceedings, and told Deputy Sheriff Henderson not to "talk that way to God's anointed." The men were found sane, but officers advised them to leave town. Brother Brooks said nothing. Joshua merely laughed quietly as he went out the courthouse door.

1908, wrote me: "——— was a young girl in my history class, very attractive. After a two days' absence from class I asked her brother, also a student, what had become of his sister. He was evasive, obviously embarrassed. But I found out that ——— was too taken up with the Holy Roller meetings to think of school. One day a bit later this girl went to the college president's office and asked if she might pray for him. He assented and called in Prof. Crawford and one of the lady teachers. They told me how beautifully, how fervently she prayed for them, to do more for the spiritual welfare of the students. The next day I found this girl in my room, sobbing. I tried to reason with her. She was adamant. I was glad to know her mother had come to be with her son and daughter, but alas, the mother soon became a victim of that satanic influence. . . . As I recall it, both mother and daughter were later committed to the asylum."

In the meantime Mr. Hunt—but apparently not his women-folk—had discovered that he wanted no more of Joshua and his sect. In the meantime, too, prints of a photograph that had been taken many weeks before began to circulate in Corvallis. The name of the Unbeliever who took this picture has been lost to history, but his little Brownie camera had a good lens. The picture was what today would be termed a candid-camera shot, and it was taken during one of the spiritual orgies of the cult on Kiger Island. The film was small but as clear as crystal, and the picture was as candid as could well be imagined. It showed Joshua, quite naked, amid nothing less than a bevy of naked and local matrons and girls, some of them standing, some rolling in the lush wild grass. Several were easily identified. The film, it is said, was soon worn out in making prints.

No movie ever made created such a furor as this two inches of silent, static film. There was an immediate uproar, as enraged fathers and injured husbands had their kids and wives packed off to the state hospital and to the home for wayward girls. Some fifteen of Joshua's sect were at once taken out of circulation, while others got warnings to which they paid little if any heed.

Then, on the coolish evening of January 4, 1904, a band of silent men called at the house where Joshua and Brother Brooks had quarters. None of the men were masked, nor was there any attempt at concealment of the affair, and nearly all of the mob were citizens of high standing. Without a word this band took the two long-haired boys to the edge of town, where a pot of tar was heating over an open fire. They were made to strip, then given a coat of tar and feathers,[3] and told to keep out of Corvallis.

3

Brother Brooks was never again seen in town after the party at the tarpot. It was different with Joshua. Mrs. Hunt and her

---

[3] I am told by one who was present that the mob was particularly careful to see that Joshua's coat of tar and feathers covered all of him.

young daughter, Maude, searched for and found the feathered prophet hiding miserably in the woods. They brought him to their home. The sticky coat was removed, and a few days later Joshua dropped his Biblical name long enough to marry Miss Maude Hunt. The marriage proved something of a local sensation, for it isn't often that the daughter of a respected pioneer family ties up with a man who has just had tar and feathers scraped off his hide. The marriage, too, doubtless eased the minds of many Corvallis males; they could well believe that now the prophet's search for a second Mother was done.

But the search *wasn't* done. Leaving his new wife at the home of her parents in Corvallis, Joshua went to Portland to commune with a married woman who had been a follower in the palmy days of the Kiger Island colony. She and the prophet were presently taken *in flagrante delicto* by her husband, who swore out a warrant in which he called the prophet's holy search by the vulgar name of adultery.

Police had been waiting for something tangible like this to work on. But now they couldn't find the prophet, and to stimulate the search for him O. P. Hunt, the prophet's own father-in-law, offered a reward of $150 for his arrest. Maude Hunt Creffield secured a divorce. Things looked dark for Joshua the Second.

Nearly three months thus passed with the prophet supposedly at large. Then, one day in June, young Roy, adopted son of O. P. Hunt, made a startling discovery. Crawling under the Hunt home in search of a tin can to carry worms on a fishing trip, the youngster was frightened near out of his wits when he suddenly found himself looking into the great, blazing eyes of a bearded man.

Backing out of the hole as fast as he could, the lad ran screaming to his foster father. Mr. Hunt came and peered into the hole, then called police.

The cops came and hauled the prophet from his den under

the house. He was, as one of the officers remarked thirty years after, a sight to behold. Naked as to clothes, and dirty as a hog, the prophet was hairy all over as a water spaniel, and most wonderfully endowed by Mother Nature withal. His beard grew down to his stomach and was bushy as a clump of black alder. But he was as thin as a fence rail. He was weak, too, and could scarcely stand.

"You're Creffield, ain't you?" asked a doubtful cop, no doubt recalling folk tales of surviving specimens of *Pithecanthropus erectus*.

"I am Joshua." The voice that came from the long beard was weak, yet obviously the voice of a prophet.

It was a weird tale that the officers and Mr. Hunt pieced together. For more than two months the prophet had lived day and night in his lair under the home of his ex-father-in-law, unsuspected by menfolk of the house. He had existed on jars of fruit and scraps of food that Mrs. Hunt and other faithful (who were admitted to the secret) could smuggle to him. He had thrown away all his clothes before he entered the den. The only covering he had when taken out was a ragged and filthy quilt.

Creffield was put on trial before Judge Sears in Multnomah County court in Portland. He readily admitted what the court charged were improper relations with the former Corvallis matron, but he said that such things were not at all improper in a man of God such as he. "Christ," he said in the usual manner of mountebanks, "broke the Sabbath day and the Jews put Him to death. I've broken your laws, and you will undoubtedly do the same to me. Like Christ, however, I will rise again and ye all shall suffer."

The jury was made up of forthright men. In twelve minutes, or about the time it took them to go to the jury room and back, they brought in a verdict. It was "Guilty." Judge Sears asked Creffield if he had anything to say before sentence was pronounced. He did. He had a lot to say. In a rambling yet fervid harangue, during which he misquoted considerable Scripture and called the saints to witness, he told the court and the jury that he forgave them, for they knew not what they did.

"Two years in state's prison," said Judge Sears, a man of few words.

"God bless you," replied the prophet, and impious deputies laid hands on him and whisked him away to Salem. He was dressed in at the pen as Number 4941 on September 16, 1904.

4

Fifteen months later the prophet was released. The warden, of course, couldn't know what a baggage of trouble and tragedy he was turning loose. His beard gone, his hair cut close, Joshua left the scene of his triumphs and trials, going at once to Los Angeles, then as now a lodestone for prophets of all kinds. He didn't stay long, but was soon in San Francisco. How he lived during this period of exile is not known, but one should consider that no prophet has ever starved in California.

Very soon Corvallis learned that Joshua was writing letters to seventeen-year-old Esther Mitchell, she who had attended the prophet's meetings on Kiger Island. He wrote her that God had at last made it clear to him—that Esther and no other was to become the second Mother. This had been revealed to him in a message direct from Heaven. What young Esther replied is not known, but events that were soon to pile up would indicate she was favorable to the message. The prophet also sent a letter from San Francisco to Mr. Hunt, his former father-in-law at Corvallis.

God has resurrected me [wrote Joshua]. I have now got my foot on your neck. God has restored me to my own. I will return to Oregon and gather together all of my followers. Place no obstruction in my way, or God will smite you. Joshua II.

That was clear enough. And from San Francisco, too, the prophet wrote his ex-wife, Maude Hunt, then living in Seattle with a brother and a sister-in-law, Mr. and Mrs. Frank Hunt.

Maude replied that she would re-marry Joshua if he would come to the Puget Sound metropolis.

The prophet, now in full beard again and ready for anything, came north, stopping neither at Corvallis nor in Oregon but going direct to Seattle. He and Maude were married by an orthodox minister. And now he made plans for a triumphant return to the state that had used him so shabbily. He would, he vowed, go to a primeval spot that he knew on the Oregon coast and there establish a colony for the faithful, a true Garden of Eden in which the flock could live in a manner best suited to them and their beliefs, free from the profane gaze of scoffers.

It would take a little cash, obviously, to purchase this Eden, which he had visited, and he suggested that Mr. and Mrs. Frank Hunt dispose of their Seattle property and buy the land for the glory of God.

So hypnotic was this bearded man with the startling eyes that the Hunts did just that. They sold their Seattle house and bought the strip of land in question. It was south of Waldport, Oregon, fronting the Pacific, and in 1906 was a very remote place indeed. The Hunts and Maude were to go to the spot as an advance party. Joshua would in the meantime sound the call to the faithful, telling them that they would remain away from Eden at their own peril.

"Peril?" asked Frank Hunt, who was not yet fully apprised of the powers of a genuine prophet.

"Peril, yes," replied Joshua, and added, "Brother Hunt, I have called down the wrath of an angry God on these modern Sodoms of Seattle, of Portland, of San Francisco, of Corvallis itself. Have no fear, Brother Hunt. My faithful will return to the fold—all of them. They will leave all behind them—their scoffing fathers, their brothers, their husbands—and come to our Eden." And then he let go an awful curse.

"A curse, O God, on San Francisco, on Portland, on Corvallis, on Seattle."

This tremendous curse was loosed on the morning of April 17, 1906, just as the Eden advance party got aboard a train at Seattle on the way to Newport, Oregon, nearest railroad station to the Garden.

Next day, the eighteenth, Joshua again laid foot on Oregon soil. He avoided Corvallis, where he would have had to change cars, by getting off the train at Airlie and being taken in a livery-stable rig to Wren, twelve miles west of Corvallis, where he boarded the train for Newport. He was met at the depot by his wife and the two Hunts, who were all but speechless and who told him in awed tones of telegraphic dispatches that day reporting the total destruction of San Francisco by earthquake and fire.

Joshua smiled, probably smugly. "I knew it," he said quietly, "I knew that God would respond. The other cities of the plain will be next. We must rouse the faithful before it is too late."

And rouse they did. When a man with a big long beard has friends who can shake a big city to pieces, well, it is time to pay heed. And Joshua had sent the word through the mails to Corvallis. Within twenty-four hours trainmen on the Corvallis & Eastern Railroad wondered at all of the traffic, all of it female, heading for the end of the line at Newport. There were middle-aged women with babies, middle-aged women with grown daughters, middle-aged women alone, and young girls who, it turned out, had run away from home. Most of all, trainmen were struck with and remembered the slim beauty of fair-haired Esther Mitchell, soon to be in headlines throughout the West.

There were two trains daily out of Corvallis, and for the next several days every train brought a few more girls and women. All had to be ferried across Yaquina Bay, thence on foot or in buggy to the Garden of Joshua.

The cynical folk around Waldport put no stock in the prophet, not even after the terrifying results of his great curse became known. Waldport was openly hostile. But ninety miles

east, back in troubled Corvallis, Joshua's trumpet call had
sounded loud and clear. Young girls in their teens started for
school and disappeared. Husbands returned home at evening
to find their wives gone, at least one of them carrying a six-
week-old babe with her. Still another husband found a note
pinned to a pillow in his home. It told him his wife had heard
the call.[4]

Down in the Garden, Joshua was receiving more revelations.
One message told that Corvallis itself was to be the next sinful
city to be destroyed. Another directed all members of the cult
to burn their clothing and to wear a sort of "holy" wrapper.
A big fire was set going and into it screaming, moaning women
and girls heaved all their vile finery, and forthwith dressed
themselves in the wrappers that Joshua provided.[5] And the
prophet's search for the second Mother went on wonderfully
well. . . . Praise Joshua and great day in the morning!

Living conditions in the Garden were pretty bad. Lean-to
and wigwam huts were made. Everyone slept on the ground.
Food was cooked over open fires and was plain. Between forty
and fifty girls and women and the two men made up the colony.

By April 26 at least one man in Corvallis had learned the
whereabouts of Joshua. This man's young daughter had disappeared and investigation showed she had walked most of the
way to Newport, then down the coast road to the Garden. The
youngster, all alone, had done more than eighty miles of the
trip on foot. Her father, one of Corvallis' highly respected
citizens, set out to find her.

This man meant business. At Newport he paused long enough

---

[4] This note, which survives, is a fair example of how strong was Joshua's
call: "I don't want to leave in the daytime because the children will see me and
cry to go with me. I must leave while they are asleep. I have taken $2.50 of
your money. This will not pay all my fare and I will still have to walk 90 miles
or more to where I want to go." Walk she did, and alone, over the Coast
Range mountains, where bear and cougar stalked the road.

[5] Considerable research has failed to reveal where or how Joshua got these
wrappers, but one who saw them at close range tells me they were like heavy
cotton bathrobes.

to purchase a thirty-two-caliber revolver and a box of cartridges. Going down to the water front to get transportation
across Yaquina Bay, he barely missed the ferry which was just
pulling away from the dock. On the ferryboat he saw the
bearded prophet amid a group of wrappered females. Without more ado this man pulled his gun and aimed it at Joshua,
while the women screamed. But the gun only clicked—clicked
five times in a row.

Out on the ferryboat Joshua smiled gently at the puny attempts of mere man to kill him. "See," he told his women. "You
see. No man can kill Joshua." And the women were certain they
had witnessed another example of the prophet's power.

Not so the man on the dock. "It was the god-damn fool who
sold me them cartridges and gun," he complained to friends.
"The gun is center-fire, and the cartridges rim-fire. That's why
that ——— is still alive."

But the men of seething Corvallis, now thoroughly aroused,
were getting ready to lay the prophet low. Singly and in twos
and threes they took train to Newport. Armed with rifles and
revolvers, they crossed on the ferry and went to Waldport.
Here they learned that Joshua must have been forewarned. He
was last seen heading for Newport, alone, and had no doubt
hidden in the woods to let the several posses pass.

This information was hurriedly telephoned to Corvallis. In
that town was George Mitchell, twenty-one-year-old brother of
Esther. Taking a revolver, he went to Albany—thinking he
might catch the prophet there waiting for a train to Portland.
Mitchell learned he was too late. The prophet was already gone.
With him was his wife, Maude, and the two had bought tickets
to Seattle. Young Mitchell had to remain overnight in Albany
for another train. He arrived in Seattle on the morning of
May 7, 1906.

Whether or not Mitchell knew where in Seattle to look for
the prophet has never been clear. What is clear as daylight is
this.

About eight o'clock on this May morning Joshua Creffield and his wife, now both dressed in orthodox fashion but the prophet in full beard, left the cheap rooming house where they had taken lodgings and walked down Second Avenue. At Cherry Street they turned and walked to First Avenue. In front of Quick's Drugstore was a weighing machine. The prophet's wife stepped onto the machine, while Joshua stood looking into the store window.

Young Mitchell had sighted the couple. He stepped quickly up behind the man, placed the muzzle of his revolver at the prophet's left ear, and fired. Joshua the Second slumped quietly down to the sidewalk.

The small and wiry woman turned and screamed. She flew at Mitchell like a cat and tried to take the gun from his hands. Mitchell retained the gun but made no attempt to escape. In a moment Maude left him and bent over her husband, whose blood was now running in a stream across the sidewalk. The prophet had died without moving, without even a shudder.

Mitchell stood idly, holding the gun in his hands. Without a word he handed it to a policeman who had hurried from a near-by corner.

Mrs. Creffield at first was frantic, but she calmed. "This man," she told the surprised cop, pointing to the figure on the sidewalk, "this man is my husband, Joshua the prophet. He will arise in three days and walk."

"Sure, sure," said the officer, who was used to all kinds of people. He called the wagon and an ambulance.

At the police station George Mitchell was calm, even happy. He asked for a telegraph blank and sent a message to O. P. Hunt at Corvallis, who, it will be remembered, was again the prophet's father-in-law. "I got my man," read the wire, "and I am in jail here."

In spite of protests of the widow and of Mr. and Mrs. Frank Hunt, who had hurried from Eden to Seattle, the body of the late prophet was turned over to the Bonney–Watson undertakers. These kindly men stuffed cotton into the hole in the prophet's ear, and laid him away tenderly in Lakeview Cemetery on May 9. Only the widow and Bonney–Watson employees were at the grave. No services were held.

That was how they laid Joshua the Second away in the ground. But his work was far from done.

5

As King County (Seattle) prepared to prosecute George Mitchell for the murder of Edmund Creffield, all eyes turned to the Puget Sound city where the trial would be held; and the late prophet's Garden of Eden, three hundred miles to the south, was forgotten. Things were going badly there. On May 15, a week after the shooting, George Hodges, timber cruiser of Salado, Oregon, had been looking over some fine old Douglas fir not far from Waldport on the coast. It was a cold, windy day. When he emerged from the timber onto the beach he saw something that liked to have caused him to swallow the *Climax* he was working on.

Hodges couldn't know, of course, that he was in Garden of Eden country, and he brushed his eyes when he saw five women and young girls, one of them with a baby in arms and all dressed in outlandish wrappers, camped on the beach. One look told him they were starving. Their cheeks were pinched and some were too weak to stand. They were grouped around a frayed and torn old tent and they told the startled timber cruiser that they were followers of Joshua, the prophet who recently had destroyed San Francisco.

Hodges was a man who read the papers. He began to get the drift of what he had stumbled into. And where was this Joshua, he asked. The women said that Joshua had gone north to Queen Charlotte Islands, off the north coast of British Columbia, where he was seeking out a new Garden of Eden for his followers.

"But this prophet of yours, he is dead," Hodges told the women. "He was shot and killed in Seattle a week ago."

The women laughed crazily at that one. Joshua dead? He could not be killed. They had seen a man try it with a revolver. You couldn't kill Joshua.

Convinced that the bedraggled women were completely out of their heads, and learning that they had had nothing to eat in two weeks except a few crabs and mussels, Hodges left them what provisions he carried in his pack and went to Newport. He then telephoned authorities at Corvallis, giving them, in true land-looker style, the line, range, and section of the Garden of Eden. Expeditions of brothers, husbands, and fathers set out at once to bring their womenfolk home.

Up in Seattle the trial of George Mitchell was getting under way. It brought out some sensational stuff and it would have made front pages all over the country had it not been for Harry Thaw, concurrently on trial in New York City for slaying Stanford White. The revelations concerning the late and lusty prophet Joshua, as brought out by Mitchell's defense counsel, made the Thaw case a Dorcas Society meeting in comparison.

William D. Gardner, superintendent of the Oregon Boys and Girls Aid Society, testified that "a large number of young girls" had been sent to his institution from Corvallis by their parents; that most of these girls had confessed to "criminal relations" with the prophet, but were really not criminal at all because the prophet was searching for the Mother of a Second Christ. Certain practices of the prophet had been particularly revolting and would have made a chapter or two for Herr Doktor Krafft-Ebing.

"Creffield was a degenerate of the worst sort," shouted John Manning, district attorney of Portland, in a letter to Kenneth MacKintosh, who was prosecuting Mitchell, and added, "He practiced unspeakable brutalities on ignorant and unsophisticated girls."

A Corvallis citizen testified that Esther Mitchell, sister of the defendant, had been sent to the Boys and Girls Aid home to get her away from Joshua. When released, she immediately took up with the prophet again. "She is obsessed," concluded the witness.

Esther herself attended the trial of her brother. Day after day she sat there, and spectators remarked on her lack of emotion—or was it something else?—as she watched and listened with a dead-calm face.

Another witness told of a broken home due to Joshua. His daughter, he said, had left Oregon State College in the last term of her fourth year because Joshua had told her that all learning was the work of the Devil. "She even destroyed the graduation dress she had been working on all winter," this witness said. The mother also was obsessed. She had destroyed all the family dishes except the plain white crockery; further, when he wanted something to eat, the witness said, he had to get it himself. All this was Joshua's doings.

Evidence to be given on several days of the trial was such that the court was cleared of spectators. "No such testimony has ever been given in a King County court," the Seattle *Post–Intelligencer* observed.

George Mitchell conducted himself with quiet dignity. He was the hero throughout the trial. A large delegation came from Corvallis, including Mr. O. P. Hunt, the late prophet's father-in-law, who attempted to give bail for Mitchell and who was a stanch supporter of the youth during the trial. Women heaped flowers on the defendant every day until the judge ordered that this should stop, so far as the courtroom was concerned.

Mitchell's statement was simple. "I came here to kill this man because he ruined my two sisters. I have completed my work." He seemed the happiest person in the room.

From the first it was clear that the Messrs. Silas M. Shipley and W. H. Morris, counsel for Mitchell, were attempting to indicate justifiable homicide as well as temporary insanity, which latter was just then coming into popularity as a defense in criminal trials. Nobody, one could guess, was surprised when the jury, out an hour, returned a verdict of not guilty. George Mitchell was all but mobbed by friends and well-wishers. It was noticed, though, that his handsome, sad-faced sister, Esther, left the courtroom without going near him.

The trial ended on July 10. Two days later George Mitchell and brothers Fred and Perry went to Seattle's King Street station to take the four-thirty afternoon train to Oregon. The waiting room was crowded with summer tourists and with perhaps seventy or eighty persons who had come to Seattle from Corvallis purposely for Mitchell's trial. It was a jolly gathering.

Fred Mitchell spied Esther standing near a pillar in the big depot, nonchalant and aloof. Another man recalls seeing her there. A jaunty new sailor hat sat on her ash-blonde head. Her skirt was a bit short, coming almost to the tops of her shoes. Around her throat was a white satin ribbon, done in a big bow, its ends streaming down over a white shirtwaist. She carried a light coat over one arm.

Fred left his two brothers and went to Esther, asking her if she wasn't going to bid good-by to George. The slim girl assented with a nod. She and Fred joined the others. She took George by the hand but did not respond to his greeting, and the four Mitchells walked toward the gate of the train shed. The station announcer was now calling the train for Portland and way points.

And now the silent girl moved quickly as a panther. Reaching her right hand under the coat on her arm, she brought out a small pearl-handled revolver—just the sort a woman would buy. In a move so quick that Fred Mitchell had no time to think or act, she placed the gun's muzzle behind George's left ear and pulled the trigger. George sank to the marble floor without a word.

In the noisy, crowded station the gunshot made little impression, but Patrolman John T. Mason had seen the move. He took the smoking gun from Esther and placed her under arrest. The man on the floor was already dead.

At the Seattle police station Esther remained calm and dry-eyed. She said the killing had been a matter of course. Her brother had killed God in the form of Joshua Creffield, hadn't he? Well, that is why she had killed her brother. Shot him in the same place he had shot Joshua, she pointed out.

It took no questioning at all by police to learn that Esther and Maude Creffield, the prophet's widow, had planned to kill George Mitchell should he be freed by the court. Detectives were sent to bring Maude to the station. The stories of the two women agreed in everything: Maude had bought the gun; it was decided after some discussion that Esther should do the killing. She loaded the gun herself and put it in the bosom of her shirtwaist. Maude had objected, saying that perspiration might prevent the gun from firing. Esther then wrapped the gun in a handkerchief and put it in her waist. She would have done the shooting on the day the trial ended, she said, but no opportunity had presented itself. It was the same on the day after the trial. She knew her brothers were to leave town on the following day. She was at the station, waiting.

This new sensation fairly rocked both Seattle and distant Corvallis. When a girl who had been chosen to be the Mother of a Second Christ picks a crowded railroad station to kill her own brother—well, the Harry Thaw case was moved off page one for a few days.

Both Esther and Mrs. Creffield were held. Tried on a charge of murder, Esther was found not guilty because of unsound mind. She was committed to the Washington State Asylum.[6] Maude Creffield was being held in the county jail for disposi-

---

[6] Colonel A. E. Clark of Portland, Oregon, defended Esther Mitchell without charge. He remembers her as "a girl of fine appearance and of high intelligence, except for her one tragic delusion."

tion, but she took care of the matter herself. One morning the
matron, a Mrs. Kelly, found the young woman stiff in her
bunk, quite dead. An autopsy revealed much strychnine in her
stomach.

Three years later Esther Mitchell was released from the
asylum. Two days afterward a thin and tragically beautiful
girl came into the editorial offices of the *Morning Oregonian* at
Portland and asked Miss Amanda Otto, secretary to Editor
Harvey Scott, if she knew where George Mitchell was buried.
Miss Otto immediately recognized the girl as Esther Mitchell,
and replied that she would see if she could find the information.
She left the room a moment. When she returned, Esther was
gone.

Some weeks later the unfortunate girl—she was only twenty
years old—died at the home of friends not far from Waldport,
scene of the late Joshua's erstwhile Garden of Eden.

6

Memories of the Creffield–Mitchell cases are scattered over
three hundred miles of the Pacific Northwest. Railroadmen in
Seattle recalled the exact spot where George Mitchell stood
when he was shot. At Corvallis middle-aged and elderly people
sometimes gaze with mixed emotions at Kiger Island. Old-
time court attachés at Portland remember how different, and
how sad, the prophet Joshua looked once his beard and long
hair were cut by the jailhouse barber. And now and again some
visitor to Waldport will ask to know the exact spot of Joshua's
Garden of Eden.

CHAPTER TWO

THE GREAT HOMESTEAD MURDERS

THE EVENING OF March 8, 1900, was wild. A storm howled down out of the Cascade Mountains and swept through the Columbia River gorge as Mr. Norman Williams, a homesteader, drove a two-horse team out of the Fashion Livery Stables, finest establishment of its kind in Hood River, Oregon. Beasts and man alike bowed their heads to the wind. So black was the night that H. D. Langille, one of the Fashion's proprietors, lighted a lantern a few moments after Williams had left, and followed the team. He found it in front of Thompson's boardinghouse near by.

Langille proffered the lantern to Williams, remarking that the twenty miles to his homestead was a long way to go on so dark and miserable a night. By the lantern's feeble, flickering rays the liveryman could see a young woman, who looked to be quite handsome, on the wagon seat; another and much older woman came down the steps from the boardinghouse and got into the seat beside the girl. Neither woman spoke.

Williams thanked Langille for the light, picked up the reins, and drove out of Hood River into an inky darkness from which the two women never returned. Nor were they ever seen again, dead or alive.

Hood River folk did not realize anything was amiss, that evening of the eighth of March. Next morning at about half past eight Williams, alone now, returned the team to the Fashion Stables. That was all, just then. Williams returned the team and went away. Nobody could know that two women had disappeared as completely as though they had never lived—almost.

Four years, lacking a month, passed. In the meantime President McKinley had been assassinated at Buffalo, and Theodore Roosevelt was in the White House. The Boer War was over, the Russo–Japanese affair just getting under way. Horseless carriages were making their appearance in the larger cities in increasing numbers—even Hood River had two of them—but they were yet a long way from being a threat to livery stables in backwoods Oregon. The Fashion Livery was still doing business at the old stand.

Then one day in February of 1904 an unassuming young man of about thirty got off the morning train in Hood River. He asked the station agent to direct him to a livery stable. A few minutes later he walked into the Fashion, now operated by Bert Stranahan. The stranger said he wanted to hire a horse and buggy to go to the homestead of Norman Williams, and added that he didn't know where the place was. "Can I get somebody to drive me?" he asked.

It was a mild, sunny day, much nicer out of doors than in. Bert Stranahan said he'd go, and he hitched a fine black mare into a rig. Just as they were about to get into the buggy the stranger asked if there was a spade around the stable they could take with them. "I might want to do a little prospecting," he said.

Now Bert Stranahan had lived in Hood River a long time and he had never heard of any gold being found on a valley ranch. But in 1904 livery-stable keepers were just as used to odd people and queer requests as are taxi drivers today. Stranahan wouldn't have batted an eye if the stranger had re-

quested an electric liver pad and a stereopticon. He got a spade
and shoved it under the buggy seat.

There wasn't a great deal of conversation on the twenty-mile
drive. The stranger did say that his name was Jackson, and
after a while he offered the information that he used to know
Norman Williams "back in Iowa." Stranahan said "That so?"
or its equivalent, and the horse jogged along for another mile
or two.

The road became steeper on its climb to the Parkdale district. Mr. Jackson talked some more, but it was chiefly questions. He wanted to know something of how Williams stood in
the community. Stranahan racked his mind to find out, and replied truthfully that Williams didn't have much of a reputation one way or the other. He was just a common everyday
homesteader in homesteading country. Nothing unusual about
him, far as Stranahan knew. Come to think of it, he hadn't seen
Williams in a long time. Damned if he could recall when it was.

On arrival at the Williams homestead it was immediately
evident that the place had been deserted for a long time. The
rude shack, the disheveled barn—they had the look and the
smell of disuse and neglect. Dead grass, long yellowed, grew up
in front of the doors. Boards on the barn were loose. There is
even a "feel" about such places—a sad, nostalgic flavor, haunting, elusive, yet profound.

The mysterious stranger lost no time. Taking the spade, he
began prodding the earth, first between the house and barn,
then around both buildings. Knowing nothing of these odd doings and being a man who minded his own business, Stranahan
sat in the buggy listening to the stranger, who seemed too
young to mutter but who audibly was doing just that. "No,
not here," he mumbled, making a pass at the ground with his
spade, then moving. "Not there, not there," he repeated.

Finally this Mr. Jackson disappeared into what looked to
have been started as a henhouse and never quite completed. It
was a jerry-built job, now badly dilapidated. In a moment

Jackson came out of the hut. His manner was changed. His words came quicker. His face seemed tense. And now he addressed Stranahan direct for the first time since they arrived at the homestead. "I think I'll dig in here," he said, indicating the henhouse and speaking just as if the digging was something they had understood and discussed. "The dirt seems loose," he added. He ducked back into the shack, then out again. "You might as well unhitch the horse," he said. "We'll likely be here all day."

Stranahan, naturally mystified but still minding his own business, took the mare out of the shafts and put her in the barn. Then he went over to the henhouse. Inside, the ground was indeed loose and there was a visible depression, roughly of an oblong shape. Jackson was already digging, methodical and unhurried. But his face was tense, Stranahan noted.

In a decent while Stranahan offered to spell the man off. He took the spade and dug in, finding that the dirt came up easily. The hole—for it obviously had been a hole—was better than two feet wide, perhaps six feet long. Stranahan dug for ten minutes or so.

It was a queer business, this going out to an abandoned homestead and digging and not knowing what you were digging for; so when Jackson silently reached for the shovel, Stranahan put the matter out in the open.

"What the hell are we supposed to be digging for?" he asked.

"That I don't know," Mr. Jackson replied. (Stranahan noted that the man's eyes were sort of set and stary. Was he bughouse?) "That I don't know," he repeated. "All I know is that something tells me this is the right place."

Stranahan decided it was time to take a smoke. Leaving Jackson at his digging, he strolled out of the shack and filled his pipe. The place was in deep shadow now. Twilight was coming down from the flanks of Mount Hood. He could see a lamp glimmering in a small house half a mile away, the only light visible in the valley. He returned to the henhouse.

By now the hole was down more than four feet. Jackson was digging faster and the loose earth made quite a pile in the small enclosure. Never a man to take stock in the metaphysical, Stranahan recalls that for the first and only time in his life he felt as if he were alive and awake but playing a part in a most unreal dream. He took the spade without a word from either man and dug.

Down went the excavation, five feet, five and a half. Suddenly the spade struck something hard. Pulled out, it proved to be a length of rived cedar a foot wide, two inches thick, and five feet long. Stranahan could see Jackson's face in the twilight. It looked like chalk. "I think," Jackson said, almost in a whisper, "I think we are going to find what, what——" He broke off, then asked, "Have you a lantern?"

Stranahan said he had. He went to the buggy and brought it back, lighted. Jackson was down deep in the hole, feeling in the cool dirt of the pit with his hands. Stranahan passed the light down to him, and watched. The man had something in his hands. "Looks like burlap—sacking," he said, holding the lantern close. "Yes, it's burlap. We'd better quit now. Leave everything as it is until daylight. It's liable to be very important."

Still mystified and still minding his own business, Stranahan hitched up the horse. The two men drove to the light that blinked from across the valley. It was a rancher's place and the two men found food and lodging. Bert Stranahan finally dozed off, marveling at the odd things in the life of a livery-stable proprietor in a small back-country town.

Breakfast was at six, and long before seven the two men were back at the henhouse. In the clear light of morning they could see some pieces of badly rotted burlap at the bottom of the hole. Jackson had brought his suitcase, which he had emptied of its usual contents, and now he put it down, open, on the edge of the hole. He got into the excavation and, using the greatest care, lifted out the burlap and placed it gently in the

suitcase. It was dark and moldy. Pieces of it fell away. Looking at it closely, Stranahan could see what appeared to be a
dark stain—even darker than the rotten sacking—and a few
small hairs matted into the stain.

Without a word Jackson closed the suitcase, and the two
men walked to the buggy. Stranahan thought it was about time
he knew what was afoot, and told the stranger so.

"My name isn't Jackson," the man explained. "I am George
R. Nesbitt." He seemed to think that the name might convey
something to Stranahan. It didn't and Stranahan said it didn't.

They got into the buggy, and as they drove down Hood
River Valley toward town Jackson, or Nesbitt, opened up. He
said his home was in Harlan, Iowa, and he had come to Oregon
to try to find his younger sister, Alma, and their mother.

Stranahan recalled vaguely that he had known of some woman,
or women, by that name who had once lived on a homestead
somewhere in the region and might still be living there for all
he knew. Nesbitt continued his story. In 1899, or five years
before, Alma had come to Hood River, Oregon, to take up a
homestead next to that of Norman Williams. This move had
been urged by Williams in letters to Alma. Williams, who was
thirty years older than the girl, had known her since childhood, and her family as well. He had lived near Harlan, the
Nesbitts' home.

As the horse jogged along, Nesbitt continued his narrative.
Alma had been an adventurous as well as a romantic girl, he
said. For months, back in Iowa, she had talked of little but of
how she wanted to become a "pioneer woman," one who could
go into the wilderness, file a homestead claim, and tame the
ground. It became almost an obsession with her, and the letters
from Williams, who already had settled on his Parkdale homestead, finally fetched her West. She had filed on and secured
one hundred and sixty acres next to Williams' place.

That had been early in 1899. A few months later Mrs. Nesbitt, mother of Alma and George, also came West. For the next

few months letters had come to Iowa regularly from mother
and sister. Things were going well with them, they wrote. They
related how Williams had helped build a small house on Alma's
claim, how Alma had hired men to do stump grubbing and
plowing, and how Alma and her mother had worked hard with
their own hands at planting apple trees. The two women appeared happy, and they wrote of further improvements they
planned to make on the place in the spring of 1900.

Then, on March 8, 1900, the letters had ceased. "A letter
with that date, and mailed not in Hood River but in Portland,
was the last we heard of them," Nesbitt concluded.

"Well," said Stranahan, getting back to the subject that
still troubled him, "what did you expect to find at Williams'
place? And, by the way, what *did* we find?"

"I hardly know what I expected to find," Nesbitt said in a
queer voice, "and I'm not sure that we have found anything.
But I'm going to take the matter up with authorities."

On the long drive back to Hood River, Nesbitt was as nervously
talkative as he had been moodily silent on the way out. He went
into such detail as he could about his lost sister and mother.

He related how, back in Iowa, Norman Williams had been
"sort of sweet" on Alma, although she was little more than a
girl and he was middle-aged. Nothing serious, though. Then,
in 1897, Williams had come to Oregon. His letters to Alma had
been filled with the fanciful color and romance of pioneering
the land in the Last Great West. The romantic Alma saw Indians behind every tree and she could hear the rumble of covered-wagon wheels. *They* were what she thought she wanted.
So Alma came; then her mother came.

"That last letter we had—four years ago, come March—
was written at Winters' rooming house, 60½ Grand Avenue,
Portland, Oregon," Nesbitt said. "In it Alma and Mother said
they were coming home to Iowa. Didn't give any reason. Just
said they were coming home. We back there were mighty
pleased."

"Haven't you tried to find them before this?" inquired the practical Stranahan.

"Of course we have," Nesbitt said; and he told how he had written letters to Williams at Hood River, asking what had become of the girl and woman. After a lapse of several weeks Williams had replied that the two women had "gone away" and he hadn't the least idea of where they went. In reply to a second letter from George Nesbitt, Williams had unburdened himself. He wrote that Alma had promised to marry him. Everything had been arranged, including the date. Then, so Williams wrote, Alma had taken to going around with an un-named man. "A younger man than me," Williams had written, "and good-looking." He also intimated that Alma had fallen into loose ways. And the second letter concluded by repeating that both women had gone away together, without saying why or where.

"For four years we have done everything we could to find them," Nesbitt said. "We inserted notices in many newspapers throughout the West. We offered a reward. We wrote to post-masters and chiefs of police of many towns and cities. And now, after four years of waiting and hoping, I've come to Hood River."

"You must have suspected something, to start right in dig-ging that way," Stranahan said. "How come you asked me to take the spade with us?"

"I can't tell you why. I don't know myself. I just had a feel-ing. It seemed to me—well"—he fumbled for words to express himself—"I guess it was just one of those strong hunches we have sometimes. I just couldn't get a shovel out of my mind. Something said to me, 'Take a shovel; take a shovel.' Sounds queer, I know, but I simply can't make it any clearer."

2

Next day George Nesbitt, toting the suitcase with its con-tents of rotting burlap, went to The Dalles, seat of Wasco

County, and told his story to District Attorney Menefee and Deputy Fred Wilson. The men looked at the burlap. Under a reading glass—the only scientific aid in The Dalles of the time —the dark stains looked like blood or like any other nearly black substance. Matted solidly into the stain were perhaps five or six silver-gray hairs. They might have come from a dog, possibly from a fox; both were plentiful in the Hood River Valley. Fred Wilson remembers that the mildewed, moldy mass struck him as mighty poor evidence of any sort.

But Wilson also was struck by the quiet earnestness of George Nesbitt. He sent the burlap by express to Dr. Victoria Hampton, a brilliant young woman of Portland whose profession was then known as that of "chemist and microscopist." This was a daring thing to do, in 1904, for the profession was a new one, at least to Oregon, and Dr. Hampton was a woman. In 1904 Oregon was pretty much of a man's world.

Nesbitt now swore out a warrant for the arrest of Norman Williams. The man was located without much trouble. He was working in a sawmill in Bellingham, Washington, three hundred miles away, and living with a woman. "Meet my housekeeper," Williams said to the sheriff and Deputy Attorney Wilson by way of introduction.

Williams expressed surprise, seemingly sincere, that he should be wanted in connection with a betrothed who had "thrown me over to run away with another man." He readily agreed to go to The Dalles without extradition and to do what he could, which he feared wouldn't be much, to clear up the mystery, if that's what it was.

Deputy Wilson arrived at The Dalles on February 11, 1904, with Williams in custody. Williams turned out to be a tall, well-built man, rather good-looking and younger than his sixty years—the kind of man one would turn around on the street to look at. Over six feet. The tall man's face broke into smiles when he was confronted with George Nesbitt. With a clear countenance, as Fred Wilson remembers it, he denied any knowledge of what might have happened to Alma and her mother. He said he had never set eyes on the women since the morning he had driven them back to Hood River village from the homesteads at Parkdale and taken them to the railroad depot, where they had caught a westbound train.

That had been in March four years before, Williams continued, and the books at the Fashion Stables no doubt would show the exact date. (The books did; and the date was March 9, or the morning after the stormy night when Williams had driven *out* of Hood River with the two women in the wagon.)

Williams went on with his story, told it in an apparently straightforward manner. He related that Alma had obviously tired of him after their engagement. He felt sure she had fallen in love with some man whose name he did not know but whom Alma had met during a short period when she worked as a domestic at The Dalles. She had "worked out" the winter of 1899–1900, Williams said, in order to get ready cash with which to buy farming tools. During this same period Williams had worked at a small sawmill in the Parkdale district. But in the spring a homestead didn't look so attractive to Alma.

"When she and I went out to the homesteads together the first time in the spring of 1900," Williams related, "I could tell that she didn't want to settle down and be a rancher's wife.[1] She had got notions. No back-country ranch would do for her."

The man's story was convincing enough. His face and eyes seemed to soften as he spoke of Alma, and the watching attorneys fancied they detected sadness untouched by bitterness when he told of Alma's faded love. "I'd marry her today if she'd only come back," he concluded.

They locked Williams in Wasco County jail and held him

---

[1] In Oregon, then as now, "ranch" may mean any sort of farm or rural home from a two-acre stump ranch with a few chickens to one of the great cattle ranches of thousands of acres.

in $10,000 bond, which he made no attempt to raise. "It'll all come out all right," he smiled.

3

Now began the unraveling of a mystery without any aid from professional detectives. The only sleuths in this case were George Nesbitt, a farmer from Iowa, and young Deputy District Attorney Fred Wilson, a home-town boy who had never in his life worked on a crime of any kind—much less a disappearance as mystifying as this one appeared to be. I can think of no comparable case that called for so many matched and interlocking links, let alone ones forged by two rural and strictly amateur detectives.

First thing the two back-country sleuths did was to take a train for Portland, the Oregon metropolis. Here they went to the rooming house at 60½ Grand Avenue operated for many years by Henry D. Winters. This was the place where Alma had written the last letter to her brother in Iowa, in March of 1900. Proprietor Winters got out his four-year-old register, now covered with dust. There in the clear, flowing hand of the days before typewriters became common were two signatures: "Alma Nesbitt, Hood River, Ore.," and "Mrs. Louisa Nesbitt," with a ditto mark.

George Nesbitt scanned the writing. He declared that both signatures were in his sister's hand. The women had registered on February 8, 1900, and had remained until March 8. The latter date, it will be remembered, was that of the last letter written by Alma to George. It was also the date Norman Williams had hired the two-horse team at Hood River.

Proprietor Winters remembered the two women well. He said that a man had called on them and the three had spent some time in the rooming-house parlor. They had talked a long time, and Winters was positive they were having some sort of argument. Concerned land, or property, he thought, for he had heard mention of a homestead. The discussion had become rather heated.

Winters' testimony was offered the two sleuths without prompting. And it was something. The next step was a lot more. Acting on what Wilson says today was nothing more than a hunch—the way a man bets on a horse sometimes— Deputy Wilson and Nesbitt went to Vancouver, Washington, just across the Columbia River from Portland. Vancouver, then as now, was a noted Gretna Green. In the Clark County recorder's office they learned that on July 25, 1899, or some six months before Alma's disappearance, she and Norman Williams had been married by a justice of the peace. This find made Williams out a liar.

In the meantime District Attorney Menefee, back in The Dalles, had learned that Williams also had married a woman in Dufur, Oregon, in 1898, and had left her without troubling about a divorce. So Williams was a liar and a bigamist, if nothing worse. The pattern was still far from clear, but something approaching a motive for murder began to take shape.

Next the amateur detectives located one J. R. Reese, a laborer in the Hood River Valley. Reese told of once doing some day labor for Norman Williams. It had consisted of cutting an immense amount of brush and scrub timber and of grubbing a good many stumps on the Williams homestead. That had been, Reese said, sometime in April of 1900, or in the month after the women disappeared.

Later that summer, Reese continued, he had occasion to visit the Williams homestead again. The brush and stump pile, which he described vividly as "the god-damnedest pile of stuff you ever see," had been burned. This, of course, had not been strange, for it is customary to burn brush and stumps.

The sleuths canvassed the scattered homesteads of the valley for someone who had known Alma Nesbitt. They found an acquaintance in a Mrs. Mary Riggs, homesteader. Mrs. Riggs said she had talked with Williams a number of times "since

Alma and her mother went away" and she had always asked
him about Alma. At least four times, she said, Williams had
replied that he had received letters from Alma, that she and
her mother were well. Mrs. Riggs, who had considered Alma
and herself to be rather close friends, thought it mighty queer
that the girl had left the valley without even saying good-by
to her.

Detective Fred Wilson next visited Norman Williams in
his cell. He showed him, for the first time, the rotting burlap
that had been dug up beneath the henhouse. Williams smiled.
Yes, he said, that sure was blood on that sacking. A mare of
his had foaled a colt on it. It was mare's blood. Why had it
been buried so deeply in the ground? Williams smiled again.
The henhouse, he said, had been built over the hole of an
old outhouse. Into this hole Williams had thrown the sacking.
Later he had moved the outhouse, placing it nearer the barn,
and had then filled the hole. He had built the henhouse on the
site.

Wilson and Nesbitt made a return trip to the Williams
homestead to check the man's story about the outhouse. The
dilapidated remains of such a structure were, as Williams
had said, near the barn. But at the small sawmill four miles
away, where Williams had worked at odd times, the sleuths
gathered information in conflict with what Williams had told.
Mill employees recalled that Williams' mare had indeed foaled
a colt, but at the sawmill and nowhere else.

Neighboring ranchers, including Mrs. Riggs, vowed that
at no time had there been an outhouse where the henhouse now
stood. One neighbor remembered an interesting incident. He
had called at Williams' place one day. It was raining hard and
had been raining for several hours. Yet Williams had a pile
of several sacks of oats in the open, on the ground, in the
approximate place where the henhouse had later been built.
Seemed strange, this witness had thought, that a rancher should
leave good oats out in the rain when a barn was handy.

The amateur detectives did much more investigating, but the results were not made known until the trial.

Despite the quiet manner in which Wilson and Nesbitt had gone about their work, the disappearance of Alma Nesbitt had by now become an Oregon sensation destined to spread as the trial progressed. It had that something about it—the man driving two women, one of them young and beautiful, out of Hood River and into a dark from which the women had not returned. And almost overnight, in the press, Alma Nesbitt became the Lone Girl Homesteader, the pioneer covered-wagon woman right down to date. It was the kind of copy to make front pages and headlines in the Far West.

Williams went on trial in the old Wasco County courthouse at The Dalles on May 24, 1904, more than four years after the two women were last seen in Hood River. Their disappearance into the night of March 8, 1900, had not made a ripple at the time. They had few acquaintances and almost no close friends in the district. Now, however, Oregon witnessed the power of the press with a good story as it hadn't been witnessed since Harry Tracy and Dave Merrill shot their way out of the Oregon penitentiary and into the paper-back dime novels in 1902.

The Dalles was packed with the biggest, liveliest crowd seen there since the eastern Oregon gold rush of the 1860s. Seattle, Spokane, Portland, even San Francisco, newspapers sent reporters and sketch artists[2] to cover what was already "The Great Homestead Murders Case." *The Morning Oregonian's* reporter was Leslie Scott, and he wrote that "the nodding plumes and gay ribbons show that the female contingent is out in full force." The courtroom overflowed. Fortunately the day was warm and Judge William Bradshaw, a humane man,

---

[2] As many of us remember, in the days before half tones were common, sketch artists were very important at big trials, and almost without exception they made the accused, if a male, look like a close friend of the Devil himself; if a woman, like an angel. Norman Williams, being male, was made to appear particularly horrible by artists in attendance at his trial.

permitted open windows, thus allowing those in the yard to see and hear. The milling crowd, that soon became very quiet, packed the yard and flowed into the street.

In his opening statement Fred Wilson, now playing the part of prosecutor instead of detective, told the jury that the State would attempt to prove: (1) that Norman Williams drove the two women to his ranch on the night of March 8, 1900, and there murdered them in cold blood; (2) that he buried their bodies in the ground, covering the hole with a pile of oats from March 8 until such time as he had gathered a great pile of brush and stumps; and (3) that this pile was used as a funeral pyre.

As a motive, prosecution said, the State would prove beyond any doubt that Williams had another wife living when he married Alma Nesbitt; that Alma may have discovered this fact, or in any case had planned to leave Williams; and that Williams wanted Alma's homestead for himself.

Important to the State was the testimony of H. D. Langille, the onetime partner with Bert Stranahan in the Fashion Livery Stables. Langille related how Williams had hired the team and told of seeing two women in the wagon. That had been late at night. Ordinarily when he worked late, Langille said, he did not show up at the stable next morning. But on this occasion, and for reasons which now escaped him, he was on duty next morning at the stable. He testified that he had been standing at the front of the stable and had seen Williams driving into Hood River by the Parkdale road, the same road he had taken on the way out the night before. "There was no one in the wagon but Williams," Langille said on oath, "and Williams drove direct to the stable. That was about half past eight."

Prosecution now brought out a blackboard and on it Prosecutor Wilson drew a rough chalk-line map of Hood River village to show that Williams could not have driven to the

Hood River railroad station without first having passed the Fashion Stables.

Next the chief train dispatcher of the Oregon Railway & Navigation Company testified that the only westbound train to pass through Hood River on the morning of March 9, 1900, had done so at five-thirty-three, or some three hours before Langille had seen Williams driving into town.

It will be recalled that Williams had claimed the last he ever saw of the two women was when he put them on a westbound train on the morning of March 9.

Prosecution next sprang what the press termed a bombshell. The bomb was in the form of John H. Hall, United States attorney of Portland. Hall told the jury how, late in 1900, a Norman Williams had brought to his office a document purportedly signed by one Alma Nesbitt in which she relinquished her homestead in favor of Williams. The transfer had been made, the federal man said. Then, he continued, a clerk in his office got to thinking. He had remembered Alma Nesbitt, a very handsome girl, at the time she herself had filed her original homestead claim. He became suspicious of the signature appearing on the relinquishment. He confided his suspicions to Mr. Hall, and Hall had then sent to Washington, D. C., for the original homestead application, on which he knew the woman's genuine signature would appear. This document proved beyond any doubt that the relinquishment was a forgery.

Hall continued his testimony. He had gone to Norman Williams, he said, and accused him of the forgery. Williams admitted having signed Alma's name, but said she had given him permission in writing to do so. Asked to produce such permission, Williams said it had been stolen from him together with letters from Alma. "At the time Williams was arrested on a charge of murder," Hall concluded, "my office was looking for him. He was under indictment for forgery."

The links in the chain were becoming tighter. Reporters at the trial noted how the prisoner, at first so calm, if morose, now moved about in his chair, changing his position every little while.

Dr. Victoria Hampton, the Portland chemist and microscopist, was called to the stand. Here was the sensation of the trial. Dr. Hampton was young and stunning. She was a scientist, but she was also a woman; and the conjunction was almost unheard of in the Oregon of 1904. The boys in the press box wrote their heads off.

Amid a silence so tense that Fred Wilson remembers it more than thirty-five years afterward, the young microscopist took the stand.

"The stains on this gunny sacking," she said in a clear, musical voice, "are of human blood."

The prisoner was seen to twitch. The jury was bug-eyed.

"Matted in the stains," Dr. Hampton went on, "I found several hairs, white in color—or nearly white. They are human hairs. They were torn from the head before death."

The hush was tomblike. Scientific testimony was new to The Dalles, Oregon. Jurors were amazed at this sort of witness, and they had a number of questions to ask Dr. Hampton. She explained, clearly and to the point, how she had arrived at her conclusions. The jury seemed satisfied, as well as highly pleased; but one of the members wanted to know just how it was that she could tell the hairs had been pulled from the head *before* death. Dr. Hampton explained that microscopic examination had shown the roots still clung to the hairs. If they had been pulled after death, there would be no roots adhering.

In a series of understatements the boys in the press box wrote that the testimony of Dr. Virginia Hampton had "made a profound sensation on jurors and spectators alike." One wonders how it affected Williams.

The State closed its case with Dr. Hampton.

Now Henry E. McGinn, Oregon's most noted criminal law-yer of all time, loosed his eloquence, which was very great. He called no witnesses at any time. He did not put Williams on the stand. He rested his case solely on the premise that the State had not shown a corpus delicti—which, as he explained carefully to the jury, meant that the State had not proved that *anybody* had been murdered, much less Alma Nesbitt and her mother.

"Gentlemen," cried the dramatic McGinn, "the State of Oregon has not proved, and cannot prove, death in this case. The prosecuting attorney knows it. There are suspicions, gen-tlemen, grave suspicions, but nothing more. You cannot hang a man on mere suspicion, especially when there is such serious doubt of death as there is in this case."

Here McGinn went into many legally famous cases of the past. Some of his citations went to prove that neither judge nor jury would condemn a man, no matter how damning the circumstantial evidence, unless a corpus delicti—the body—were shown. Other citations showed how this or that man had been hanged for a crime of which he was later, and too much later, proved to be innocent.

"For all you and I know, gentlemen," cried McGinn in his closing, "and for all prosecution knows, Alma Nesbitt and her mother are today alive and well, living for reasons of their own in some obscure place. You can't find this man, this Norman Williams, guilty of a crime that *you don't even know has been committed.*"

It was a dramatic and a forceful plea, one of the best ever heard in an Oregon courtroom but the jury could and did find Norman Williams guilty as hell. In less than four hours they brought in a first-degree verdict.

An appeal was taken to the state supreme court, but the learned judges denied a rehearing. The Oregon court's denial has been cited again and again in the intervening years and in almost every state in the Union.[3] Said the court, in part:

The strict rule contended for by defendant would operate completely to shield a criminal from punishment for the most atrocious crime, and afford him absolute immunity if he were cunning enough to consume or destroy the body . . . or completely hide it away or otherwise destroy its identity. But the death of the person alleged to have been killed is a distinct ingredient in the case of the prosecution for murder and must be established by direct testimony or presumptive evidence of the most cogent and irresistible kind. . . . Where, as here, the circumstances point with one accord to the death of the person alleged to have been murdered, the finding of fragments of a human body, which are identified as part of the body of the alleged victim, will be sufficient, if believed by the jury, to establish the fact of death, when this is the best evidence that can be obtained under the circumstances: *People v. Alviso,* 55 Cal. 230; *McCulloch v. State,* 48 Ind. 109; *Commonwealth v. Webster,* 5 Cush. 295 (52 Am Dec. 711); *State v. Williams,* 52 N. C. 446 (78 Am. Dec. 248); *Gray v. Commonwealth,* 101 Pa. 380 (47 Am. Rep. 733). No universal rule can be laid down in regard to the proof of the corpus delicti. . . . The body of the crime may be proved by the best evidence which is capable of being adduced, if it is sufficient for the purpose. . . . There was sufficient evidence, without commenting on it, in the case at bar, in our opinion, to establish the death of the alleged victim within the rules of the law referred to.

More than a year after the trial The Dalles was again crowded with the curious, many of them to witness the hanging—the last public affair of its kind in Oregon. Williams made a good subject. He walked firmly to the gallows and shot through the trap promptly at 6:00 A.M. on July 21, 1905, thus ending the Great Homestead Murders case, although Norman Williams lived on in a ballad.

> Oh, Williams built a fire
> And he throwed the bodies in;
> He thought he'd covered up
> His bloody trail.

---

[3] The Oregon court's denial was cited by prosecution against Hauptmann in the Lindbergh baby kidnaping case.

But he left a couple hairs
A-buried in the ground, and
They hanged him at the
Wasco County jail.

Today the case is forgotten except by Hood River old-timers, who still mention it on wild March evenings, and by lawyers the country over, to whom this homestead drama is known only as 46 Ore. 287 (80 Pac. 655).

CHAPTER THREE

ROCKY MOUNTAIN DYNAMITE MAN

IT WAS SNOWING lightly that evening, which was December 30, 1905. The small village of Caldwell, Idaho, lay under a thin blanket of white, marking the steps of Frank Steunenberg, ex-governor of Idaho, as he made his way the short distance from the Saratoga Hotel to his home. When he was about two blocks from his house a stocky figure passed him in the gloom, walking briskly in the opposite direction. He probably did not recognize the passer-by, who was new to Caldwell, and it wouldn't matter in another two minutes anyway.

There was a picket fence around the Steunenberg home. Mr. Steunenberg opened the gate, passed through, and turned to close it. At that instant a tremendous explosion shattered the quiet dark of the village, and the former governor of Idaho was literally blown to pieces.

So great had been the explosive charge, whatever it was, that the blast was heard by farmers miles out of town, and the windows on the front of the Steunenberg house were blown into jagged bits of glass that were found protruding from interior walls.

This mighty blast was to have other reverberations. It was

a bomb that rocked the United States. It soon brought into the national spotlight a young Idaho attorney, William E. Borah. It brought fame to Clarence Darrow. In Big Bill Haywood it produced either a saint or a monster, depending on the point of view. And it put Harry Orchard into the Idaho State penitentiary for life.

At almost the same instant the bomb went off at the Steunenberg gate, Orchard strolled into the Saratoga Hotel, which Steunenberg had left five minutes before, went into the bar, had a drink, helped the lone bartender to tie up a small gift package for some friend, then went upstairs to his room.

Orchard was cool enough, and why shouldn't he be? Steunenberg was simply the thirty-first man he had killed in his time. But Orchard had never been arrested in his life. He had apparently never even been under suspicion. There was nothing to fear. But now in the safety of his hotel room he made a small mistake, and when he left the Saratoga two days later he was on his way to jail and prison.

2

Albert E. Horsley, who became John Dempsey and T. S. Hogan and finally Harry Orchard, was born in Northumberland County, Ontario, Canada, on March 18, 1866. He was one of eight children of English and Irish parents and went regularly to church but never got beyond the third grade in public school. When twenty-two years old he followed a trend of the place and time by going to Saginaw, Michigan, then one of America's great lumber-making centers, to work as a logger.

His early life was not particularly interesting. Returning to Ontario after a season in the woods, he married and became an employee, then an operator, of a cheese factory. He became infatuated with a married woman. He slapped a good piece of insurance on his cheese factory, set it afire, collected the insurance, and he and his beloved ran away from their families.

The couple parted in British Columbia. Orchard[1] went to Spokane, which is next door to that part of Idaho known as the Coeur d'Alenes. In the 1890s the Coeur d'Alenes composed one of the busiest lead- and silver-mining districts in the United States and included the lively mine towns of Kellogg, Mullan, Wallace, Burke, Gem, and Wardner. Shortly after his arrival in Spokane, Orchard was sent by an employment office to work a milk route at Burke.

The mining country of northern Idaho is beautiful. Distinctive, too. Deeply wooded with pine, the mountains rise abruptly and are intersected with deep, narrow canyons through which run small, swift streams. The first thing Orchard had to learn, on his job of delivering milk, was that this region was "union country"—meaning the Western Federation of Miners—and that a miner who did not join the union was "run down the canyon," a process that might mean merely deportation but more often included a beating-up and sometimes death. He had to learn, too, that the Mine Owners Association, far from giving in to the union, was fighting it, both openly and secretly, and was thought to be preparing another open-shop drive on a large scale. It was known that all the mine towns were infested with "finks," as company detectives were called, who were "getting evidence" to be used against active union men.

Orchard naturally sided with the union, which did not prevent him—as it did not many another good union man—from wanting to be a capitalist. He saved his money from his milk-route wages and in the fall of 1897 bought a one-sixteenth interest in a new mine at Burke, the Hercules, for five hundred dollars, paying two hundred dollars down. Now he went into the coal and wood business on his own and did very well, due to his genial manner and wide acquaintance with the mining population. In fact, he did so well he couldn't stand the prosperity. He began drinking hard liquor and he gambled more

---

[1] He used so many names that we might as well call him Orchard and be done with it.

than his income warranted, especially in a town that was alive with tinhorns—sure-thing gamblers who posed as honest workingmen.

Unable to keep up his payments on the Hercules, he sold his interest and got a job as a mucker in the Tiger–Poorman mine at Burke, a strong union job with more than four hundred active members. He presently learned that real trouble was brewing, if the Coeur d'Alenes were to remain union. Ed Boyce, union head, was counseling members to buy firearms and learn to use them. "The operators are going to bring in thousands of scabs," Boyce said, "and we must prevent it, or at least drive out the scabs."

On April 29, 1899, things came to a head. The Burke local of the union called a special meeting for seven o'clock in the morning. The hall was packed and speakers reported that the Bunker Hill & Sullivan mine in Wardner, not far away, had resumed work after a shutdown with a crew of nonunion men. The speakers called for direct action.

Direct action came immediately. A few minutes after the meeting was done, a gang of masked armed men held up the Northern Pacific passenger train at Burke and ordered the train crew to add a string of boxcars. This was done and some four hundred men, most of them armed with either rifles or revolvers, climbed aboard. The train pulled out for Wallace, junction point on the way to Wardner and the Bunker Hill & Sullivan mine. At Frisco Magazine, near Gem, the train was stopped. Willing hands broke into the big powder house and put eighty boxes of dynamite on the train. Another stop was made at Gem and more miners, many armed, got aboard.

Meanwhile all telegraph wires out of Burke and Gem had been cut but not until a code message had been sent to Mullan, mining town on another branch railroad. And now at Wallace the results of this message were in evidence. At the Wallace depot were five hundred, possibly six hundred miners. More than half were armed. They climbed on. Here at Wallace the

Northern Pacific train crew protested against moving the train
farther toward Wardner, the objective of the trip, pointing
out that the rails to Wardner were not Northern Pacific but
belonged to the competing Oregon Railway & Navigation
Company.

"Hell," said the mob's leaders, "what difference does that
make?"

Apparently it didn't make any difference. The train was
switched over to the other rails, while twelve hundred men
shouted and sang.

"It all seemed," says Harry Orchard, "like a gigantic picnic,
or a Fourth of July celebration. I doubt if any of us that day
thought we were breaking a law by stealing a train and forc-
ing its crew to run us where we wanted to go, and regardless
of other trains. I had a loaded revolver in my pocket, like
hundreds of others, but I never thought for a moment that we
were doing anything except the proper and the natural thing.
Everybody was joking. It really seemed just like a big picnic,
a clambake, a barbecue."

Down through the winding canyons went the long train
filled with more than a thousand hard-rock miners, running
on a one-track line and with no knowledge of what other
trains might be abroad and moving. The man in the cab kept
the whistle wire down much of the time as they heaved around
curves and bounded through canyons, and when the woods
were not filled with the lokey's moan they resounded to songs
sung in nearly ever accent common to the United States and
most of Europe. Moving pictures did not amount to much in
1899; but here was a moving picture, traveling at thirty miles
an hour through some of the most picturesque scenery in the
country—a full cargo of trouble on wheels for the Bunker Hill
& Sullivan mine.

The leaders had the mob in good hand. The train came to
a stop at the Wardner depot, and the miners dismounted and
formed ranks. Ten men armed with "long guns," rifles, were

deployed ahead to draw the fire of any guards who might be on duty, and the main body began a march direct on the mine buildings. The mob, of course, contained a number of half-wits and these soon made themselves known. Seeing a group of men armed with rifles near the mine buildings and not recognizing their own advance party, they opened fire—killing one and wounding several of the advance guard and driving others to cover, before leaders could stop the suicidal action. The Bunker Hill & Sullivan Company's mine guards had already fled.

A call for volunteers to dynamite the mine was made. Harry Orchard stepped forward and with others packed the eighty cases of strong powder from the train to the mine buildings. They packed it carefully in two tiers, where "it would do the most good," then lighted the fuses and ran. The big buildings went up with a roar that shook the earth for miles. And Harry Orchard had got his first experience in the medium he was to use with so much art—that of giant powder.

Attention was now given to other company structures. Men broke into the nearly deserted boardinghouse, sprinkled kerosene, and fired it. The same was done to the mine superintendent's home. During this action a stray employee of the company was shot and killed but it was an incident. The mob got aboard the train again, which had been held under guard, and left the blazing town of Wardner to burn to ashes.

Orchard and others returned to their jobs in the Tiger–Poorman mine at Burke, but not for long. "It occurred to me, after the affair was over," says Orchard, "that you can't steal railroad trains, dynamite mines, and burn villages, without some reaction."

The reaction came soon. The governor of Idaho, Frank Steunenberg, declared Shoshone County to be in the hands of outlaws and called on President McKinley for federal troops. They were sent under command of General H. C. Merriam and included a regiment of Negro soldiers to act as guards of the bull pens. These concentration camps were made up of old stables, warehouses, boxcars, even of open stockades, and into them were herded miners by the hundred.

With arrival of the first troops Harry Orchard and other quick-thinking men quit their jobs and, without troubling to ask for their wages, hit out on foot over the Coeur d'Alene Mountains and didn't stop until they had got to Thompson's Falls, Montana, twenty-five miles as the crow flies but more than twice as far on foot.

Leaving the Coeur d'Alenes to settle the uprisings as best they could,[2] Orchard first made his way to Butte. For the next two years he ranged all over the Far West, working in mining camps in Montana, Oregon, California, and Utah. In 1902 he settled down for a time in the Cripple Creek district of Colorado, where he had a job in the Vindicator mine. Just for the hell of it, he married again.

3

Orchard became a member of the Free Coinage Miners Union, a local of the Western Federation at Altman, and he soon learned that here, as in Idaho, the Mine Owners Association was making a drive against the union. A year later, in 1903, most mines in the Cripple Creek district were shut down by something approaching a general strike. The usual rioting broke out. National Guard troops were sent in to "restore and keep order," which union leaders translated as meaning protection of scabs and strikebreakers. The Vindicator, a very rich mine, was closed. Orchard, with a few cronies, figured out a way to get into the mine undetected; and here they did quite a bit of high-grading, which meant working the richest veins they could find, packing as much of the rich gold-bearing

---

[2] So rigorous were the measures taken against Coeur d'Alene miners that Congress ordered an investigation. This dragged on for months in 1900 and resulted in a divided report, the majority finding that charges of brutality made against the troops were not justified and a minority of seven condemning the actions of the troops and authorities as barbarous.

metal as they could get into their clothes, and taking it out for sale to gold buyers who were really fences for stolen property.

During his secret high-grading in the Vindicator, Orchard noted a considerable stock of dynamite that had been left on one of the levels when the mine was closed. He mentioned this to the president of his local union, and this official offered him two hundred dollars to put cap and fuse to the powder and set it off. Orchard tried, but the attempt failed when he was surprised by a guard. A bit later, however, he rigged up a set piece that worked.

Placing a big stock of powder near the lift on the seventh level of the Vindicator, he made a sort of target out of giant caps—detonators—on the front of the powder deposit. Next he set a revolver in a vise, aimed directly at the cap-target. He cocked the gun and wired the trigger to the guardrail at the lift entrance of the level. Whoever got out of the cage at this level and moved the guardrail would pull the trigger.

It worked perfectly. A day later the Vindicator's mine superintendent and a shift boss got off at the seventh level. They moved the guardrail, and never knew what happened; they were scattered all over the mine walls.

Orchard now went to Denver to meet Charles H. Moyer and William D. Haywood, respectively president and general secretary of the Western Federation of Miners. He related to them how he had made the lethal set piece in the Vindicator.

"Fine work!" the ebullient Haywood chortled. He gave Orchard two hundred dollars. "Stay here in Denver a few days and enjoy yourself," Big Bill continued, and cautioned Orchard not to make any show of the money. "Then go back to the mines and tear something loose."

The Rocky Mountain Dynamite Man was in the making.

Orchard went back to the mines and prepared immediately to do some tearing loose. "I got some roofing pitch," he relates, "and melted it. I took a dozen sticks of giant powder and tied them up in burlap, winding them tightly with twine. I put this bundle into a bucket and ran the warm pitch around it. When it had cooled, I hacked it up a bit so it looked just like a chunk of coal. I then made a black powder fuse and filled it full of caps. Bored a hole into the chunk, then put in the fuse and sealed it over so it would not be noticed. I made a couple of these jobs, and got an old union man named Dempsey to throw one of them into the coal bunkers of the Vindicator mine." It wrecked the bunkers.

During a lull in the mine war Orchard's conscience, or something, got to troubling him. He tentatively approached a detective of the Mine Owners Association with the idea of confessing, but nothing came of it. The general strike in Colorado was now in full swing. Many union members had been arrested and charged with derailing trains to and from the mines. Orchard, working closely with union officials, devoted some time to preparing witnesses to furnish homemade alibis for the men arrested. More important, though, was that his work brought him into contact with George A. Pettibone.

George Pettibone appeared on the surface as the genial, witty, and kindly operator of a small store in Denver. His former life had been anything but humdrum. As a striking miner in Idaho, back in 1892, he had stolen two hundred pounds of dynamite, packed it to the top of a hill back of the Helena–Frisco smelter, mounted it on a float, and sent it away down the flume that led into the building. "The whole smelter," said a witness, "went up like an umbrella." For this crime Pettibone had served eight years in prison, and was of course black-listed by the Mine Owners Association. Although he now worked no more in the mines, he was a paid-up union man and was very active in the affairs of the Western Federation.

Pettibone was also something of a chemist. At his Denver store he showed Orchard the secret of making what he called Greek fire; it was composed, as Orchard recalls it, of stick

phosphorus, bisulphide of carbon, benzine, alcohol, and turpentine.[3] Pettibone and Orchard stirred up a batch of this,
and Orchard tested it in a secluded spot outside Denver. It
worked very well, he says, and never failed to start blazing
immediately the bottle containing it was broken. He was getting a second batch of it ready for use on a mine structure,
but orders came to refrain for fear purchase of the materials
in its making would be traced.

But Big Bill Haywood wanted something torn loose right
away, for he was always a direct actionist. A huge man of ele-
mental forces, careless, impatient, tremendously vital, he was
the toughest fighter the American labor movement has produced. Blow for blow was his idea. Or, maybe, two blows for
one. He was a big package of primitive instincts. Now he told
Orchard that money for strike support wasn't coming in at all
satisfactorily but that it would pick up immediately things
were torn loose, somewhere or other. He gave Orchard small
amounts of money from time to time, and Orchard continued
the work of preparing alibis for arrested strikers charged
with sabotage. He also organized miners into political clubs.

At this period Charles H. Moyer, president of the Western
Federation, was arrested—seemingly on general principles—
and detained in jail. The miners held Governor James H.
Peabody of Colorado responsible for Moyer's arrest and for
the presence of the militia. Orchard thought it would be a good
idea to bump off the governor and apparently received encouragement from union officials. Thinking, with Orchard, was
acting. He took a gun and waited near the governor's home
on several nights running, awaiting opportunity to blow his
head off; but he did not get what he considered a good chance
—dogs and women and children got in the way.

---

[3] The classic Greek fire, used by the Byzantine Greeks in medieval warfare,
was vomited through long copper tubes at the enemy or was hurled in pots and
barrels. Scholars report that naphtha, sulphur, and niter entered into its
composition.

However, there was other work that needed doing. One Lyle
Gregory, a mine detective much hated by union men, had
appeared in the district. Pettibone, so Orchard says, suggested
that he catch Gregory and "perform a mutilating operation
on him" as a warning to others. So, with another gorilla
named Steve Adams, Orchard went out to find Gregory. They
trailed him around Denver most of one evening, and finally
to a saloon. Seeing no chance to perform the suggested operation within the city limits and catching sight of Gregory coming out of the saloon, Orchard up and shot him dead; then he
went away from there.

Killing the mine dick was hailed as fine stuff, but Big Bill
now felt that "something ought to be blown up." The ranks
of the union were wavering and Bill thought a really good uproar would serve to hold the boys together. Orchard always
had an idea. This time he proposed that the railroad station
at Independence, Colorado, would be a mighty nice place to
blow up. He pointed out that the mine at Independence was
being worked by strikebreakers who went off shift at two-thirty
in the morning and who five minutes later would be congre-
gated at the railroad station, waiting for the train due at that
hour. Haywood thought the suggestion a good one.

"I went to Cripple Creek that afternoon," says Orchard,
"with a couple of small bottles of acid and some other rigging.
I broke into a powder magazine and took two fifty-pound boxes
of dynamite and hid them within easy distance of the Independence railroad depot. Late that night I prepared a bomb
under the station platform. The mechanism was a simple job
and consisted of the powder, some caps, a bottle of acid, and
a little windlass which, when turned, would pull the cork from
the bottle and permit the acid to run out. This would explode
the charge.

"But setting the bomb in place took some work. I had to
crawl a long way on my belly under the platform. It was dark,
and cold. Hooking up the windlass to the cork was a ticklish

job. But I managed it. Then I attached one end of a long wire to the windlass, and backed out from under the platform with the other end. I ran this wire into the bushes and up to an abandoned ore house on a siding. Then I sat down to wait.

"Through the dark I could hear the strikebreaking miners —quite a crowd of them—coming out of the mine and going to the depot. The train was on time. I heard her whistle for the station at two-thirty-five, and a moment later she hove in. Just then I pulled on the wire. A second later the charge went off with a tremendous roar."

Twenty-six men were killed instantly by the blast and twice as many maimed, some for life.

Orchard now took a deserved rest. Pettibone sent him some money and he made a pleasure trip through Wyoming, doing a little hunting and fishing, and returned to Denver after a few weeks. The depot bombing had been a fine thing for the union, Big Bill said, and now they had a very important job for Orchard to do. It was to "get" Fred Bradley, an official of the Mine Owners Association.

Mr. Bradley and his association, according to Haywood, were the spearhead of the attack on the Western Federation of Miners. "They won't be satisfied," he opined, "until the union is driven out of every camp in the West." Bill told Orchard that he had already sent two men to get Bradley, but they had failed. Orchard said he would undertake the job. In August of 1904 Pettibone, who seemed to be handling most of the money for the Federation, gave Orchard two hundred dollars and a shiny new valise, and the Rocky Mountain Dynamiter left Denver for the Pacific coast.

4

Using the name John Dempsey, Orchard went to San Francisco—where Mr. Bradley made his home. Bradley had gone to Alaska and would not return for several weeks. Dynamiter Dempsey decided to do his waiting in ease. He went to what

was then known as Caliente Springs and made himself com-
fortable in this high-toned resort, doing a little drinking and
gambling to while the hours away, and returned to San Francisco to find his man at home.

Engaging a room near the apartment house where Bradley
lived with his family, Orchard–Dempsey struck up an acquaintance with a man who ran a small grocery and liquor store in
the neighborhood. Through this man he was introduced to the
domestics who worked at the Bradley home and from them
learned something of the family and its daily routine.

Setting a bomb did not at first seem feasible, so Orchard
tried another tack. "The desperate and horrible means I conceived to carry out my plan," he says, "I would gladly let
die in my breast." He arose at two one morning, and after seeing the Bradley's milkman leave a bottle of his product at the
door he went across the street, took the cap from the bottle,
and added a good unhealthy dose of strychnine to the milk.
He replaced the cap and returned to his own room, from which
he could watch the Bradley family when they sat down to
breakfast.

The Bradleys had their morning repast at the usual hour,
and although Orchard watched closely he saw nothing un-
toward at the meal. At first he was mystified, but later that
morning he learned what had happened. The Bradley cook
had gone to the neighborhood grocery to get a quart of milk.
This being unusual, the grocer had remarked on it; and the
cook told him she had tasted the milkman's milk that morning
and had found it "awful bitter," as well it might have been.

So Orchard went back to his old favorite, dynamite. He
had to do some fancy planning on this one to make sure that
Bradley would be the first occupant to come out of the apartment. No use wasting good bombs.

Orchard got the bomb ready. He crossed the street one
night and put a small screw eye into the inside door of the
double doors that led from the apartment building to the

street. Next day, in the afternoon, he called Bradley at his office by telephone. Representing himself to be a mine owner with property to sell, he made an engagement to meet Bradley at the latter's office at nine the next morning.

Bright and early next morning Orchard was up and watching through the windows while the Bradleys ate breakfast. When he saw Bradley start on his second cup of coffee, Orchard put the bomb under his coat, went downstairs, crossed the street, and in a jiffy had the bomb connected by string to the screw eye he had put in the door. Then he went back to his room.

Less than five minutes later Bradley put on his coat and went downstairs. He opened the door. The explosion blew away the entire front of the building, three stories of it; and it put Bradley in a hospital for many months, where his hearing and eyesight were despaired of. But he lived.[4]

On the day before the bomb went off Orchard had taken his valise to a downtown saloon and checked it. With the job done, he sauntered downtown, got his bag, and looked for a rooming house in a different part of town. He found one. He was pretty tired from loss of sleep, what with sitting up for the milkman and all, so he undressed and got into bed for a nap. Just as he was dozing off there came a terrific pounding on his door. "What do you want?" Orchard demanded, thinking that he knew what was wanted well enough. No reply except more pounding and "Come out of there!"

"I was sure it was police," Orchard recalls, "and as I started to dress I wondered how they had traced me so quickly, or how they had traced me at all for that matter." He dressed and opened the door to find that some cruel landlord was moving the landlady, her furniture, and her roomers into the street

[4] The blast was laid to a gas main and years later, after Orchard had confessed, was the subject of a lawsuit by the gas company for return of the money it had paid in damages.

because of nonpayment of rent. "Gave me a bad turn for a moment," Orchard remembers.

Pettibone had sent Orchard money several times during the past few weeks, and now he suggested that the dynamite man return to Denver. He did. This time it was to be Governor Peabody of Colorado. A mug by name of Art Baston had been "working on Peabody," Haywood said to Orchard, but wasn't getting anywhere. Seemed that Baston, once a terrible man indeed, had got married. "They don't seem to work so good after they get hitched," Big Bill observed to Orchard, who also was married part of the time.

Orchard made a try. After several days of experiments in the country with time and contact bombs he devised one he thought might turn the trick, even though the governor was always well bodyguarded. It was a contact bomb, to be set in the street where Peabody would be sure to trip it. Orchard made several attempts to get the infernal machine in the right place at the right time, but something always happened to prevent.

Next victim selected by what Orchard always refers to as the "Inner Circle" of the Western Federation was Judge Luther M. Goddard, a justice of the Colorado Supreme Court. This time Orchard used some imagination; the bomb was to be placed in the snow, of which Denver had plenty in the winter, and was to be set off when the judge picked up a woman's purse, a fine-looking purse, ostensibly lost by some passer-by.

Orchard studied the judge's habits for a week before placing the bomb. The judge turned out to be a man of quite regular routine. He left his home every morning at the same hour, almost to the second, and on the way to his office never failed—during Orchard's observations—to take a short cut across a vacant lot. The path through the snow here was well marked, indicating that others besides the judge used it. Orchard planned to place the bomb as soon as he saw the victim leave his home, only a short block from the open lot.

On this morning Orchard, the bomb and purse under his coat, was watching. He saw the judge come down the steps from his home, and turn to walk his usual way. Working quickly but unnoticed, Orchard went into the lot, placed the bomb and covered it with snow, and left the purse fair in the path. Then he walked away, watching over his shoulder from time to time to mark the judge's progress.

Just as the judge was about to turn into the path across lots, a man hailed him. It was some old acquaintance or other, and the two men talked a moment. Then, while Orchard watched from a distance, the two men walked *around* the block.

So Judge Goddard did not find the purse. But one Merritt W. Walley, a citizen of Denver on his way to work, did. Walley came right along within three minutes, walking briskly. He turned into the vacant lot, saw the purse, and . . .

"The explosion also shattered several large windows in the neighborhood," the *Rocky Mountain News*, Denver paper, reported.

5

He who for some time had been John Dempsey now became Thomas S. Hogan, and for a few months, until the excitement about Mr. Walley subsided, Mr. Hogan was engaged in selling insurance—"fire, hail, and cyclone"—to Midwestern farmers. But it wasn't very pleasant work and, besides, there were more important things to be done. The war, and it was nothing less than a war, between the Western Federation and the Mine Owners was being continued without letup. In August of 1905 Orchard–Hogan returned to Denver to confer with Haywood, Moyer, and Pettibone. Moyer was now out of jail.

Big Bill said that Frank Steunenberg, the ex-governor of Idaho who had called for federal troops during the Coeur d'Alene riots, ought to be torn loose. If that could happen, Big Bill told Orchard, Bill would see that anonymous letters, calling attention to Steunenberg's death, were sent to "Governor Peabody of Colorado, Sherman Bell, and others who are attempting to crush the union"—promising that they were to get the same dose, every one. "The only thing those men understand is violence," Big Bill shouted, "and that is what they are going to get."

So on August 25, 1905, Thomas S. Hogan–Orchard packed up his shiny valise again and left Denver. This time he went to small Caldwell, Idaho, where ex-Governor Steunenberg was living, and registered at the Saratoga Hotel, letting it be known that he was in the sheep business.

Frank Steunenberg was a large, rather silent man, simple in manner and dress, who had come up from the ranks, a member of the typographical union who still carried a card. A strong sympathizer with labor, and a Populist when that party was active in the 1890s, he had served two terms as governor. It was during his second term that he called for federal troops, as already related. He had known that this action would mean political death for himself, but, he said, "for many years the county officers in the Coeur d'Alene region had been either in sympathy with or intimidated by criminals. There could be no compromise with crime." On the expiration of his second term he had refused to try for reelection, and had retired to private life. In August of 1905, when T. S. Hogan registered at the local hotel, Steunenberg was living quietly in Caldwell, devoting himself to a sheep ranch.

Orchard–Hogan, on making inquiries about the local sheep situation, was told that Steunenberg dealt in sheep, which, of course, Orchard already knew. But Steunenberg was then in Boise, staying a few days at the Idan-ha Hotel there.

Taking his valise, which you may be sure contained a good workable bomb, Orchard went to Boise and to the Idan-ha. He got a look at his victim, learned the number of his room, and set about to plant the charge under his bed. The bomb this time was arranged to be set off by an alarm clock; but in setting the clock under the bed in his own room as a test,

Orchard decided that the ticking was too loud. It was sure to be discovered if set in a quiet room.[5]

While Orchard was figuring out another plan, Steunenberg checked out of the Idan-ha and left town on a business trip of some sort. Orchard learned it would be at least three weeks before the man returned to Caldwell.

Orchard was no man to sit around, inactive. He decided that while waiting he would go along to Portland, Oregon, to see the sights at the Lewis & Clark Exposition, then in its closing weeks. "I always dreaded to do these murders," he says, "and usually put them off as long as I could, or rather as long as I had money." He went to Portland and the fair, then on a trip to Puget Sound—thinking, he says, that someday he might buy a farm near the Canadian border and go in for a little smuggling.

It was December when the old dyno man returned to Caldwell. He was still T. S. Hogan, sheep buyer and seller, and he again put up at the Saratoga Hotel. Working with his room locked, he now prepared a contact bomb containing ten pounds of dynamite to be set off by a string pulling a cork from a bottle of acid.

He had already looked over the lay of the land and considered it the best bombing chance he had seen. The Steunenberg home was the only house on its street. There were several members of the family, so Orchard studied their comings and goings. And one evening in mid-December he knew that Steunenberg was downtown and almost ready to start for home, on foot. Taking the bomb, Orchard set it beside the only path that led to the front of the house and then stretched a stout cord from the bomb to a small stake he drove on the other side of the path. Half an hour later he watched while the ex-

---

[5] In 1940 the Idan-ha was still doing business at the old stand, filled with the fine flavor of the McKinley–Roosevelt period, and retaining a pioneer charm of which Boise, with its increasing tonnage of glass block and chromium, should be glad. One bomb of the Orchard special-hotel size would have made rubble of the Idan-ha.

governor started for home. The minutes passed, very long and quiet. There was no explosion. Investigation later that night indicated to Orchard that the intended victim had stepped over the cord without suspecting its existence.

Steunenberg left town next day and was gone almost two weeks, but on Saturday afternoon—it was December 30— Orchard, who was playing cards in the Saratoga's bar, saw him come into the hotel lobby. Orchard quit the game. He went across the street to the post office and returned by way of the hotel lobby. He saw that Steunenberg was still there, talking with two men. But it was now after six o'clock and he was sure that Steunenberg would soon start home for supper.

"I went up to my room," Orchard says, "and took the bomb out of my valise. I wrapped it in a newspaper, put it under my arm, and went downstairs. Mr. Steunenberg was still in the lobby. I went outside and hurried as fast as I could to his residence, and laid the bomb down close to the gatepost. I then tied a cord into the screw eye of the cork and ran it around a picket of the gate. I had it fixed so that when the gate was opened it would jerk the cork from the bottle and let the acid run out and set off the bomb.

"I fixed it so that even if he did not open the gate wide enough to pull the cork he would still strike the cord with his feet, and this would do the job as well. I brushed some snow over the bomb and hurried back to the hotel."

Next, as the reader knows, Orchard passed Steunenberg when the man was about two blocks from his home, and the explosion occurred at about the same time Orchard reached the Saratoga. After a quick drink in the bar, he went to his room. It was here and now that he made his slight mistake. Let him tell it in his own words.

"I was going to take some things out of my room and throw them away. There were some bits of dynamite, some pieces of fuse, several giant caps, and a bottle or two of acid. I emptied the acid into the sink and put the bottle into my side pocket,

planning to take it downstairs and throw it away. It wasn't
two seconds after I put that bottle in my pocket when a flash
like a pistol shot rang out in the room and the coat was nearly
all torn off my back."

Little wonder. What had happened was this. In his pocket
Orchard had a spare detonator or two, giant caps. The bottle
he had just put into this pocket was not quite empty. A drop
or two of acid remained. It dribbled out, reached the caps,
and—off came the old Rocky Mountain Dynamite Man's coat,
blown, as you might say, by his own petard.

Now when one's own coat is blown off one's own back it is
usually if not always wholly unexpected. "I immediately understood what had taken place," says Orchard in what, despite his
terrible coolness, must be an understatement, "*and it almost
unnerved me for a moment.*"

One grants that it would have "almost" unnerved anybody.

But no one apparently heard this second and minor explosion. The entire town was undergoing an excitement such
as it had never known. Orchard went downstairs and ate a
good solid supper. It is possible that his unconcerned manner
even then attracted attention, but he did not realize it at the
time. And although he was seemingly cool enough, both inside
and out, he seemed to be at a loss to know what to do. As the
precious minutes slipped away, he did nothing.

"Something, I cannot tell you what, came across me," he
explains. "I got to thinking of the many incriminating things
in my room. Besides the fuse and caps, I recalled that I had
some sugar and some chloride of potash in my things. I also
had an amount of plaster of Paris, a batch of screw eyes, and
an electric flashlight. I knew all these things would be hard
to explain if found, but still I sat there and didn't do anything
about them. After that cap went off in my pocket, I seemed
to lose my reasoning power. I simply left everything where
it was."

There was a train out of Caldwell early that evening, too,

but Orchard didn't take it; and by the time a later train was due he felt sure that anyone trying to take it would be held on suspicion. He remained in the Saratoga, doing nothing, not even touching that room filled with all the requisites of a dynamite man.

Although most of Caldwell was up all night, Orchard–Hogan went to bed and slept well. Next morning he committed a mistake even worse than mixing acid and explosive in his pocket. As T. S. Hogan, the sheep man, he walked up to a group of local men who were standing in front of the hotel and discussing the one topic of interest—the bombing of Caldwell's best-known citizen. In a matter-of-fact way he asked if anyone in the group could tell him where he might buy a band of wethers (sheep). It all sounded just a little too casual. Local police took Orchard aside and questioned him about his business in town. His replies were so logical that he was released with an apology.

On the same day, though, Orchard was sighted by Harvey K. Brown, the high sheriff of Baker, Oregon, who happened to be in town. "I know that feller," he told a local officer. "He isn't T. S. Hogan. He is Harry Orchard who used to be active in the miners' union." [6]

Orchard was put under arrest. He denied any knowledge of the bombing, but police went to his room in the Saratoga and there found the miscellaneous array of articles which not even an angel with wings could have satisfactorily explained in Caldwell that day. Orchard was held in the local jail as a suspicious character.

By this time rewards totaling $15,000 were being offered for apprehension of the killer or killers. The news had gone out over the wires, and now, among many others attracted by

---

[6] Sheriff Brown was later the victim of an explosion similar to that which killed Steunenberg. The gorillas got him near his home with a set bomb. It was generally believed that this act of terrorism was directly due to Brown's identification of Orchard.

the excitement, a remarkable sleuth came to Caldwell. He was James McParland, head of the Denver office of Pinkerton's National Detective Agency.

McParland was one of the most successful and by all means the oddest detective in the United States. He was the man who, a whole generation before the Steunenberg case, had broken up the Molly Maguires, the notorious secret terrorist order in the Pennsylvania coal fields. The public of 1905, if it thought of McParland at all, thought of him as long since dead, or at least superannuated. He was far from either. Nearly seventy now, he retained the drive and subtlety that had brought the Mollies to the scaffold way back in the 1870s. He appeared now in Caldwell, Idaho, wearing gold-rimmed glasses, an enormous mustache, and a cutaway coat.

It has never been quite clear how McParland, a private detective, got an interview with Harry Orchard in Caldwell jailhouse. But he did, and from Orchard he got a confession of the many killings with which the reader is acquainted. Orchard says that he was ready to confess, that McParland made him no promises whatever of immunity. Nor did anyone else. "I was afraid to die unless I unburdened my conscience," Orchard explains.

Whatever prompted the confession, the result was implication of Moyer, Haywood, and Pettibone of the Western Federation of Miners. At the time of Orchard's confession these men were in Colorado, hence beyond the jurisdiction of Idaho authorities. To be tried they must be extradited. To be extradited a man must be a fugitive. None of these men was a fugitive. They were merely charged with being accessories to the crime of killing Steunenberg. Under general interpretation of the laws it would be impossible to extradite an accessory; but the United States Supreme Court had often held that the right of a state in which a crime had been committed to try an *abducted* person could not be questioned, whatever the means used to secure his presence.

So, with a request for extradition from Governor Gooding
of Idaho in their possession, sheriffs went to Denver and asked
for extradition of the three men. Governor McDonald of
Colorado granted it. But the sheriffs knew they would have to
be careful if they were to bag their men; the law had usually
if not always been interpreted to mean that a fugitive from
justice facing extradition "may challenge the fact by habeas
corpus immediately upon his arrest."

The Idaho sheriffs looked at the calendar. February 17,
1906, three days hence, would be a Saturday. Courts would
be closed until Monday, and it would be difficult if not impossible to get a writ of habeas corpus until then.

The sheriffs waited until Saturday, then acted. Moyer,
Haywood, and Pettibone were quietly taken into custody in
Denver, put aboard a special car, and whisked away to Idaho,
where they were to lie in jail at Caldwell and Boise for eighteen
months before their trials even began.

6

The long delay in beginning the trial of Moyer, Haywood,
and Pettibone was occasioned by another trial, a mere curtain
raiser to the main event, when one Steve Adams, who had been
associated with the Western Federation officials and with
Orchard, was tried for the murder of a man named Tyler in
the Coeur d'Alene mining region. Both prosecution and defense hoped to use Steve Adams; but nothing came of either
hope, and the big case finally got under way.

Counsel for Moyer, Haywood, and Pettibone was headed
by E. F. Richardson of Denver, and he was to be assisted by
Edgar Wilson and John Nugent of Boise, Fred Miller of
Spokane, and Clarence Darrow of Chicago. The prosecution
was in charge of Owen M. Van Duyn, district attorney, and
James Hawley and William E. Borah. Anyone who ever saw
the two men in action will know that Borah and Darrow stole
the show.

The real show was further delayed when defense counsel asked for a writ of habeas corpus. This was denied, lastly by the United States Supreme Court—which denied it eight to one, Justice McKenna dissenting in a sharp note in which he referred to moving the three men as "kidnaping."

The case, even before it got to trial, created wider interest and more bitter feeling than anything since the Haymarket affair of the 1880s. There was no sitting on *this* fence. Either you were for Moyer, Haywood, and Pettibone or you were against them. The President of the United States, even, was not immune to the hysteria. In a private letter that was made public, Theodore Roosevelt wrote that whether or not these three men were guilty of the Steunenberg crime they were "undesirable citizens." This letter made a noise. Writing in his paper, *The Appeal to Reason*, Eugene Debs made a vitriolic attack on the President. Union men all over the country began wearing buttons on which was inscribed "I Am an Undesirable Citizen." Labor unions staged monster parades of protest. Meetings were held in all large cities and in all mine towns. A large defense fund was collected.

The trial was held in Boise and began on May 9, 1907. Present were special representatives of fifty-four daily newspapers and of perhaps a score of magazines and other periodicals. The eminent Professor Hugo Münsterberg, Harvard psychologist, was brought West by the prosecution. His testimony was to the effect that, amazing though Orchard's confession was, the man was telling the truth. Clarence Darrow, for defense, remarked that Orchard was, among other things, "the most monumental liar that ever existed."

Boise and all Idaho were tense as the trial progressed, for this was no common murder case. Back East, Debs was calling editorially for "the workers to form an army and march to Idaho to free these martyrs to the cause of Labor."

First to be tried was Haywood. The prosecution rested its case almost wholly on the confession of Orchard, for there was little brought out that could have been termed specific corroborative evidence. Orchard told his story and he stuck to it. Not even the uncanny cross examination of Darrow failed to shake it in the least.[7] Orchard remained as cool as ice, answering all questions in a direct and polite manner. Apparently the man did not have a nerve in his body.[8]

Darrow was of defense counsel but he quickly turned defense into an offense. He sought to show by many witnesses that Orchard had a personal reason for killing Steunenberg, that Orchard had owned an interest in the Hercules mine in north Idaho, that because of his activity in the Coeur d'Alene mine riots he had been forced to sell this interest for a small sum and flee the state when troops entered the district and began making arrests. These troops, Darrow recalled to the jury, had been sent there by Governor Steunenberg. And Darrow showed that the Hercules mine had become a big money-maker. The implications of personal revenge were clear.

Again, Darrow sought to show that Orchard was a bigamist, a hard drinker and gambler, a man who had dealings both with detectives of the mine operators and with officials of the miners' union—all of which Orchard had confessed. From here on Darrow demonstrated with all his eloquence that the trial was merely one more battle in the age-old struggle between capital and labor. William Borah objected. "This is a murder trial," he said, "not a debate."

---

[7] In 1922, or fifteen years after the trial, James H. Hawley, of prosecution counsel, remarked of Orchard's confession: "I found every statement to be true and correct. Even in little incidents, which were not brought before the court but with which we tested him, I found that not even in the slightest particular was his recollection at fault, or had he magnified the charge. He is the most extraordinary man I ever encountered, in probably as long a life of criminal prosecution as any man in this state was ever called upon to engage in. . . . And Orchard went on the witness stand with never a promise or even an intimation of immunity. . . . He went on the stand for the sole purpose of rectifying these great wrongs that he had in part committed."

[8] I have often wondered, idly enough, what would have been the effect on Orchard if, when he was on the stand, another giant cap had let go in his coat pocket. Doubtless he would have remained the one calm person in the courtroom.

In summing up for the jury Chief Defense Counsel Richardson spoke for nine hours, Darrow for eleven. Prosecution, as related, rested its case pretty much on the confession of Orchard. When the lawyers were done, Judge Clement Wood charged the jury. There was no pettifogging. Judge Wood's instructions to the jury were clear as crystal.[9] "Under the statutes of this state," he said, "a person cannot be convicted of a crime upon testimony of an accomplice, unless such accomplice is corroborated by other evidence."

It took a fair and a very brave man to speak those words to the Haywood jury. Fair, because radicals had been subjecting the judge to columns of vile abuse in their publications. Brave, because the powerful Mine Owners Association of Idaho and other Western states wanted a conviction at any cost.

Judge Wood's charge left no doubt in the minds of the jury. After being out a few hours on July 28, 1907, they brought in a verdict of not guilty in the case of Idaho versus William Dudley Haywood.

George A. Pettibone was the next defendant tried. He also was found not guilty. The case against Charles Moyer was dismissed. Harry Orchard was sentenced to be hanged, and the sentence commuted to life imprisonment.

Long before the trial was over, the Industrial Workers of the World (the celebrated I. W. W., the Wobblies), which Haywood had helped to found in 1905 and which he was to lead with roaring success until 1918, were taking the headlines away from the Western Federation of Miners, although the Federation's troubles in Butte, in 1914, resulted in much shooting and the dynamiting of the union hall there.

Of the principals in the Steunenberg case only the old

---

[9] This just and brave man died December 22, 1940, in Boise, at the age of eighty-four. Born in Winthrop, Maine, he studied law at Bates College, and went to Idaho in 1881 as assistant district attorney for the Territory. He retired from the bench in 1911 but continued active practice until 1934.

Rocky Mountain Dynamite Man remains, tending his chickens and turkeys in the prison with the same care that he always applied to any task before him, reading Adventist literature, and writing his memoirs of thirty-five years in the penitentiary.[10]

---

[10] Strong arguments for a pardon for Harry Orchard have been made in the past by James H. Hawley, Frank R. Gooding, and other persons prominent in Idaho. Mr. Hawley contended that Orchard, because of his exposure of conditions within the "Inner Circle" of the Western Federation, was "entitled, not only as a matter of right, but as a matter of law, to a full pardon."

CHAPTER FOUR

KITTY GING'S BUGGY RIDE

IT WAS NO MERE WHIM of preachers in the 1890s that produced the countless sermons against livery stables and fast rigs. Anyone who makes a study of crimes involving women during this period must be struck by the numbers of females who never returned from buggy rides. An even greater number of females, so ancient rounders say, returned from buggy rides in a condition which was, as a vivid phrase of the time had it, worse than death. But leaving "sin" as compared to crime out of the matter, it would appear in retrospect that a pretty girl's progress from the livery stable was often direct to the morgue.

That was the way it went with Kitty Ging, and I know of no better way to set the scene of the time and place than by quoting the gifted prose of a contemporary account:[1]

Minnesota's winter was tardy in cementing its fetters of ice and snow about old mother earth in the year 1894, and when the third day of December had marked the page of history, the virgin snows of an early winter had not yet painted the landscape with its robe of Parian white.

[1] *The Ging Murder and the Great Hayward Trial,* by Oscar F. G. Day, Minneapolis, 1895.

A few miles from the business center of Minneapolis lie two sheets of water that have been taken into the park system of that fair city. Lake Calhoun and the Lake of the Isles were frozen over, and hundreds of the youth and beauty of Minneapolis disported themselves upon steel runners beneath the light of the crescent moon. Around the eastern shore of Lake Calhoun winds a wide driveway, until it passes the lake, and then loses itself in its windings toward the country, until a mile away it passes between tall trees and through dismal swamps.

An electric car line passes along the left side of the road for a distance, then branches off to the right, and cuts through high banks where the hill has been pierced. A few residences nestle among the trees on the adjoining hillsides, but for the most part the scene is lonesome and drear, and in the light of a waning moon it is doubly so. Farther out the road rises to a slight hill, and then passes through a tamarack swamp. All is silent, nothing is to be seen but the light twinkling from the window of a lonely residence upon the hill.

The waning moon descends to the horizon, until its crescent shape is cut into fantastic patterns by the top branches of leafless trees. Ever and anon, wafted by the faint breezes, comes the faint voice of the merry skaters, and often the quick, sharp report of the cracking ice is heard, as old Boreas rends its frozen surface with his icy hand. It is nearly 8 o'clock when the report of a firearm is heard. Few hear it among those hundreds of skaters, and it is hardly noticed. It is probably some merrymaker, firing off his revolver as he walks down the road. Then all is silent again.

Suddenly the sound of hoofs is heard upon the frozen ground, coming from a distance out the road. Then there is the rumble of an electric car, the flash of its lights as it passes around the end of the lake. A passenger alights and proceeds up the road. It is William Erhardt, a young man returning home to that lonely house on the hillside. He has proceeded but a short distance when he hears the sound of hoofs, sees a light colored horse coming on the gallop, drawing a light buggy with its top up. He steps to one side to let it pass, wondering why a man should be driving at such a pace.

It is a lonely road, and a lonely hour, but the young man has traversed it many a time, and he walks on merrily. Suddenly he sees a dark object lying at the side of the road in front of him. For a moment he is startled and falters. Then he gains courage to proceed. Closer and closer he advances; gradually the object assumes a shape. Horror steals upon him! A human body lies before him in the road.

It is the body of a woman, lying partly on its side, partly upon its face, one arm under it, the other outstretched. The cheek is on the frozen ground, beneath the face is a pool of blood still streaming. Erhardt leaned over the body and felt the hand. It was clothed in a black mitten, and the wrist was warm.

Such was the end of Kitty Ging's last buggy ride, in a fast rig hired at a livery stable.

The actual killing of Catherine M. Ging, an up-and-coming young businesswoman of Minneapolis, was not very interesting. What sets it apart from the general run of murders were the fantastically elaborate plans of the person responsible for it. Three people knew of these plans, in whole or in part, and I can think of no more cold-blooded person in the annals of crime than the man in whose horrible mind the plans were conceived.

2

William Erhardt, the young man who found the warm body in the road, was just returning to his home on Excelsior Road from his work as baggageman at the Soo Line depot in Minneapolis. He immediately thought of the galloping horse and buggy which had passed him a few minutes before, and thought with some reason that the dead woman was the victim of an accident. So, too, did Dr. William Russell, hastily summoned, who arrived on the scene, "driving his fast rig," half an hour later. About eight inches from the corpse's feet was the mark of a woman's heel in the dust of the frozen road; this mark ended in a scrape, as if the woman had landed upon her feet and then pitched forward to fall. Dr. Russell pronounced her dead. The body was taken to the Hennepin County morgue, and the coroner's office notified.

Hours before the police suspected anything more than another fatal buggy accident, and hours before they knew the victim's full name, a livery stable knew for certain that foul play had doubtless happened to Miss Catherine M. Ging.

Miss Ging's body had been discovered near Lake Calhoun

a little past eight o'clock. Less than an hour later Lucy, a buckskin mare, drawing a covered buggy, trotted carefully and happily down Nicollet Avenue in downtown Minneapolis, some four miles from Lake Calhoun, turned the corner at Grant Street, and walked into the Palace Livery Stable— where she stopped in the proper place on the barn floor, as befitted a veteran livery horse.

The reins were wrapped around the whipsocket. The buggy was empty. This was nothing unusual at livery stables, for their customers often left their rigs to return alone and the horses became very clever in turning out for traffic they happened to meet. Without another thought in his mind Harry Gilbert, the man on duty at the Palace, unhitched Lucy and put her in her stall. But when he went to take the robe out of the buggy it was not there. Moreover, he noted a peculiar odor. Bringing a lantern, he saw a pool of clotted blood on the seat cushion.

Gilbert looked at the rig more closely. Inside the buggy top were splashes of blood; the back cushion was bloody, so was the bottom of the vehicle. One of the bows supporting the buggy top appeared smeared with blood as if by a hand.

Gilbert consulted the stable register. It showed that the rig had been taken out by Catherine M. Ging, who Gilbert knew was the stylish dressmaker with an establishment in the Syndicate Block and who lived at the Ozark Flats, an apartment house. The horse and buggy had been delivered to her at the West Hotel at seven o'clock that evening. It was now a little past nine. Gilbert went to the telephone and notified police.

At the city morgue Coroner Willis P. Spring examined the corpse. It was of a woman close to thirty years old, he judged. It was dressed in black woolen over which was a sealskin sack, in 1894 the height of elegance. The hands were mittened. On the head was saucy sailor hat. Underclothing had a laundry mark: Ging. Coroner Spring found a bruise on the lip, a broken nose, a bruise over the right eye. The left eye had been pushed from its socket. In putting it back into place, his fingers encountered a small hard object which proved to be a bullet. Examining the back of the skull, he found that the bullet had entered close to the right ear.

Meanwhile detectives were sent to the scene of the accident, crime, suicide, or whatever it was. They could find nothing of interest except that the buggy from which the woman had fallen or been thrown had turned around about fifty feet beyond where the body was found. No clues were discovered.

Other police, with the address given them by the Palace Stable, went to the Ozark Flats at Hennepin Avenue and Thirteenth Street. George and Harry Goosman, proprietors of the Palace, were already at the Ozark, making inquiries about their customer who had met with foul play or an accident.

It was now a little past eleven. Harry T. Hayward, son of the owner of the Ozark Flats, came in. He had just taken a Miss X home from the Grand Opera House, where they had been to see a popular play,[2] and now he was going to his own apartment in the Ozark. From police he learned that Miss Ging was dead. At this time nothing was said as to how she came to her death, for the officers did not yet know of the coroner's discovery of the bullet. A Miss Ging had been found dead near Lake Calhoun; that was all police could say.

Hayward showed real concern and immediately spoke of Mary Louise Ireland, the young niece of Miss Ging who lived with her aunt at the Ozark. Miss Ireland was awakened and notified. Hayward then went to the police station to learn particulars. Miss Ging had been a very dear friend, he said.

At the police station Hayward stated that in his opinion the woman had been murdered, and murdered for her money. He intimated that she often carried large sums of money with her and was careless in showing it. When the coroner's report

---

[2] The play at the Grand that night was Hoyt's *A Trip to Chinatown*.

became known, Hayward gave an odd exclamation. "She has been murdered!" he cried. "She has been murdered and I am done up—my two thousand dollars is gone!" [3]

The young man quickly explained that he had lent the dead woman money with which to enlarge her dressmaking shop and to add a millinery department. Police may have thought it was a little soon to bring *that* up, but they said nothing. "And," as Mr. Oscar F. G. Day, original historian of the Ging murder, observed, "the long night wore away, and still that silent body lay upon its cold marble slab at the county morgue. Nowhere was there light. Deep, dark, impenetrable mystery was over everything."

3

Catherine M. Ging, known to friends as Kitty and Kate, was twenty-nine years old, "commanding of mien," says a contemporary newspaper description, and rather good-looking. Certainly she was dashing. Her black hair was curly. Her big eyes were gray. She had a fine complexion. She was five feet seven inches tall, weighed one hundred and fifty pounds, and was "exceptionally well formed." The nineties had a word for it—Junoesque.

Born in small Auburn, New York, she had come to Minneapolis to open a dressmaking shop. She catered only to the well-to-do and wealthy, and was doing very well indeed. She herself was a walking advertisement, for she was a perfect clotheshorse and the clothes she wore were always in the mode. The wives and daughters of local timber barons and flour kings were coming to her shop in increasing numbers. Minneapolis bankers and businessmen knew her as a shrewd but honest and hardworking woman of drive and ability. She

---

[3] The expression "done up" seems odd. Obviously it means he was "done in," as we say, to the extent of two thousand dollars, or "done out" of two thousand dollars. It appears many times in the transcript of the case; so it must have been in the vernacular of half a century ago, although I can find no other example of its use.

was unmarried. "No breath of scandal had ever touched this young woman's skirts," declared the Minneapolis *Tribune*.

For almost a year before her death Kitty Ging had been keeping company with Harry T. Hayward. Hayward was a country boy twenty-nine years old and had been born in rural Macoupin County, Illinois. He had come to Minneapolis with his family. His father, W. W. Hayward, was reputed to be wealthy from real-estate operations in the Twin Cities and owned a number of buildings—including the Ozark Flats, described as a "fashionable apartment house." An older son, Adry, worked in his father's office in the Oneida Block.

Harry was the favorite of the family. There is no clear record that he had ever done an honest day's work in his life. When he had money, he gambled; but apparently was not much given to women or liquor. He had mortgaged a valuable piece of property given him by his father and invested the money attempting to understand the art of faro, a game he seems never to have mastered from either the banker's or the player's side of the table. He was tall and handsome, wore a fancy mustache, and was a good dresser and fast talker. He lived something of a double life. He was well known and liked by a number of business and professional men and their families.[4] And he was equally well known in Minneapolis professional gambling circles. That was Harry T. Hayward as he appeared on December 4, 1894.

The murder of Kitty Ging made a noise in the papers. It is difficult to convey a sense of her occupational status to generations who have long since forgotten about dressmakers (and milliners) in the sense of the 1890s, or who never have known what a dressmaker was. The young professional dressmaker of that day occupied a unique place in society. Usually styl-

---

[4] Newspapers of the time and place attempted to make Hayward out a cultured gentleman, but the stenographic report of his utterances is filled with such things as "I ain't positive of that," "He don't know," and "the furtherest one." His culture, apparently, barely stopped him short of double negatives and "drown-ded."

ishly dressed herself, and elegantly bonneted, more often than not good-looking, she had a dash and a freedom of action and manner that few other women possessed or were permitted to possess. Single, or at least a widow, and easy to meet, the dressmaker almost always attracted men. Hence her more stodgy clients secretly envied her and whispered to one another that she was "bold" and "risqué." No real scandal needed to touch a professional dressmaker; she was what today is known as "glamorous" without any scandal.

Harry Hayward was helpful to the police. He explained in some detail the cash loans he had made to Miss Ging, and directed them to friends of the dead woman who might have other information. A close friend was Miss Ella Vedder. Miss Vedder knew little of Miss Ging's business transactions, but she told police of a happening that might be significant. On a Sunday in the previous April, she said, she and Miss Ging, with Harry Hayward and Thomas Waterman—who often formed a quartet for buggy rides and suppers—had taken a drive around Lake Calhoun. Not far from the spot where Miss Ging's body had been found, the four young people were held up by a masked man and robbed of their valuables. The girls had managed to secrete the rings which they wore. Miss Vedder had no opinion as to whether there could be any connection between the holdup in April and the murder in December.

Police looked up Thomas Waterman, Miss Vedder's male friend. He related the same holdup story, substantially as Miss Vedder told it. He had seen Miss Ging and had talked to her on Monday, the day of the murder; but he had no suspicions as to motive, unless it were robbery.

Mary Louise Ireland, Miss Ging's niece, who worked in the dressmaking parlors, reported that on Monday afternoon her aunt had received a note delivered by a messenger boy, had torn it up after reading it. Bits of torn paper in a wastebasket were pieced together but seemed to have no significance. A dry-goods clerk and an unemployed man who had known Miss Ging were interviewed by police, and were dismissed.

The mayor of Minneapolis, William H. Eustis, took an immediate interest in the mystery. He asked Harry Hayward to come to his office to give such help as he could to direct detectives in their investigation. Hayward responded at once. The mayor and police asked if Hayward had any suspicions. For a few moments "his handsome face was buried in deep thought." He twirled his blond mustache. Then he named a man who lived in the Ozark Flats. This man cleared himself without difficulty.

During his interview with the mayor and police Hayward volunteered the information that Miss Ging and he had "been in love" for many months. His story:

She had known he was a gambler and often gave him small amounts of money to play for her, win or lose, and he displayed written statements of such sums in the woman's handwriting. But she had quit gambling. She was ambitious and wanted to enlarge her shop. To do this she needed seven thousand dollars, which, with three thousand dollars of her own money, would give her the supplies required, furnish the place of business, and allow for working capital. He had lent her seven thousand dollars, and produced notes signed by Miss Ging acknowledging the debt. He produced other notes, also signed by Miss Ging, which, he said, were receipts for money he had "deposited" with the woman to keep for him. Thus the dead woman had owed him ninety-five hundred dollars at the time of her death.[5]

Asked if these loans had been made without security, Hayward said Miss Ging had assigned to him two life-insurance policies of five thousand dollars each. He held the policies, he said.

---

[5] It was recalled later that on first hearing of Miss Ging's death Hayward had made a remark that "my two thousand dollars is gone." Not ninety-five hundred.

At this point the mayor proposed, oddly enough, that all present go to the morgue to view the remains. Hayward made no objection. The group stood around the dismal slab while the shroud was removed from the girl's face. Hayward looked, imperturbable. "Poor girl . . . poor dead girl," the mayor heard him say softly. "If you only could speak now, you could tell us who it was."

Back at the mayor's office again, Hayward had one more item to offer. He was quite sure, he said, that on the day of the murder Miss Ging had drawn a large sum of money from her deposit box in a downtown bank. He thought it might amount to ten or twelve thousand dollars. This delayed mention of what looked important to his hearers seemed odd to them, but Hayward was not held.

Now there appears on the scene a young man one would like to know more about; but he is present only for a fleeting moment in the yellowed record, then vanishes for good. He was F. A. Briggs, variously described as "a young journalist," "a newspaperman," and "the young editor of a sensational newspaper." Briggs came to police of his own accord. In an issue of his paper of several months previously he had disclosed, he said, the gambling operations of Harry T. Hayward. After publication of the article, which had been in the nature of an exposé, Hayward had threatened to have Briggs beaten up. Personal friends told Briggs that the man Hayward had hired to do the beating-up was "the engineer at the Ozark Flats."

Police appear to have paid no heed to Briggs. It is possible that police didn't care for a young man who was running a sensational newspaper, what with exposing local gambling and all, but in any case they did not trouble to look up the engineer at the Ozark Flats. At least not then. The police and mayor, in fact, were not getting anywhere at all. The break came from another quarter.

It came in a letter that sat Albert H. Hall, assistant county attorney, straight up in his chair. It was from Levi M. Stewart, one of the city's most prominent men, a retired attorney who had made a fortune out of Minneapolis real estate.[6]

Three days before the murder of Miss Ging, so Mr. Stewart wrote, Adry Hayward, older brother of Harry, had come to Stewart's office. Stewart was an old friend of the Hayward family and had often acted as adviser to Hayward, Senior, and his sons. Adry was greatly excited. He related to Stewart that his brother Harry and a confederate were planning to kill one Kitty Ging, a dressmaker, in order to get money from her life insurance. Harry had managed to have Miss Ging display large sums of money in front of many people, to give semblance, after the murder, to the theory that she had been robbed and killed. Harry had "fixed it" so that he would appear to have lent her large amounts of cash, to divert possible suspicion from the assignment to him of her insurance policies.

All this information had been given to Mr. Stewart three days before Miss Ging's body was found, given by a brother of Harry Hayward. Mr. Stewart, while considering Harry to be a "dishonest rogue," did not believe he would rob and kill. He had told Adry that it was nothing more than some of Harry's "big talk," for which he was noted. Stewart counseled Adry to forget the matter. All a bluff, he said. But now, with the murder a fact, Stewart saw how tragically mistaken he had been. Hence the letter to Attorney Hall.

Hall took the letter to his superior, State's Attorney Frank M. Nye. Its contents were not made known, but Harry Hayward was formally arrested. He chafed at this only, he said, because he had planned to accompany the body of Miss Ging to Auburn, New York, for burial. A few hours later Adry

---

[6] Old-time Minneapolis folk will remember Levi Stewart, usually known as Elder Stewart. In spite of his wealth his tastes were very simple and for years he lived in a modest cottage, surrounded by trees, in a full block of downtown Minneapolis, probably as valuable as any piece of property in the Northwest.

Hayward was arrested and charged with firing the shot that killed Miss Ging. Before being locked up he was questioned. Mayor Eustis, who was present, long afterward remembered that Adry disclosed little and was obviously trying to shield his brother. At this time Adry did not know the information he had given Elder Stewart was in possession of the officers. Next day, however, on advice of Elder Stewart, Adry told detectives substantially the same story he had told Stewart before the murder.

Adry related that his brother had made the proposals of murder to him early in November. The victim was to be a woman and at first her name was not mentioned. Harry had offered his brother two thousand dollars to commit the act. Adry had refused. Later Harry told him Miss Ging was the woman he had in mind. Hardly a day passed, now, that Harry did not mention his plans to do away with the girl. And on Friday, November 30, Harry told Adry that at last he had found a man with nerve enough to do the job. This man was Blixt, engineer at the Ozark Flats—the second time this man's name had come up. It was on this day that Adry had gone to Elder Stewart.

Police took the engineer, Claus A. Blixt, and his wife into custody. Both appeared to have perfect alibis. Blixt was put through quite a sweating. Was he plain dumb, or devilishly clever? Police could make up their minds on but one thing. They agreed that never had they seen so uncommunicative and imperturbable a Swede as this Blixt with the walrus mustache, and this opinion was also shared by Sheriff Holmberg and Deputies Megaarden, Anderson, and Ege—Scandinavians all. Mrs. Blixt was released, but police thought some further sweating might help her husband.

Mayor Eustis had taken the notes and insurance policies from Harry Hayward. Now he studied them and he noticed that witnesses to the notes had been one Witherspoon, and nobody else but Claus A. Blixt. Witherspoon, elevator man at the Ozark Flats, was brought in. He related the circumstances of how Harry Hayward had asked him to witness the signatures of Hayward and Miss Ging. He had no knowledge as to what the transactions were about. The mayor sent for Blixt, who was brought to the West Hotel—where the mayor had set up a sort of extracurricular office of investigation.

Blixt appeared to Mayor Eustis as a "sluggish, simple individual." The mayor treated him kindly, even jovially, and presently the man was pouring out his life story, from his birth in Sweden to his work as engineer at the Ozark Flats. Much of his life had been spent on a farm at Spring Garden, Goodhue County, Minnesota, not far from Cannon Falls. Since leaving the farm he had worked as a streetcar conductor, a bartender, a farm laborer; but mostly, of late years, he had been a stationary engineer. He was forty-one years old, had been married three times, and apparently adored his third wife.

"Now tell me, Claus," the mayor said, "what did you do from seven o'clock, Monday night, December 3, until you went to bed?"

Without hesitating, Blixt stumbled through his story of Monday night. He had gone to South Minneapolis after supper to collect a debt of one dollar and a half. The man wasn't at home. On the way back to the Ozark, Blixt had stopped in a bar for "a few beers" and at a jewelry store to leave a watch to be fixed. And so to bed. Over and over again the mayor had him repeat the story. Blixt never faltered. But the mayor was convinced that he wasn't telling all. The man's mouth was notably dry. He was "spitting cotton." [7] Blixt was returned to solitary in the jail.

A day later Blixt asked to be taken to the mayor's office. Had something to tell, he said. And tell he did. His story:

---

[7] Most readers doubtless have read of the ancient method, said to be used by Chinese, in which several suspects are stood in a row and each forced to hold a small quantity of dry rice in his mouth. After a few minutes each of the suspects discharges the rice into the hand of an officer. If the rice is moist, the suspect is released; if dry, he is placed in jail.

Harry Hayward had arranged for Blixt to meet him on the west side of Lake Calhoun at eight o'clock on Monday night. Blixt was there. Hayward came, driving a buckskin mare; and in the buggy was Miss Ging, dead. Hayward had shot her ten minutes before, and Blixt had heard the shot as he waited. Under Hayward's direction Blixt had got into the buggy, and Hayward got out. Blixt, bearing the victim, drove along Excelsior Road until he got to the Tillney place. Then he turned around and drove back toward town, heaving the body out of the rig where it was found.[8] He then drove into Minneapolis, abandoned the bloodstained rig near Dupont Avenue, and took a streetcar home.

The mayor thanked Blixt politely and observed, "Claus, you are doing very well. You have told us part of the truth. The trouble is, you see, Harry Hayward could not have been at Lake Calhoun at eight o'clock, or anywhere near eight o'clock. At eight o'clock he was taking a young lady to the play at the Grand Opera House."

Blixt blinked a bit but said nothing. He was returned to solitary, where a good fat Bible was given to him. Twenty-odd hours later he again asked to be taken to the mayor's office.

As he entered the room in charge of police, Mayor Eustis grasped his hand and shook it warmly. "I am always glad to see you, Claus," he said.

"Mayor," the man gasped, "I shot the girl!" Then, and while a stenographer took it down, Claus Blixt, the honest and dim-witted farmboy turned engineer, made a long confession— the confession that was "made to stick" and which not even the many wiles of attorneys failed to shake in any detail.

Before and after Blixt's confession Mayor Eustis and both county and city officers were literally besieged with would-be witnesses. As in all such cases many were publicity-loving cranks who attempted to make something out of things seen

---

[8] This spot is not far from the present entrance to the Minnekahda Club.

and heard in order to get their names into the newspapers.
These were soon weeded out, and more than forty men and
women volunteered or were brought to the courthouse to give
small pieces of apparently unrelated evidence which, when
pieced together with the confession of Blixt and the admis-
sions of Adry Hayward, showed Harry Hayward to be more
of a monster than a man.[9]

These witnesses included a round dozen of insurance agents,
several bankers, a trance medium, a couple of gamblers, a bartender or two, an elevator operator, employees of Miss Ging's
shop, the mother and father of the Hayward boys, a prominent attorney, a crossing watchman, a jewelry-store clerk, a
pawnbroker, livery-stable employees, and young boys and
girls who had been skating on Lake Calhoun on the night of
December 3.

The prosecuting attorney for Hennepin County was Frank
M. Nye, a State-of-Mainer with a fierce mustache, a sound
knowledge of law, and a vast liking for fine-cut tobacco. He
took a sizable chew of his favorite brand and prepared to
marshal what at first must have looked like a chaotic haystack
of tangled evidence. The trial began in late January. Harry
Hayward was the first to be tried and his father permanently
impoverished himself to secure as counsel a battery of legal
lights headed by the redoubtable W. W. Erwin, called the
Tall Pine of Minnesota, probably the most celebrated criminal
lawyer in the Twin Cities of the day.

4

The trial proved that the dim Blixt had been a frightened,
unwilling tool in the hands of Harry Hayward. It absolved
Adry Hayward from any part in the crime. It showed that

---

9 The irrepressible Ignatius Donnelly, author of *Caesar's Column* and of *The
Great Cryptogram,* ex-Congressman, and in 1894 running a newspaper, came out
with an editorial advising that Harry Hayward be hanged at once. If Hayward
were acquitted, Donnelly said, the public had better turn to and hang Hayward's attorneys. Donnelly was never short of ideas.

Kitty Ging, for all her shrewd and excellent qualities as a businesswoman, had been a pitiful dupe for Hayward. "When a woman of thirty falls in love," Hayward had often remarked to his brother, "she is a fool, an easy mark." And the trial served to strip Harry Hayward of his irresponsible, hail-fellow covering and to exhibit a mind and character that were fearful to contemplate. If nature really does imitate art, then the unbelievably cruel and callous villains of novels and melodramas made a perfect model for Harry Hayward. But not even in the rankest fiction does one often meet the equal in all-around duplicity and cold-bloodedness of this country boy turned tinhorn gambler.

Courtroom oratory in 1895 was in fullest flower—one reason why the stenographic report of the Hayward trial ran to four hundred and ninety-six large pages of small, close type. Here, for instance, are a few of the nine hundred and sixty-five words which Assistant Prosecutor Hall used to describe the legally unimportant fact of the finding of Miss Ging's body:

> There on that lonely road but a moment or two before, the spirit of Catherine Ging had taken its flight, ushered without warning, without thought, on her part, into the presence of her Maker while the silent stars looked down in pity from the gray heavens overhead, and the winds blowing from the frozen bosom of Lake Calhoun sighed her requiem as they passed through the tops of the tamarack trees.

But it was no such oratory that convicted Harry Hayward. One after the other, in deadly monotony, the witnesses trooped to the stand, had their brief say of dull, hard facts, and left nothing undone—not even an ounce of doubt—except a job for the public hangman.

Miss Ging and Hayward met first in January of 1894 when she rented a flat at the Ozark—owned by Hayward, Senior—where Harry also lived, almost wholly on the family's bounty. She was of stunning appearance, a fine businesswoman; and it is probable that she had never been in what is rather loosely termed "love." Hayward, as said, was a handsome, strapping fellow who had acquired the thin polish of a tinhorn gambler. And—but it is always futile to attempt to know what attracts a woman to a man, and vice versa. Hayward took Kitty Ging to supper, to the theater, for buggy rides, and the evidence indicated that the woman, even though she may not have known it, paid for all these outings.

Hayward was not long in finding out that the girl had ready money. He bragged to her how easy money could be made at gambling. She gave him money, as said, to place for her in faro and roulette. Sometimes he allowed her to win; more often she lost—really lost. Doubtless she loved Hayward, loved him wholeheartedly. She must have loved him much, almost to insanity, to do the things she did later in the year. As for Hayward, he simply never could have loved anyone but himself. All he did was to "make love" to the girl. She was always ready to make him loans, not one of which he ever repaid.

The reader knows that on a buggy ride around Lake Calhoun in the summer Hayward, Miss Ging, and two other young persons were "held up" by an alleged highwayman. It is easy to believe, and considerable evidence was collected (but was not permitted in court) to show that Hayward himself staged this robbery through an accomplice, with the hope that Miss Ging would be carrying a large sum of money that day.

Hayward learned from Miss Ging that she held a mortgage of eighteen hundred dollars on a small flour mill at Hamel, a village near Minneapolis. Conversation brought out the fact that the mill had no fire insurance. Acting as her agent, Hayward had a policy written. Not long after, the mill was destroyed by fire "of undetermined origin." Miss Ging received the insurance money. Hayward soon had the money himself.

How much Hayward "borrowed" from the girl who was so shrewd in business dealings but so trusting in friendship will never be known. It was more than three thousand dollars. It may have run to twice that figure. And all or nearly all of it

went into the bank, the faro banks. Hayward was always broke,
or near it, and twice was so short as to pawn things.

Meanwhile Kitty Ging was pining for marriage, but Hayward put it off. Miss Ging's niece, Mary Ireland, testified she
often saw her aunt attempt to fondle this ratty male; but it
only bored him, at best, and sometimes he was rough, telling
her to "lay off," pushing her aside. From the evidence given,
one is prepared to believe there were never intimate relations
between the couple.

The summer thus wore on, with Hayward borrowing whatever ready cash Miss Ging had and also becoming tired of her
endearments. It was probably at this period that he began lay-
ing plans for a job which would accomplish several things. It
would rid him of the obligations for the money of which he had
bilked Miss Ging. It would rid him of Miss Ging herself. And if
he played it well and carefully it would give him what he liked
to call "a wad of dough" from the life insurance he would have
his victim take out and assign to him.

The build-up for the crime was most elaborate and occupied
much of Hayward's time for five months. He casually took the
girl to a trance medium whom he had previously "fixed," and
this seer told Miss Ging that whatever transactions she had
with Hayward would be wonderfully successful. He urged her to
enlarge her dressmaking shop and, while her ready ambitions
were contemplating the sort of place this would be, he consulted
twelve different insurance agents about the best sort of policy
"a friend of mine should take out to cover a big loan." He
brought up the matter of death by suicide; death by accident,
such as drowning; death while defending one's self against robbery, rape, or other assault. He also learned about the niceties
of assignment of policies and other affairs usually set in small
type. By the time he was done he could have written quite a
treatise, and authoritative, on What a Man Contemplating
Murder of a Policy Holder Ought to Know.

Next he managed a complexity of ostensible financial dealings between himself and Miss Ging. But these dealings were on paper only, and his great influence over the usually shrewd girl is indicated by the plain idiocy, so far as she was concerned, of all the documents she signed.[10] She put her name to notes that said she had borrowed from—not lent to—Hayward certain sums of money. With her knowledge and connivance he wrote her formal demands for return of these phony loans, dating the letters as best suited his purpose; and she replied to these demands, in writing, stating that she could not then pay. He had her engage a safe-deposit box and arranged for her to be seen putting large rolls of alleged currency into the box, along with his letters demanding payments of the notes she had signed. On several occasions, in front of friends and waiters in a popular restaurant, she displayed, no doubt at his bidding, large sums of alleged money.

Likely most of this currency was counterfeit. "Green goods" were alluded to several times during the trial and, although nothing definite was established, it was common talk that Hayward was "playing around" with a counterfeiting gang.

He next proposed that he and Miss Ging take out life-insurance policies in favor of each other. The girl did so, taking two policies of five thousand dollars each, and Hayward made certain that she signed riders conveying the insurance money to him. He, too, made motions of taking out a policy. Like everything else he laid hand to, it was a fake.

During these arrangements and many more Hayward was also preparing what was to be the instrument of death. This was the dim-witted Claus Blixt. Each day for more than two months he spent some time with this man, the furnaceman at the Ozark Flats. Blixt was basically honest, but he had little mind of his own. Hayward bullied him into setting fire to a

---

10 In its account of the Ging–Hayward case, which you may be assured overlooked no possibilities, *The National Police Gazette* referred to Hayward as "The Minneapolis Svengali" and stated that he had held Kitty Ging "in the awful bonds of his hypnotic power."

barn on Hennepin Avenue and gave him ten dollars. He then scared the daylights out of Blixt by promising him "ten years in the state pen for arson" if Blixt did not do his bidding.

His bidding, of course, was the murder of Kitty Ging. But Blixt proved more difficult than Hayward had thought possible. Arson, even robbery—but murder, no. Blixt was horrified at the thought. Hayward must have been discouraged for a time, for he went to work on his brother Adry. Adry was a plodder, a man of little ambition and no imagination. After telling him several wild tales of the men he had killed "in Chicago and other places," Harry said that killing a human did not result in haunting memories. It was no more than killing a dog, he said. Finally he made the out-and-out proposition: if Adry would kill a certain woman, Harry would give him two thousand dollars.

At first Adry did not believe that his tall-talking brother was in earnest. But Harry continued to urge and to bully him by turns and finally said all right, never mind, he had found a man—a man with nerve—who was going to do the job. He even told Adry it was Blixt. This was when Adry went to Elder Stewart a few days before the murder and was told to forget it.

Harry Hayward never really got the assent of Blixt to the murder. On December 1 he went to Blixt and told him that on Monday night next he must perform the duty—his duty, which was to kill a woman. If he did just as Harry said, it could never be detected; and there was two thousand dollars in it for him. If he didn't do it, Hayward was going to kill Mrs. Blixt. The promise of money seemed not to move the simpleton, but threats about his wife scared him no end. He begged with tears in his eyes that his wife be left out of everything.

Hayward went ahead, doubtless knowing that now he could impose even murder on the man. To give Blixt a look at the woman he was to kill—and also a look at some ready cash— Hayward had Blixt come to the Oneida Block, ostensibly to get a throttle valve needed for the Ozark furnace. Here Blixt saw

Miss Ging and "a big pile of money on a table" and was asked to witness the signatures of Hayward and the girl on one of the many fake notes between them, about which Blixt knew nothing. Then Hayward took him on a shopping trip to buy the valve.[11]

Events now moved swiftly and smoothly toward the night of Monday, December 3.

5

Early on Monday morning, before even the early-rising furnaceman was out of bed, Harry Hayward went to see him. Tonight was the night, he said, the girl was to die. Blixt pleaded that he hadn't the heart to kill anyone, and he might as well have pleaded to a horned toad. He wept. Hayward replied by saying that he still had a good mind to kill Mrs. Blixt, if Blixt didn't do as he was told, then left the trembling man.

Hayward had a busy day. He called several times on Miss Ging and the two talked in private. He called on brother Adry and told him, "You'd better not stay at home tonight, for something is going to happen and your wife's word wouldn't help you in court." Just why this move was made isn't clear, unless it was to give Adry an additional feeling of having knowledge of a crime.

In front of friends and acquaintances on this day Hayward made remarks that his sweetheart, Kitty Ging, was being untrue to him, that he had learned she had taken buggy rides with other men. (To make sure that Kitty Ging would appear to be going out with other men, the rat Hayward got Kitty herself to warn Palace Livery Stable men "not to say anything to

---

[11] This shopping trip must have been quite an event in the life of the moron Blixt. He related every move in detail. Among other things that day "we bought the throttle valve at First Street and First Avenue. Then we went straight to a saloon, where there was a horse with a mustache like a man. When we come to that place we went in to look at it, and there was a lady following us in the big room, and she showed us a pig with doll's feet on, and after we looked at that took us further and we looked at alligators."

Hayward" about her hiring a buggy that night.) Hayward also remarked to friends that Miss Ging owed him a good deal of money and that he was worried about it. He took the Thomas Waterman already mentioned in tow that day and got him drunk, meanwhile moaning to Waterman about the fickleness of women and of Kitty Ging in particular. He was going to paint her as black as he could.

He met a Miss X, daughter of a well-known professional man of high standing, and told her he should like to call on her that evening. If he had finished his affairs in time, Hayward said, he would like to take Miss X to the play at the Grand Opera House that evening. Miss X was pleased and it was agreed that he should call on her, as he had done several times in the past.

Hayward made one more call, just before suppertime, on Miss Ging. They talked perhaps fifteen minutes, alone. What plans she *thought* she was helping to carry out will never be known, but she agreed to whatever they were. She promptly telephoned the Palace Stable and asked that her favorite horse, the buckskin Lucy, and a covered buggy be sent to the West Hotel [12] for her at seven o'clock.

At about the same time Kitty Ging was ordering the rig for her last buggy ride, Hayward again showed up in the furnace basement of the Ozark. "Put on your coat and come," he ordered Blixt. He put a revolver in the man's hand. It was loaded. He gave the man six extra cartridges, of the same caliber but of different length than those in the gun. "After you have killed her," he told Blixt, "you are to take out all the cartridges, both used and unused, and put these others into the gun. Throw the others away, into the furnace. Put the revolver

---

[12] This gaudy and well-built hotel was the center of the town's social and political life in the 1880s and 1890s and continued in use, although of lesser importance, until the late 1930s. When I first visited Minneapolis in 1914, it was still elegantly formidable with its brass and marble inside and its exterior of mixed Gothic, Renaissance, and Late General Grant motifs; but even then it had a flavor of the long-ago.

under the pillow of my bed in my room." Hayward then left, telling Blixt to follow him.

Blixt, bemused with a loaded gun in his hand, kept Hayward in view in the falling winter night. Hayward went out Hennepin Avenue to Kenwood Street, then turned across a vacant lot. Somewhere near Lyndale Avenue, Blixt saw a horse and buggy standing. It was Miss Ging and her rig. Blixt stood by while the man and woman talked briefly. Miss Ging apparently had not expected a third party, but she made no protest that Blixt heard. "Get in," Hayward commanded. Blixt and the woman did so. "Now drive around by Hennepin," Hayward said, "and out to Lake Street, then follow around the west side of Lake Calhoun. I will meet you. I will have a team, and when you meet the two horses we will exchange and I will take you back." This seems rather involved, but it was as near what Hayward said as the frightened Blixt could remember. Just before the two got into the buggy Hayward said to Miss Ging, "This man is one of the gang. He's in it, too." She nodded, and they drove away.

This happened after seven o'clock, possibly twenty minutes after. Hayward must have covered a lot of ground from now until eight. It is known that he went to the Ozark, went to the rooms occupied by his mother and father and passed the time of day with them. Said he thought he would go out for the evening. See a show, maybe. He then left. At two or three minutes past eight he was ringing the doorbell at the fine residence where Miss X lived with her family, many blocks from the Ozark.

Miss X was charmed. While Hayward talked with her father, she quickly got ready; and before the curtain went up at half past eight, Mr. Hayward and Miss X were sitting in two orchestra seats in the Grand Opera House. Hayward seemed to make it a point to greet many acquaintances in the audience, and to bow low to a number of women.

Lucy, the buckskin, trotted along at an even gait toward

Lake Calhoun and the tamarack swamp.[13] The vague empti-
ness of Blixt's head was filled with horror and fear. He tried
to think of something to say but couldn't. Kitty Ging asked
him "if Harry is out buying green goods," to which Blixt muttered that he didn't know—or something. All the while, Lucy,
the buckskin, was speeding along.

"And we kept going right on [said Blixt] and she kept looking for Harry at all times, and every little while she stuck out
her head, and I kept thinking it over every little while how I
could do this, and kept thinking that I would get out of the
buggy and run and leave her, and so I was thinking a way
that I should do that, get out of the buggy and leave everything, and then I thought of my wife, and that he would kill
her if I did, sure, and that is why I stayed in the buggy. And
after that she kept looking out and I could a killed her ten
times, but I could not. It was fighting with me, and at last I got
too far and she stuck her head out like this—and I raised my
revolver and shot, and I never looked where I shot or nothing,
but it just happened that I shot her where he asked the doctor
would it kill the quickest, and when I shot her, she braced back
in the buggy seat, like this, and . . ."

With a dead woman in the buggy seat Blixt became panic-
stricken. He hauled Lucy up in a quick turn and they started
back toward town on the dead run. All the man could think of
was to get that awful deed of his out of the buggy. Reaching
down, he grasped the girl's feet and heaved her out while Lucy
fled on. Somewhere near Dupont Street, Blixt stopped the
horse; tied the reins around the whipsocket; and got out, bidding Lucy go on alone. The mare turned around and looked at
the man a moment, then put her nose toward home and trotted
off.

---

[13] In giving evidence at the trial of Hayward, Harry Gilbert, barnman at the
Palace Stable, referred to Lucy as "a clever pretty mare, and a good roader."
No taxicab company will ever know the pride livery-stable men took in their
horses and rigs.

Blixt made his way to a streetcar, stopping once—for an alibi—to talk with a crossing watchman. Soon as he got to the Ozark he changed the cartridges as instructed by Hayward, put the gun under Hayward's pillow (where Hayward got and cleaned it next day), then went off to collect a small sum from a man and to leave a watch at a store for repairs—all for alibi purposes. Then he returned home and went to bed.

Hayward saw Miss X home after the theater, then went to the Ozark Flats. He had made several mistakes already. Being confident that his brother Adry would never say a word was one error. Having Blixt witness the signatures on the fake notes was another. Speaking of being "done up—my two thousand dollars is gone" immediately on hearing of Miss Ging's death was suspicious. His complete reliance on the silence of Blixt, the moron, was certainly an error of judgment. These few errors made hash of Hayward's long and elaborate preparations.

Hayward was convicted without difficulty in a trial that occupied most of seven weeks, and he was hanged—"on a red-painted scaffold," shouted the *Police Gazette*—at twelve minutes past two o'clock on the morning of December 11, 1895. Dr. Frank Burton, county physician, said it took him thirteen minutes to die. In the highly important matter of his last words, the local papers did not agree. The *Tribune* reported that the rat chattered, "God, for Christ's sake, have mercy on my soul!"—while the *Journal's* man, who may have had imagination as well as the usual whisky, distinctly heard him say, "Pull her tight. I'll stand pat."

In his autobiography, published in the Minneapolis *Journal* in 1930, ex-Mayor William H. Eustis stated that before the trial was over Harry Hayward admitted his guilt to W. E. Hale, one of his attorneys, who then quietly withdrew from the case.

CHAPTER FIVE

TROUBLE AT CAMERON DAM

THE TROUBLE THAT CAME to Cameron Dam began elsewhere. In 1901 John F. Dietz, his wife Hattie, and a numerous family were living in an otherwise unoccupied logging camp of the Chippewa Lumber & Boom Company on the Brunnette River in Sawyer County, Wisconsin. They had moved here from Rice Lake, in adjoining Barron County, where Dietz had farmed and worked in the woods.

Near the camp on the Brunnette was a dam, known as Price Dam, used by the company for storing water for log-driving purposes; that is, for floating logs downstream from the forest to the sawmill. In the spring of 1902 John Dietz was hired by John Ryan, boss of the company's Chippewa drive, to act as a watchman at Price Dam during the periods when its gates were shut to impound water—to "get a head of water," as loggers put it.

In the meantime the Dietzes, in the name of Mrs. Dietz, purchased from the widow of Hugh L. Cameron a piece of land on the Thornapple River, and there in 1904 John Dietz and his family moved. Across the river at this point was a dam, the Cameron Dam, one end of which rested on Dietz land. On the

94

other side of the dam was a camp of the Mississippi River Logging Company.[1]

John Dietz was a large, able, and husky man, a Wisconsin native who was used to hard work. Two of his boys were big and husky, too. They cleared the land of stumps and brush. The makings of a house were already present in an old logging camp once used by Hugh Cameron's lumberjacks. This was a stanch affair, almost a fort, built of big pine logs and chinked with moss and clay. With a little work the Dietz men and women had a serviceable backwoods home, the kind that no wind would blow away. The barn was of the same solid construction, roofed with cedar shakes almost two inches thick. Dietz and his boys erected a few outbuildings, and in a slight hill back of the house they dug a deep root cellar. The old logging road was the way to the county road, thence to the village of Winter.

Not long after he moved to Cameron Dam, Dietz sought to collect wages he claimed the company owed him for services as watchman at the other dam, Price Dam, on the Brunnette. The company's superintendent, Mulligan, advised the company there was no foundation for this claim, that Dietz had been paid in full at the time he left Price Dam. Mulligan and Dietz had heated arguments and at least once came to blows.

Now Dietz posted a notice at Cameron Dam forbidding trespass on his land at the east end of the structure. When the company's men came to close the dam gates to store a head of water, Dietz warned them away. He also told the company superintendent that no more logs would go through the dam until he, Dietz, had been paid a toll of eight thousand dollars for the eighty million feet of logs he estimated had gone through since he acquired his land. When company lumberjacks allowed that they'd go ahead and sluice the six million

---

[1] For all narrative purposes the Mississippi River Logging Company, which cut the timber, and the Chippewa Lumber & Boom Company, which drove the logs to the mills, are one and the same. Henceforth I'll refer to them simply as the company.

feet of logs already behind the dam, Dietz appeared with a
rifle and told them to get out and to stay out until the company had settled with him.

Now in Wisconsin you drove logs in the spring or you didn't
drive them until the next spring. You had to have high water.
With better than six million feet of logs ready to go, the company needed to work fast. It got an injunction restraining
Dietz from interfering with operation of the dam. Dietz ignored
it, saying he "didn't take any stock in courts," and continued
to keep a sharp watch on the dam. Sawyer County now issued
a warrant for arrest of Dietz and sent two deputies, William
Giblin and William Elliot, to make the arrest.

In 1904 it was a sixty-mile trip over rough roads from Hayward, county seat, to the backwoods home of John Dietz.
Armed to the hip with revolvers and rifles—for Dietz was said
to have made powerful strong threats against any who might
try to interfere, claiming that Sawyer County laws were only
for the rich—the deputies were joined on the way by two employees of the lumber company and a farm hand. The two
lumberjacks were on their way to the company camp at Cameron Dam.

This aggregation was traveling in a wagon pulled by four
horses. The boys were lolling on bags of oats in the wagon, taking life easy, until they reached a point some three miles from
the dam. One of the horses snorted. Deputy Elliot sat up and
thought he saw a figure of a man dodge behind a stump not far
from the road. An instant later he was sure of it. The man
stepped into the open, a rifle at his shoulder. "Hands up, you
sons of bitches!" he shouted. Then he began firing.

At the same moment a second man appeared from behind
another stump and he, too, began firing at the wagon. The
horses reared up, then broke into a run. Bullets flew thick. One
took off the hat of the farm hand, a man named Giauque, and
he tumbled out of the wagon. Another bullet neatly cut the

suspenders off Deputy Elliot, shearing them clean through right under the nickel buckle that said "Hercules" on it and causing the galluses to fly out like a released spring. Two more bullets struck one of the lumberjacks on the seat of the wagon.

The team and four survivors galloped off, leaving the poor Giauque in the road. The two gunmen now came up to him; ordered him to start running back, in the general direction of Hayward; and followed the order by shooting branches from over his head as he ran.

The deputies made no further attempt to serve the warrant on Dietz; but they identified the two gunmen, in spite of blackened faces, as John Dietz and a neighboring homesteader, Valentine Weisenbach. A night or two after this affair, while loggers of the lumber company were at supper in the camp at Cameron Dam, a bullet crashed through a window and wounded one Tracy, a common lumberjack.

What happened next would indicate that John Dietz was already a man much feared by the so-called law-enforcement officers of Sawyer County. Valentine Weisenbach was promptly arrested on a charge of assault with intent to commit murder, was tried, convicted, and sent to the penitentiary. In denying a new trial for Weisenbach, Wisconsin's supreme court was "astonished" that John Dietz, whom the court held to be "the most significant figure in this affair," was not arrested, was not even brought to testify at the trial of Weisenbach. All the evidence at the latter's trial indicated that Dietz had been the directing head of the attack on the wagonload of deputies and lumberjacks.

John Dietz was now generally termed an "anarchist" in the neighborhood. This was not true, of course, but there was some reason for terming him an outlaw. Dietz was also a member of the Masonic order. An attempt was made by brother Masons to have the argument between him and the lumber company arbitrated by five past grand masters of the lodge, who would sit as a board. Dietz refused. The six million feet of logs remained in the water, behind Cameron Dam.

Early in 1905 the company got another injunction, this time from a federal court, and two United States marshals attempted to serve the papers on Dietz. He was wary. He refused service and drove the officers from his land. A warrant for arrest of Dietz, charging contempt of court, followed, and this time a posse of twenty-five United States deputy marshals went out to what was becoming known, with some reason, as Dietz's Stronghold and Fort Dietz. Dietz was ready. He told the whole posse to go to hell. Instead they returned to Hayward, where they were something of a laughingstock.

2

For the next five years John Dietz and his two rugged sons, Leslie and Clarence, ably helped by Mrs. Dietz, daughter Myra, and young Helen, managed to hold the fort against all attacks. And the attempts to arrest Dietz were many, if only halfhearted. In July of 1906, for instance, the Dietz men and women were engaged in getting a load of hay from the field to the barn. Sharp-eyed young Helen spotted some men in the woods surrounding the clearing and told her father. John dropped his fork and got a gun. He took his stand and shouted for all trespassers to get off his land.

Who started shooting is anyone's guess, but shooting there was. Clarence Dietz fell wounded. Leslie Dietz, who had fetched a rifle, opened fire and shot a deputy named Rogich, wounding him severely. Rogich swore out a warrant for arrest of Leslie Dietz. Nothing was done about serving the warrant.

The years flew by. Local administrations changed in Sawyer County and sheriff followed sheriff, each bequeathing to his successor a sheaf of warrants, injunctions, and other legal hocus-pocus concerning the persons of John and Leslie Dietz. But no real attempt to serve any of them seems to have been made. True, sheriffs Peterson, Giblin, Gylland, and Ackley, and United States Marshal Pugh, all made calls at or near the Dietz farm; but neither Dietz nor his son was ever anywhere near being in custody.

In the meantime Dietz had turned lumberman himself. He and his sons hauled a quantity of logs out of Cameron Dam, engaged a portable sawmill, and sawed the logs into enough lumber to make twenty-eight piles, which stood in the clearing back of the Dietz buildings. In the meantime, too, the lumber company, in a last effort to settle the controversy, paid Dietz the full amount of his claim for wages at Price Dam, many years before. This totaled $1717, but it made no difference with the plans of Dietz. No logs, he said, would ever go through Cameron Dam at less than ten cents a thousand feet toll. So the company, doubtless on the reasonable assumption that Sawyer County was not equal to the arrest of John Dietz, carried on its logging operations by hauling its logs overland from the Thornapple to the Flambeau River, thence down the latter to its sawmills. What finally began the train of events leading to the downfall of the Defender of Cameron Dam was an incident that had nothing to do with logs or the dam.

John Dietz believed in education. Of little schooling himself, but a great reader with retentive mind, he was a better-educated man than many townfolk in Winter, the nearest village to the Dietz home. But it was ten miles to Winter. The roads were bad at all times, almost impassable in spring and fall. In 1910 Dietz engaged a young man just out of college, Frank Gates, to tutor the Dietz children in their home.

On September 6, 1910, Dietz and son Clarence drove to Winter for the purpose of collecting from the school board an allowance for rent, fuel, and janitor service for the maintenance of a school in his home. It would appear that the Winter school board had agreed to pay for the services of the tutor, but balked at paying for "rent, heat, and janitor service" in Dietz's own home. Meeting C. G. O'Hare, president of the Winter town board, on the street, Dietz stopped him and demanded the allowance.

"We never agreed to pay for anything but the teacher," O'Hare said. They argued awhile. O'Hare was firm. At this point Bert Horel, clerk of the school board, came up, along with Joseph Buckwheat, chairman of the town board. The argument was continued. It warmed up, and somebody swung on somebody. Horel was knocked down by Dietz. He jumped up and felled Dietz. When Dietz came up he had a Luger pistol in his hand, shooting. Horel went down wounded in several places.

Dietz and son Clarence then leisurely untied their team from the hitching rack, got into their democrat wagon, and drove calmly out of town.

Bert Horel did not die.[2] And his name was added to the long list of complaints, criminal and civil, filed against John Dietz, and no doubt Dietz by this time thought that filing is all the Horel complaint ever would amount to.

But Sawyer County had a new prosecuting attorney and a new high sheriff, respectively J. C. Davis and Mike Madden. They looked at the stack of warrants for Dietz's arrest that ran back for a period of six years. Putting the brand-new Horel warrant in his pocket, Sheriff Madden started for the Dietz place. He was stopped by a neighboring homesteader, who warned him that Dietz and his sons had prepared an ambush. Madden went no farther, but sent the neighbor to tell Dietz to come out and give himself up peaceably. Dietz sent word to Madden to come in and get him.

Sheriff Madden and Prosecutor Davis really weren't fooling. They knew they had a clever man and a dead shot to deal with. The sheriff knew some other clever men and dead shots. He deputized Roy Van Alstine, woodsman-farmer of near Winter,

---

[2] A. C. (Bert) Horel died at Rice Lake, Wisconsin, late in November of 1932, at which time he was described as a "prominent logger."

and Fred Thorbahm, of Radisson, former lumberjack. These men had the reputation of being the best rifleshots in the county.

Making their headquarters at Van Alstine's farm, only a few miles from Fort Dietz, these two men and Sheriff Madden took turns watching the Dietz place from hide-outs in the timber. On October 1 the watchers observed that Dietz and part of his family were making preparations for a trip to town. The women put up a lunch, as was the custom in those days, and the boys were hitching up the team. Dietz himself appeared to be getting ready to go too. Waiting no longer, Madden and his two deputies went back down the road some two miles, picked out a good, likely place, and hid.

An hour later the hidden men heard the team coming. In it were only the three oldest children—Clarence, Leslie, and Myra. Madden had thoughtfully brought along warrants for arrest of the entire family, so now he stepped into the road and commanded the team to halt and the occupants to throw up their hands. What happened next is another one of those things. Sheriff Madden said later that the moment he appeared the boys reached for their rifles. The boys said they didn't do any such thing. There is no doubt about what the deputies did; they fired. And there is no doubt that firing was as idiotic a thing as they could have done.

Clarence Dietz was hit in the left arm. Myra was struck above the hips through the fleshy part of the back. Leslie, gun in hand, tumbled out of the wagon and struck into the woods, while bullets whistled close.

From the viewpoint of law and order nothing much worse could have happened than the wounding of these adolescents. No doubt the sheriff's party had reason to be quick on the trigger. The Dietz boys were known to be dead shots and not at all prone to be backward about shooting. Earned or not, even Myra had the reputation of being a mean shot. But you just can't shoot a young woman, especially a rather good-looking young woman, and not suffer certain aftereffects from a romantic public.

The arrival of the sheriff's party with the wounded young people made a noise in small Winter. Myra was taken to the hotel and given medical attention. Clarence's wounds were bandaged and he was placed in jail. Sheriff Madden immediately ordered all saloons closed and swore in and armed twelve additional deputies, giving them orders to watch every entrance to the village lest John Dietz himself come to shoot up the town and take his children. That was how John Dietz stood in Winter, or at least in the eyes of the sheriff.

Myra was taken by automobile—an event in 1910—to Hayward and from there on a cot in a baggage car to Ashland hospital, where her wounds, though painful, were found not to be dangerous.[3]

Dangerous or not, the wounds of Myra Dietz put Prosecutor Davis, Sheriff Madden, and their deputies in an unenviable spot. It was the old case of beauty in distress. The big city newspapers of Milwaukee, Chicago, St. Paul, and Minneapolis put it on the front pages, and some of the reports gave the impression that a big, nasty sheriff and a crowd of almost as big and nasty deputies had lain in ambush to shoot at three innocent children driving to town to sell a few eggs. Moreover, had wounded and almost killed two of them. The affair sounded very brutal.

Well, all this left John Dietz right where he had been—in command of his stronghold at Cameron Dam. Leslie was with him still; so was Mrs. Dietz, who many believed was a better shot with a rifle than the old man himself, and Helen, aged ten, and another younger child.

Sheriff Madden prepared to take the stronghold by siege or

---

[3] The wife of an upper Wisconsin judge was in St. Joseph's Hospital at Ashland at the same time. She recalls that Myra Dietz lay on her cot surrounded by flowers and other gifts and flanked by her bloody corset, and received scores of well-wishers daily.

attack, or both. He swore in a small army of deputies, picking the best shots he could find in Winter, Hayward, Radisson, and other near-by towns. He placed these men at strategic points along the road to the Dietz farm and around the Dietz clearing as well. He ordered the post office to stop all mail for the family, and prevented newspapermen, who were beginning to arrive from the big cities, from going to talk to Dietz.

By October 5 the sheriff had his army in position. Headquarters was an abandoned logging camp, where a cookhouse was set up and the old bunks furnished with straw and bedding. Deputies worked in reliefs, like soldiers on guard, and there were scouts, patrols, and sentinels. Such elaborate preparations for a major battle could not be made without other newspaper editors hearing of them. The press was quick to respond. On the day set for the attack almost as many reporters as deputies were at the scene, among them a brash young man from the Twin Cities named Floyd Gibbons. It was to be the noted newspaperman's first big story.[4]

On the night of October 5 the woods around the Dietz clearing were abristle with rifles, unseen by Dietz but doubtless suspected by him. The hidden men watched while Helen Dietz drove the cows to the barn for the evening milking.

3

Down in Madison, state capital, Governor J. O. Davidson had received hundreds of appeals by letter, wire, and telephone to do something to prevent the bloodshed seemingly assured at Cameron Dam. To John Dietz the governor sent two envoys— his own private secretary, Colonel O. G. Munson, and Attorney General Frank L. Gilbert. Escorted to the edge of the Dietz clearing on October 6, these two men, waving white handkerchiefs, walked alone toward the cabin while armed men in the

---

4 Years later Gibbons told a friend that the Battle of Cameron Dam was one of the most dramatic events he had ever covered.

woods watched for any hostile movement on the part of Dietz and son Leslie.

As the two envoys extraordinary approached the stronghold, Dietz appeared at a window and from there talked to the visitors. They exchanged courtesies, and a bit later Dietz came out, a gun in his belt, and the three parleyed. Speaking for the State of Wisconsin, Gilbert told Dietz that if he would give himself up peaceably he would be assured a fair trial in any county of the state he chose. Further, that all criminal charges against Dietz except for the shooting of Horel would be dropped.

Dietz seemed in no mood to surrender. He replied to Gilbert that he would not give himself up unless he were promised that the state would "clear up the other dirt," by which was meant the civil charges against him, and unless the state would compel the lumber company to "pay what they owe me for sluicing logs through Cameron Dam."

The attorney general replied that these were things that could not be promised, that they were matters of litigation for the courts to settle. Dietz said bluntly that he had no faith in courts. At the close of the interview the attorney general asked Dietz to accept a letter he bore from the governor, in which his promise of a fair trial in any county in the state appeared in writing. Dietz would not accept the letter, so the attorney general left it on a window sill of the cabin and the envoys returned to the besieging forces in the woods. No attempt to attack was made during the night of October 6. Sentinels remained at post, watching the Dietz buildings, and next morning the attorney general and the governor's secretary made another visit to the cabin. Dietz had not changed his mind. The courts, the officers, even all of his own neighbors, were against him, he said. He would make his stand and defend his home against all comers. Attorney General Gilbert then pleaded with Dietz to send his wife and younger children out to Winter Village, promising that they should have the best of care. "There is going to be trouble here," Gilbert said, "and we don't want your family to be hurt." Dietz replied he didn't think any of his family wanted to leave; and his wife said no, that they'd remain. The governor's men then went away.

One more attempt, this time by Sawyer County authorities, was made to induce Dietz to surrender. Fred Thorbahm, chief deputy sheriff, sent a note to him under flag of truce, promising to use a field gun if necessary to take the fort.[5] Dietz replied in effect that he was going to fight it out on the line he had adopted if it took all fall, and maybe all winter.

The truce was over. Raising a small American flag aloft on a pole at his cabin, the Defender of Cameron Dam and his family prepared to do battle with the forces of Sawyer County and the State of Wisconsin.

The night of the seventh was frosty, and quiet. Through an early-morning fog the watching deputies saw a figure driving the Dietz cows to the barn for milking, but they could not tell whether it was Dietz or one of his children. Gradually a bright sun beat through the mist, leaving mere small eddies of fog here and there over the clearing and the river. Shooting began a little after nine o'clock. Who fired first isn't known, and it doesn't matter much. Deputy Angus Campbell was one of the earliest to let go. With Deputies Colpitts and Rankin he had taken a stand on a slight rise of ground that commanded most of the clearing. It wasn't a very brilliant thing to do, but just for the fun of it, as he explained later, he took a shot at a grindstone that sat near the cabin door. Before his own smoke

---

[5] Thorbahm's note survives in the archives at Sawyer County courthouse, and is as follows: "John Dietz, you had better surrender it will be for the best for yourself and family you will be treated right and get a Square Deal. there is no way for you to win any other way. I have you surrounded completely and we will get you if we have to tunnell to your house or use a field [gun.] you will never get a message in or out if it takes until spring. I mean what I say. F. W. Thorbahm, Deputy Sheriff."

had cleared, a bullet fanned Colpitt's ear and another almost tore the hat off Rankin. The return fire seemed to be coming from the Dietz barn.

A few minutes later other deputies saw Leslie Dietz on the far side of the clearing. They didn't know what he was doing, but they opened fire. The youth ran like a deer back for the cabin, while bullets made the dirt fly at his feet. Another group —the woods was literally filled with armed men—sighted the old man himself between the barn and the lumber piles. They let go a volley, and Dietz was seen to fall forward onto the ground. Just as the deputies rose up to get a better view, Dietz leaped to his feet and ran for the cabin. He made it and slammed the door, while bullets thudded into the log sides of the structure.

The battle was on in earnest. Chief Deputy Thorbahm and Deputy Van Alstine forded the Thornapple above Cameron Dam and took positions on a tiny island. Deputies Britton and Holland were hidden on high ground across the river. Deputy Paulson and one other were secreted in the wooded peninsula above the dam, a point about as close as one could get to the buildings and remain in cover.

Cover was needed. Old man Dietz had last been seen running into the house, but it was now apparent that he or Leslie had got into the barn loft; for somebody in the loft had moved a few of the thick roofing shakes to make portholes, and whenever any of the dozens of attackers showed themselves bullets trimmed the bushes near by.

Not only cover but care was needed. One group of deputies, crawling through the brush to get into position, were fortunate to notice, before it was too late, two large steel bear traps, with yawning sharp-toothed jaws, set and ready to crunch shut on a man's leg or arm. It was the sort of thing to cause a man to move slowly in the woods around the Dietz place.

By now probably more than fifteen hundred persons, including some forty newspapermen and sixty armed deputies, were in the surrounding woods.

Sheriff Madden detailed four deputies—James Pomerlo, Oscar Harp, Walter Bonk, and Ernest Mewhorter—to advance, under cover of the lumber piles, to a point where they could do some good shooting into the barn loft and thus dislodge Dietz or his son, whichever it was, from this vantage point.

The four men crawled out of the timber and began their wormlike way, squirming along on their bellies in the grass. They hadn't gone far when Oscar Harp was heard to gasp, and at the same instant the report of rifle fire echoed in the clearing. Harp's head rocked back on his shoulders. Blood splurted from his mouth. The other three men of the detail jumped to their feet and ran for the piles of lumber. Poor Oscar Harp was back there in the field, quite dead.

In the shadow of the lumber piles the three deputies thought themselves comparatively safe. They paused to take stock, and Deputy Mewhorter's eye was taken by a copper wire that ran along a foot or so above the ground. "Look out!" he cried as Deputy Bonk was about to step into the wire. He was just in time. The wire proved to be fifty feet long and ran along three piles of lumber. At the other end was a double-barreled shotgun, cocked and loaded with buckshot. The deputies cut the wire.

Desultory gunfire marked the rest of the morning. The bright sun became warm as it passed the meridian, and shooting slacked as deputies grabbed quick lunches. By two o'clock all were back on the firing line, determined to blast the old man from his position in the barn—or that is where they thought he was, although no one could be sure. He had a good stock of smokeless ammunition.

Gunfire from the surrounding cover now became general, and it increased in intensity. Bullets tore shakes off the barn roof and splintered others by the score. Fire rained down on the entrance to the root cellar. Hundreds of slugs continued to thud into the log house. Its stovepipe was a sieve. All outbuildings were peppered, too. No one went after the dead man in the field, for Dietz was keeping a close watch on his many enemies. Whenever one showed himself, a bullet whizzed near. At least two deputies were sure they saw Mrs. Dietz step from behind a corner of the house, a gun in her hands, and fire.

It was plain hell on the inside of the Dietz cabin that day. One by one and in batches the dishes were shot off the kitchen table, off the shelves. Early in the afternoon Dietz came into the house, his left hand bleeding. A bullet had struck him, but his trigger hand was still all right. While Mrs. Dietz bandaged the wound, bullets continued to rake the house. A framed picture of the family on the wall was shot through and through. Bullets crashed into the family pride, an organ, splintering its sides and shooting out the stops and keys. Quilts on the beds were covered with spent bullets fallen from against the thick walls.

Rolled in a blanket, young John, aged six, was behind the stove, crying. White-faced Helen, soon to play a very brave part, looked on. Leslie was in and out of the house but was never hit, nor were any of the family except John, Senior.

In midafternoon the attacking army, which little by little was closing in, getting into better positions, saw small Helen come out the door of the house, the flutter of a white flag on a stick in her hand. All firing ceased.

Waving her little flag and walking rapidly, Helen made her way down through the clearing to the Thornapple while the silent army watched. Sheriff Madden thought it a ruse of Dietz to get deputies to expose themselves. He ordered everybody to remain out of sight.

On ran the little girl, the small flag fluttering. She crossed the narrow footbridge above Cameron Dam and made her way up through the mixed woods and clearing on the far side of the river. She never faltered but went on up the rise and into the timber, where the sheriff and others met her.

Holding back the tears with difficulty, the brave youngster told the officers that her father had been wounded and that he was ready to give himself up. "If Papa comes out," she asked, "will you promise not to shoot him?" The sheriff gave his promise, but he told the girl that Dietz and Leslie must come out of the house, their hands high, and walk to where the sheriff was. Helen started back for the cabin.

In the meantime Father Pilon, Catholic priest, left the deputies and ran toward the Dietz house, waving a handkerchief. He went inside, came out again, and ran back to the deputies to tell them that Dietz was bleeding badly and needed medical attention. Dr. G. F. Grafton of Hayward, who said he had come out to the scene because he figured he would be needed, accompanied the priest back to the house.

Dr. Grafton found John Dietz and family in the cabin. Dietz was covered with blood. He asked for a drink of whisky. By the time his hand was bandaged Deputy Thorbahm arrived. He noted that Dietz still wore a gun. Covering Dietz with his own rifle, the deputy yelled for someone to disarm Dietz. Leslie Dietz did so.

Seven guns were found on the premises, which were in truly terrible condition from the six-hour fusillade from the army. Empty shells in the barn loft indicated that most of the Dietz fire had come from there, but empty shells were found in the cabin, too, and near the root cellar. It was estimated that a total of some twenty-five hundred rounds had been fired by both sides.

Deputy Thorbahm put handcuffs on the two Dietz men; and in spite of protests from Helen, Mrs. Dietz was manacled. The family were taken to Winter and on to Hayward, where the reason soon became known why John Dietz, the man who said he would die "defending" his farm, had given up: Mrs. Dietz

was on the way to being a mother again. The poor woman broke
down and wept. "I'm sick; I'm so sick," she cried. "If I had
not kept arguing with John we all should have been killed before morning."

Incidentally, the Dietz family were not the only ones in
custody. Young and brash Floyd Gibbons, sent to Cameron
Dam by the *Tribune* of Minneapolis, was in jail at Hayward,
charged with having wrecked the telephone wires out of that
town—after he had filed his own story of the battle.

4

In May a year later John Dietz conducted his own trial in
Sawyer County court at Hayward. Conducted it very ably, so
the Wisconsin Supreme Court thought later when it denied a
new trial. "Mr. Dietz addressed the jury in his own behalf evi-
dently with fluence and force," said the high court. "An argument of this nature by a man whose liberty is hanging in the
balance may well appeal to an American jury with greater
force than the argument of a skillful lawyer."

The twelve hundred pages of transcript show that John
Dietz, the unschooled backwoodsman, indeed defended himself
with force and fluence. "If it please the court and gentlemen of
the jury," he cried in stating his case, "there can be no higher
duty devolved upon the father and husband than the protection of his home and family. This is a corporation conspiracy
that started in the spring of 1904."

His specific defense against the charge of killing Oscar Harp
was that Harp was shot by other deputies unknowingly; that
the death-bringing bullet had been fired not from the barn but
from the far side of the river; that its trajectory had been over
the lumber piles and thence into Oscar Harp's mouth and body,
until it struck a thigh bone.

Questioning and cross-questioning witnesses for the state,
Dietz with subtle skill sought to discredit them one after another. And throughout the trial he attempted to show that the

death of Oscar Harp was merely the front of a gigantic conspiracy, begun and fostered by the lumber company and entered into by Sawyer County officials, by United States marshals and courts, by the governor of Wisconsin's envoys, by Dietz's very own neighbors at Cameron Dam and Winter.

Attorney General Gilbert summed it up, correctly perhaps, in one sentence. "John Dietz is fairly obsessed," he said, "that every man's hand is raised against him."

A jury found Dietz guilty. He was sentenced to life imprisonment at Waupun. The others of the family were freed. Later the Dietz children appeared on the stage, and also were "heroes" of a moving picture which was claimed to be a true relation of the events at the Battle of Cameron Dam.

Ten years later John Dietz was pardoned by Governor Blaine; he died in 1924 in a Milwaukee hospital, with his wife, three sons, and two daughters at his bedside.

Part of the tragedy would appear to have been due to an error, or at least a misunderstanding, between Mrs. Hattie Dietz and the widow of Hugh L. Cameron, from whom Mrs. Dietz bought the land at Cameron Dam. The record shows that the dam was built in 1874 by Daniel Shaw under a charter from the State of Wisconsin. Shaw owned only the dam, but from Barrows & Leavitt, who owned the land, he secured perpetual right to build and maintain the dam. In subsequent transfers of the land a reservation always appeared in the deeds, and this reservation was "the right to maintain all improvements on said lands erected for the purposes of log driving and to operate said improvements for the purposes of driving logs on the Thornapple River and its tributaries."

But when the transfer of this land was made from the Widow Cameron to Mrs. Hattie Dietz, the reservation of the right to maintain the dam and to flow the land was inadvertently omitted. The record is clear that Mrs. Cameron owned the land she sold *only* subject to the right of the lumber company to use the dam. Thus Mrs. Dietz may have had a just claim against

Mrs. Cameron but not against the lumber company. It was a tragic misunderstanding.

The Battle of Cameron Dam is solidly entrenched in the folklore of northern Wisconsin, as well it should be.

The old Dietz place is a picture of desolation today. In the early 1930s some sort of religious group, with the idea of subsistence farming, started to found a colony there. They erected a halfhearted cabin but then seem to have thought better of it, and they went away. That left only a colony of beavers, and they appear set for a long time to come. Right handy to their dam are sizable clumps of small willow, birch, and alder—enough material to keep them in food and building timbers for many years.

CHAPTER SIX

MURDER AT BAD AXE

IN MAY OF 1909 John Wesley Sparling and his numerous family were alive and apparently in the best of health. Besides John Wesley there were his wife, Carrie, four sons, and one daughter. They lived on the Sparling farm near the hamlet of Ubly, six miles or so from Bad Axe, Michigan.

John Wesley Sparling was forty-seven years old, a hard-working, God-fearing farmer of above average intelligence. His kindly face had eyes set far apart, and his heavy black beard, in 1909, marked him as a man who held fast to the verities—a man who was not to be seduced by the passing fancy of the currently stylish mustache. Able and prosperous men in John Wesley's youth all had worn beards, hence John Wesley wore a beard.

But for all his rustic traditionalism John W. Sparling was an up-to-date farmer. His broad, level acres were plowed and harvested with the best modern machinery. There was a horse-fork in his barn for unloading hay. His barn, like his house, was spick-and-span. He paid all his bills on the day they were due, and he always had a little money in the bank. The merchants of Ubly and Bad Axe liked to see John Sparling or any of his family come into their places of business.

The four boys were Peter, Albert, Scyrel,[1] and Ray. The daughter was May, as good-looking a girl as could be found in the county.

The four boys were strapping fellows, able to swing a scythe around the edges of the fields where the Buckeye mowing machine couldn't reach, to split a cord of wood, and to heave a tumble of hay to the top and center of the biggest load the Sparling hayrick could hold. The daily work of the farm was hardly enough to keep the boys in trim, and for needed exercise it was their custom to climb the long rope of the horse-fork in the Sparling barn, hand over hand, and to chin themselves on the ridgepole before they returned to the floor. There wasn't a weakling among them.

But work on the farm was not all of the life of the Sparlings. They were sent to school at Ubly, then to Bad Axe High; and every Sunday found all the family in Ubly church.

One day in June of 1909, just when haying was getting under way, John Wesley Sparling did something he had never done before. At work in the field he complained of not feeling well. Said he thought he'd go to the house and lie down for a few minutes. He did so, and he never got up again. After a week of vomiting and purging during which he received the devoted attention of Dr. John MacGregor, the family physician, John Sparling died.

The kindly folk of Ubly and Bad Axe crowded the little church to hear the parson pay tribute to a farmer and a Christian. Sad as John Sparling's death was, it did not leave the family in bad straits at all. Peter Sparling, twenty-five, stepped into his father's shoes—or almost. Peter took charge of the actual farm work, but in all things calling for planning and judgment he was advised by his mother; and she, in turn, it soon became evident, was advised by the family physician.

Asking for and accepting the advice of a family physician

---

[1] Apparently a fancy spelling for "Cyril."

in things other than health was not unusual. In fact, it probably came nearer to being a custom of the time and place. If no
lawyer was a close friend to a widow, and even if one was, it was
common for the widow to lean somewhat on the family doctor.

Dr. John MacGregor was a man to lean on, an energetic
and upstanding figure. Six feet tall, weighing one hundred and
ninety pounds, he was an athlete as well as a physician and
often played baseball on the Bad Axe town team. He was a
Canadian by birth, thirty-six years old, handsome, and married. He and Xenophon A. Boomhower, the rising young
attorney of Bad Axe, were close friends. Just before he died
John Wesley Sparling had called Attorney Boomhower to his
bedside to will the Sparling farm and all his other property
to Mrs. Sparling.

About a month after John Wesley's death the subject of life
insurance was discussed by the Widow Sparling and Dr. Mac-
Gregor. None of the boys was insured. Presently all of them
were. The policies were for one thousand dollars each and were
written in the Sun Life Assurance Company of Canada by Dr.
MacGregor's father, who had an insurance agency in London,
Ontario, just across Lake Huron. Dr. MacGregor was the
examining physician and he must have found the boys to be
in perfect health, for all were accepted without question.

Life on the farm went on as usual, with Peter, the eldest boy,
nominally in charge and with Albert delivering milk from the
Sparling cows to the citizens of Ubly and Bad Axe. Dr. Mac-
Gregor called at the farm every few days and spent a good
deal of time with the widow, who was suffering from an eye ail-
ment. Life insurance seemed to be getting a good deal of
thought at the Sparlings'. In January of 1910 Dr. MacGregor
again examined the boys for policies, this time in the Gleaners
Insurance Company. The policies were written by Dr. Mac-
Gregor's father.

Haying time came again. Right in the middle of it, when
the Sparling fields were lined with long windrows of drying

clover, Peter Sparling had a "sick spell." He must have felt ill to leave those fields at such a time.[2] But leave he did, and he went to the house to "lie down a few minutes." Dr. Mac-Gregor was called. Five days later Peter, aged twenty-six, passed to his reward, and again friends and neighbors gathered at the Ubly church for obsequies.

Albert now became the nominal head of the family. One fine Sunday in May of 1911, when the Sparlings were in their accustomed pew in the little church, Albert began to feel ill. He managed to stick out the long service, and even stayed for Sunday school. It was well for his soul that he did; for in spite of the close attention of Dr. MacGregor, Albert died five days later after much vomiting and purging.

The *Huron County Tribune* printed condolences, and the usual "Card of Thanks" from the much-bereaved family.

It was at this period that John Sparling, a relative of this family that was getting to be known as the dying Sparlings, made a remark that will not die so long as the people of Bad Axe have memories. This John Sparling was a practicing veterinarian, a rough-and-ready character known all over Huron County for the marvels he performed with sick horses and cattle and swine and for the manner in which he handled a spaying knife. He was also a man given to forthright utterances. When he was informed of the rather sudden death of Albert, the third within two years, Doc John Sparling delivered an opinion. "By Jesus!" he said. "I don't like the way things are going. I figure all ain't well there."

So far as either the record or the folklore of the place goes, this was the first known remark on the suddenness and continuity of death in the household of Mrs. Carrie Sparling. Nothing came of the remark, though. And a bit later Mrs. Carrie Sparling bought a nice house in Ubly village.

---

[2] When a real farmer leaves the hayfield in midday, it is for no light reason. I have known farmers with cancer, with heart trouble, with lungs half gone, to stick out a good hay-day until dark, no matter the pain they were in.

Mrs. Sparling and her family did not move into the Ubly house. She remained on her farm, and so did her diminishing brood. Dr. John MacGregor and wife moved into Mrs. Sparling's village house. Folks talked a bit, then forgot it.

Out on the farm young Scyrel Sparling was now the man of the house. That is, he bossed the younger Ray in doing the necessary work. As usual, Dr. MacGregor was often at the farm treating Mrs. Sparling for her eye trouble, which seemed to get no better, and advising the widow on farm and business matters. Was it going to rain or freeze? These two guesses, on which so much of a farmer's work depends, were not left to Scyrel. Forecasts of the weather were left to Dr. MacGregor, and so were the sale of pigs and calves and the selection of the best time to plow and sow.

Not long after Albert Sparling's death Dr. MacGregor appeared in an automobile which he purchased in Bad Axe. In 1911 motor vehicles were something of a novelty in Huron County. Horses still had to be led past them, snorting with fear, and farm and town folks alike ran to their windows when one was heard tearing its way along the dusty roads.

Simply buying an automobile was reason enough for comment in those days, and to this fact was soon added the knowledge that to pay for his car Dr. MacGregor had given John Yow of Bad Axe a check from the Sun Life Assurance Company. This check was in payment of the policy held in the name of Albert Sparling; and the beneficiary was the boy's mother, Mrs. Carrie Sparling. Mrs. Sparling had endorsed the check in favor of Dr. MacGregor; and with it the doctor had bought the horseless carriage, as some of the older folks around Bad Axe still called motorcars.

If these circumstances seemed at all suspicious nothing came of them, although Doc John Sparling, the veterinarian, often was heard to mutter, while dosing a cow with soap water, that he *still* didn't like the way things were going at Carrie Sparling's place.

The fourth of August, 1911, rolled around. It was a warm, sticky day. Heat waves shimmered up and down the Sparling barn in the blistering sunlight, and cicadas ground out their interminable noise from the brush on the edge of the now stubbly oat field. The threshers were at the Sparling farm, and the barn floor was alive with the thumping of the mechanical beaters on the yellow grain. Two horses walked endlessly against the clattering treadmill, their heads bobbing up and down and covered with chaff from the oats. Rugged Scyrel Sparling, huskiest man in the crew, was working as hard as usual; but he noted, long before noon, that he was not perspiring. No oat dust stuck to his face.

Scyrel had scarcely known a sick day in his life, but now—and he wondered if it was something he had eaten—he told one of the threshing crew that he didn't feel any too good. A bit later he vomited. By the time he had got to the house he was ready to lie down. Dr. MacGregor was called.

The youth's symptoms, Dr. MacGregor thought, were "baffling." He called into consultation, at different times during the following two days, the Doctors Conboy and Herrington, both of Bad Axe. It isn't on record whether or not Dr. Conboy had heard that Dr. MacGregor was living—rent free, it was said—in Mrs. Sparling's other house. He surely knew that Dr. MacGregor had bought an automobile. It is likely that he had heard the automobile was paid for with an insurance check on the life of the late—but only three months late—Albert Sparling.

In any case, Dr. Conboy asked the ailing Scyrel certain leading questions. That is, questions as to the boy's symptoms which, if the replies were affirmative, would indicate that he was suffering from nothing but arsenic poisoning. The replies were all in the affirmative.

Dr. MacGregor was present during Dr. Conboy's examination of the patient, but made no comment until the two doctors had left the sickroom. Then Dr. MacGregor asked Dr. Conboy a question. "Do you suspect arsenic?" he asked.

"I do," said Conboy.

"So do I," agreed Dr. MacGregor, nodding his head vigorously.

That was on August 6. On the seventh Dr. Conboy again visited the sick youth, and asked a few more questions. Then he got into his buggy and drove to Bad Axe and direct to the office of Xenophon A. Boomhower, prosecuting attorney for Huron County.

"I think somebody is feeding arsenic to young Sparling," Dr. Conboy said. "I've been there twice, called in by MacGregor, and I'm as certain as I can be of anything that the Sparling boy is suffering from arsenic. You'd ought to look into it."

Attorney Boomhower acted promptly. He went right to Dr. MacGregor. "Mac," he told his old friend, "there's a mystery around here. As you already know, Dr. Conboy thinks the lad is being poisoned."

"I'm mystified about it myself. I told Conboy the thing is completely baffling. Who would want to kill him?"

Boomhower suggested that MacGregor get a nurse to stay with the boy at all times, that the youth take nothing, even food and water, except what MacGregor prescribed. MacGregor agreed it was a good idea. "I think I can get Nurse Gibbs," he said. "She has been on a case at Grind Stone City, but she's free now. I'll get her."

Nurse Gibbs, a Canadian from Ontario, was engaged. She was instructed to allow no one, not even the boy's mother, to give him anything.

But the boy grew no better. If anything, it was the other way. Dr. Conboy was called into consultation again on the tenth. "I'd give my left leg to know what is the matter with that boy," Dr. MacGregor remarked to him.

"Is the nurse here at all times?" Conboy asked.

"Yes, she sleeps on the couch here in the room. She never leaves him."

Dr. Conboy went away, agreeing that the case was indeed baffling.

Dr. Herrington was called into consultation on the eleventh, and Dr. Holdship, new to the case, on the twelfth. On the fourteenth Scyrel died, after much vomiting and purging, apparently in great pain.

At the request of Dr. MacGregor, Dr. Holdship remained at the farm that night. Working by lamplight in the Sparling farmhouse, the two physicians performed an autopsy. Next day they announced that death had been due to cancer of the liver.

Attorney Boomhower was not satisfied. Over the protests of Mrs. Sparling and the evident professionally hurt feelings of the two doctors, Boomhower sent the vital organs to the University of Michigan. Here they were examined by Dr. Warthin, head of pathology, and Dr. Vaughan. These two physicians agreed that traces of arsenical poison were patently present. Further, their conclusions as to the symptoms of the poison upon a dying person agreed with the observations of the doctors in attendance on Scyrel Sparling.

This posed a question. Was the arsenic present as a result of criminal acts by a party or parties unknown? When the report of the pathologists was made known to the attending physicians, Dr. MacGregor thought he had come upon an explanation. "After Albert died in May," he said, "I collected a large number of bottles which had contained patent medicines and threw them out. The whole family was addicted to trying patent medicines, against my advice. Many of these so-called cures contain arsenic."

Well, there it rested for a while. Dr. MacGregor continued his practice in Ubly and Bad Axe, although it may have fallen off a bit. Four deaths in one family in three years was not exactly the best of recommendations.[3]

Meanwhile Xenophon A. Boomhower prosecuted a few câses in line of duty, but he never once got the Sparling mystery out of his mind. Nor did Donald McAuley, Huron County sheriff. These two men often held talks about the strange and many deaths, and little by little they got together what they believed was enough evidence to put before a grand jury. Among other things, they had the body of Albert Sparling exhumed and a post-mortem performed by the same University of Michigan pathologists who had found arsenic in Scyrel's remains. The verdict was arsenic for Albert, too. "He came to his death in substantially the same manner as Scyrel," said the report.

On January 12, 1912, Attorney Boomhower filed an information charging Dr. John MacGregor with the murder of Scyrel Sparling. At the same time he charged Mrs. Carrie Sparling and Nurse Gibbs with being accomplices. Coincident with the arrest of these three persons Attorney Boomhower secured all the papers and books in Dr. MacGregor's safe and took them to his own office for study.

2

The trial was to be Bad Axe's biggest sensation. Seeing readily that the crowd would be the largest in the town's history and fearing that the ramshackle Huron County courthouse, one wall of which was already partially caved in, would collapse under the strain, Judge Watson Beach announced that the trial would be held in the hall over the printing shop and editorial sanctum of the *Huron County Tribune*—which may have been a contributing reason why the *Tribune's* account of the trial was so complete and excellent.

---

[3] I should like to know what, if anything, Doc John Sparling, the old veterinarian, remarked on the death of the *fourth* Sparling.

Dr. MacGregor and the two women pleaded not guilty. The doctor was put on trial in April, and Judge Beach's expectations of a large attendance were justified. There was never a foot of space to spare in the hall. Attorneys Joseph Walsh and George M. Clark acted for defense. Prosecutor Boomhower was assisted by E. A. Snow, special counsel.

Around Dr. MacGregor the prosecution wove circumstantial evidence that became thicker as the trial progressed. Step by step Attorney Boomhower, by the introduction of many witnesses, built up a continuous line of thought in the jury. Rather sinister thought. It was shown that shortly after the death of the senior Sparling insurance had been taken on the lives of the four sons, that the policies had been written by the father of Dr. MacGregor, that MacGregor himself had examined the boys twice and had found them fit both times.

Peter Sparling had died. Albert Sparling had died. Mrs. Sparling had bought a house at Ubly but *never lived in it.* Boomhower made the most of this circumstance. "And I have never been able to find record," he told the jury, "where Dr. MacGregor ever paid Mrs. Sparling a penny of rent."

Letting that one permeate the jury, Boomhower next took up the matter of the automobile. He made a point of the date when MacGregor had first talked of buying the car and of MacGregor's remark that he would pay for it "in about three weeks."

"He timed it well," Boomhower shouted at the jury. "Albert Sparling died twenty-two days after that remark was made."

Next prosecution went deeply into the financial records of Dr. MacGregor. The daybooks and other papers were produced to show that the amounts of cash paid, or given, to MacGregor by Mrs. Sparling could not "by the greatest feat of the imagination be attributed to professional services," as claimed by the defense. Boomhower, a good man with a batch of figures, estimated aloud for benefit of jury that if all of this money had been for services then the doctor must have made at least

four calls daily on the woman over a period of four years—
Sundays, holidays, and all. Even then, the attorney said, the
rate per call would be much higher than was customarily
charged by the medicos of Huron County. He let that sink
in awhile.

Next he called the University of Michigan experts to the
stand. Their testimony impressed the jury a great deal. The
two pathologists were fortunately able to explain in simple
language what they found in the vital organs of Scyrel Sparling and what its significance was. They testified at length
as to the symptoms of arsenic poisoning in the patient, and
then the jury heard the physicians who had been in attendance
describe the symptoms they discovered in the dying boy.
Everything tallied.

The prosecutor sought to show undue intimacy between Dr.
MacGregor and Mrs. Sparling. This was most emphatically
denied by MacGregor, who, on the whole, made a good witness
in his own defense. But he was tripped again and again in his
attempts to account for the various sums of cash he had received from Mrs. Sparling. He was patently the worst bookkeeper in the world. Nor could he prove otherwise than that
he and his wife had lived rent-free in Mrs. Sparling's house
in Ubly.

What its effect on the jury may have been can never be
known, but a sensation of the trial was Sheriff McAuley's testimony that Dr. MacGregor had told him that Mrs. Sparling
and all the boys were "suffering from an unfortunate disease."

Put on the stand by the defense, Nurse Gibbs told of finding
a bottle of poison in the Sparling cupboard when she was at
the house caring for Scyrel. In rebuttal prosecution held this
to have been a mere "plant," made to divert suspicion.

Dr. MacGregor and his counsel sought to make a case out
of the "constant taking of patent medicines" by the Sparlings,
indicating that sufficient poison to cause death could have
resulted from so much dosing.

But the jury had heard too much. They found Dr. Mac-Gregor guilty. The cases against Mrs. Sparling and Nurse Gibbs were never prosecuted, and were nol-prossed.

Judge Beach sentenced MacGregor to life imprisonment. An appeal was taken to the supreme court of Michigan, which affirmed the conviction and denied a rehearing. The high court did, however, offer a mild censure. It found that the course "pursued by the prosecution was improper and not to be commended." This referred to expressions of opinion made by Attorney Boomhower in his summing up of the case for the jury.

The outcome of the trial of course settled the question of guilt, at least officially, for a time. And now the real mystery of the case began.

Dr. MacGregor was sent to prison in June of 1912. In November of 1916 Governor Ferris of Michigan granted a full and unconditional pardon to MacGregor on the *ground of complete innocence.* Not only that, but the governor took the unusual course—the almost extraordinary course—of having the prisoner brought to Lansing, the state capital, by the warden and of giving MacGregor the pardon with his own hand.

In making a statement to the press at this time, Governor Ferris made a complete mystery out of the deaths of all the many Sparlings.[4] "For more than two years I have been investigating this case," the governor said. "I have had the assistance of some of the best authorities in Michigan, and I am firmly convinced that Dr. MacGregor is absolutely innocent of the crime for which he was convicted. I am satisfied that in sending him to prison the State of Michigan has made a terrible mistake."

There are no weasel words in that statement. It says that justice had not been done. It says that the murderer was still

---

[4] Ray, the youngest, and Daughter May survived.

at large—or that a father and three sons committed suicide. And the governor backed his statement with deeds. When Dr. MacGregor and his loyal wife, who never once lost faith, returned from a short visit in Canada, the doctor was appointed official physician to the state penitentiary at Jackson, where he had served four years as an inmate. He held his post until his death in 1928.

It seems unfortunate that the grounds on which Governor Ferris reached his conclusions in the MacGregor–Sparling affair have never been made known, and they must have been extraordinary indeed.

I have been unable to discover a physician who believes that the tiny amounts of arsenic found in many proprietary medicines could have caused the death of Scyrel Sparling or of his brothers and father. Nurse Gibbs can be eliminated on the ground that she was not upon the scene until three men were dead, and another ill. And Governor Ferris of Michigan, an honest man, was completely assured by a long investigation of the innocence of John MacGregor. No politics seemingly was involved.

There is no record of domestics around the Sparling home, or of hired men there.

All of which leaves implications too horrible to contemplate.

BELLE OF INDIANA

HAD IT NOT BEEN for an unfortunate hired man and a fire, Belle Brynhilde Poulsatter Sorenson Gunness might have been in business to this day; and a very profitable and interesting line it must have been. She was an extremely retiring and uncommunicative person and until fire destroyed her home near La Porte, Indiana, on April 28, 1908, she was practically unknown except to a circle of what one shudders to call her intimates.

Belle first appeared in La Porte in 1901. She was then the Widow Sorenson, relict of Mads Sorenson who died in 1900 leaving her with two children and eight thousand dollars in life insurance. From sale of the Sorenson home in Illinois the widow received another five thousand dollars. Thus she was financially well fixed when she bought a forty-eight-acre farm about a mile out of La Porte and moved there with two children of her own and another youngster, Jennie Olson, daughter of one Antone Olson.

The Widow Sorenson was forty-two years old in 1901.[1]

---

[1] She was born Brynhilde Poulsatter at Selbe, Norway, in 1859, and came to the United States in 1868. Her first marriage was in 1888.

Neighbors describe her as "rugged," which would seem wholly inadequate. She was five feet seven inches tall and weighed two hundred pounds, most of which was pure brawn. When her household effects arrived at the farm, the truckers were amazed at the ease with which she juggled heavy trunks, boxes, and crates. One of them, who may have been drinking that day, swore that he saw the woman pick the big upright piano clean off the floor of the porch, lug it unaided into the front room, and set it down as gently as she would have handled a basket of eggs. "Ay like music in home," Belle had beamed.

"Weigh three hunnert pound, easy," the awed trucker said later, referring to the piano.

In spite of her retiring disposition, neighbors soon learned that the Widow Sorenson was an accomplished farmer who could pitch hay and milk cows and who did her own butchering of hogs and calves, the meat of which she sold in La Porte. She wasn't a widow long. How they first met isn't clear; but in April of 1902 she married Peter Gunness, a Norwegian who seemed to be a jolly, honest person and became well liked by neighboring farmers. But Peter wasn't long for the world. In December, after only seven months of wedded bliss, he was killed when, as Mrs. Gunness explained the matter, he was struck on the head by a sausage grinder that fell from a shelf.

It is of course idle to speculate on whether or not the shelf had been jiggled. The La Porte coroner was called and, although later he admitted that the sausage-grinder affair "looked a little queer," he found officially that Peter Gunness, God rest his soul, had been the victim of an accident.

The Widow Gunness, who henceforth was known as Belle Gunness, was no doubt glad of the four-thousand-dollar life-insurance policy which the oddly animated sausage machine had liquidated. But she continued to live modestly, even frugally, and it soon became apparent that in spite of her forty-three years Belle was in an interesting condition. A son whom she named Philip was born in 1903. In addition, her brood included Daughters Lucy and Myrtle by her previous marriage and the Jennie Olson she was caring for.[2]

Although it was not known until later—tragically later—Belle Gunness was addicted to the use of matrimonial journals.[3] That is, she advertised in them—listing, as was the custom, her desire for a good husband and being not too coy regarding her own personality and qualifications. What Belle wanted, it seemed, was a man of Scandinavian birth, preferably Norwegian, who was kind and honest and who would help a lovable and hard-working widow to lift the mortgage on her little farm. The "kind and honest" part of the desired man's qualifications might be winked at, one gathers; but the mortgage-lifting end of the deal was nothing short of imperative. "Triflers," Belle's advertisement said coldly, "need not apply."

A photograph of Belle Gunness at this period shows a squat, powerfully built woman in a long plain dress with puff sleeves, a Gibson Girl hair-do, and an exceedingly dull and heavy face. Looking at the photograph, one is hard put to explain the undoubted attraction the woman exercised on a large number of men. To term the woman in this photograph "plain" is mere flattery. But either this picture is a gross libel on Belle or her personal charm was such that no photograph could catch and hold it.

Shortly after the death of Mr. Gunness, Belle engaged a hired man to work around her place; but she herself was still active in butchering pigs, of which she had many, and in caring for the garden. The hired men changed from time to

---

[2] I dislike to use the term "caring for" in connection with *anything* in which Mrs. Gunness was concerned, but it must suffice for the present.

[3] Matrimonial journals are still flourishing in the United States, but today they usually operate under euphemisms such as "correspondence clubs" and "acquaintance societies." In former times they came right out with it and used *Wedding Bells* and other direct-action names. Any male could get a copy free and there read all about the wondrous charms of the ladies as described by themselves. But to get the names and addresses of these jewels the boys had to pay—six for a dollar. I once knew a lumberjack who got a very good wife by mail order. I also knew a farm hand who got a frightful witch in the same manner and was forced to strangle her to regain his peace of mind.

time, some of them very suddenly indeed; but none of them
entered Belle's life very deeply until the next to last one, of
which more later.

In 1906 a Mr. John Moo arrived at Belle's farm from Elbow
Lake, Minnesota. He was a husky, good-looking man of about
fifty years of age, well dressed by country-town standards, and
a native of Norway. His object was matrimony, and he had
been fetched by one of Belle's advertisements in the wedding-
bells periodicals. With him John Moo brought one thousand
dollars to "pay off the mortgage" on his intended's farm.

John was introduced to callers and neighbors as Cousin
John, and for almost a week he was seen about the house every
day. Then, one day, he wasn't there. That was thirty-five years
ago. John Moo hasn't been seen since.

Hard on the heels of the disappearing Moo came George
Anderson of Tarkio, a village in the northwestern corner of
Missouri. George, like both Peter Gunness and John Moo,
was a native of Norway. Living in Missouri must have given
him some of the skepticism for which that state is famous:
George Anderson did not bring very much money with him to
Belle's place.

He was mighty glad he hadn't. Long afterward he related
why.

Attracted by Belle's description of herself in one of the marriage papers, Anderson had made the long trip to La Porte
with the intention of matrimony. After the usual amenities—
and by now Belle must have been getting pretty good at amenities—the woman brought up the little matter of raising the
mortgage. Really charmed by the husky Belle, George was seriously considering returning home to get what might be termed
the entrance fee and then marrying the woman.

Early on his visit at the farm, however, he suddenly awoke
in the middle of the night. "All in a cold sweat," he recalled.
Bending over him and peering intently into his face was Belle
herself, a lighted candle in her hand. What she intended to do,

if anything, George Anderson never found out. He was so
startled at the odd expression in the eyes and on the usually
phlegmatic face of his intended bride that he let go a yell.
Belle ran out of the room. So did George. He put on his clothes
and got the hell out of there as fast as he could go, and kept
going until he reached the La Porte railroad station, on foot,
where he got a train for Tarkio, Missouri.

After Anderson's departure there *may* have been a lull, a
sort of brief hiatus, between the arrivals of men with matrimonial intentions. Again, there may have been no break at all.
It is difficult to say. In any case, Belle was not idle. She changed
her advertising copy in the wedding-bells journals, and she
also engaged a new hired man—a rather dim-witted young
French–Canadian by name of Ray L'Amphere, who presently
anglicized his name into plain Lamphere. What his relations
with Belle were, other than as hired man, are not positively
known; but probably they were rather interesting, as events
were soon to indicate.

Either just before or just after Lamphere came to live and
work at the farm, young Jennie Olson, the sixteen-year-old girl
who had been put in Belle's care by the child's father, Antone
Olson, disappeared. Possibly "disappeared" is too strong a
word to use at this point, for Belle explained everything to
neighbors. Jennie had "gone to California," she said, and was
in school there. It certainly is a fact that Jennie went somewhere in midsummer of 1906. That was thirty-five years ago.
She hasn't been seen since.

During the lull in the mortgage-raising Belle began to be
something of a mystery woman in the neighborhood. Hack
drivers of La Porte told of delivering trunks to the Gunness
farm at night. One of the drivers was Clyde Sturgis. One night
he drove out there with a big, heavy trunk which was well
bound with rope. Sturgis, always a helpful man, unloaded the
trunk and started to cut the rope with his jackknife. Belle was
at him in a fury. "What are you trying to do!" she fairly

screamed. "I'll take care of this trunk." And with that she picked it up off the porch like a box of marshmallows and lugged it inside.

Added to the business of the mysterious trunks, which doubtless became more mysterious every time it was retold, was that neighbors noted Belle kept the shutters on her house tightly drawn, both day and night, for a long period. And farmers going by late at night often saw Belle herself on the prowl, around her barn or in a small yard some fifty by seventy-five feet which Belle had recently enclosed with an *eight-foot* fence of stout and fine wire mesh. Entrance to this yard was by a rugged gate of tough oak which rumor said was always locked and to which Belle alone had the key.

The cellar of the house, too, was always kept locked except at hog-butchering season. At these times a stray neighbor or two had happened to call when Belle was in the cellar, her sleeves rolled up, wielding knife and cleaver like the best man Mr. Swift or Mr. Armour ever had. The cellar was admirably rigged for such work. It contained a long heavy table of hardwood, twelve inches thick, and a large tub for scalding purposes. In the ceiling over the tub was a hook and pulley. Leather strips along the wall held a professional assortment of fine butcher's implements.

The lull in the stream of callers—if lull there was—came to an end in April of 1907. In that merry spring month Mr. Ole Budsberg, a native of Norway but long a citizen of Iola in Waupaca County, Wisconsin, packed his extension suitcase and took a train of steamcars for La Porte. Belle met him at the station in her own buggy. The loving couple had long since exchanged photographs, as is the happy custom in mail-order matrimonial circles, and they had no trouble recognizing each other.[4]

---

[4] You can say what you want to about Belle, but not that she ever attempted to seduce men by retouched pictures; the ones she sent out to prospective mates looked cruelly like her.

Mr. Ole Budsberg was a middle-aged man, the father of several grown sons. He had done very well with certain logging jobs in the white pine of Wisconsin and had saved his money. With him to La Porte he brought two thousand dollars in cash. This was, as one might guess, for the purpose of raising that apparently immutable mortgage on the forty-eight acres of the Widow Gunness.

Mr. Budsberg arrived on the farm late in April of 1907. That is thirty-four years ago and he hasn't been seen since.

2

Nineteen hundred and seven had been a rather slow year at the farm, but 1908 opened very auspiciously indeed when Mr. Andrew K. Helgelein arrived at the place in January and was made welcome by the charming chatelaine of what soon was to be known as Abattoir Acres. Mr. Helgelein was a native of Norway, but for years past he had been living near Aberdeen, South Dakota, where he successfully raised wheat.

Mr. Helgelein came with the most honorable intentions of matrimony. In his big wallet he carried no less than three thousand dollars in cash, with which to—but never mind. What had fetched him was obviously a series of letters, the last one of which happily has survived to give a good sample of Belle's literary style and general technique. It was written in Belle's own clear hand on January 13, 1908, and was inadvertently but fortunately left at his South Dakota home by Mr. Helgelein when he started for La Porte. Wrote the Belle of Indiana:

To the Dearest Friend in the World: No woman in the world is happier than I am. I know that you are now to come to me and be my own. I can tell from your letters that you are the man I want. It does not take one long to tell when to like a person, and you I like better than anyone in the world, I know.

Think how we will enjoy each other's company. You, the sweetest man in the whole world. We will be all alone with each other. Can you conceive of anything nicer? I think of you constantly. When I hear your name mentioned, and this is when one of the dear children speaks of you or I hear myself humming it with the words of an old love song, it is beautiful music to my ears.

My heart beats in wild rapture for you. My Andrew, I love you. Come prepared to stay forever.

And, by God, he did. That was thirty-three years ago and he hasn't been seen since.

Now affairs at the farm departed from their usual humdrum quiet. Ray Lamphere, the hired man, had a frightful•quarrel with Belle. He, like many another poor man, had fallen in love with her and he was jealous of the latest star boarder, Helgelein. In a terrible temper he packed up his belongings and left. In La Porte he told friends that Belle owed him back wages. He said he knew enough about Belle to make her pay him not only his wages but to keep his mouth shut, too.

Lamphere must have done a deal of talking, for it got to Belle's ears. She promptly had him arrested on complaint that he was insane and a menace to the public. He was given what passed in those days for a sanity hearing and was found sane. He made a call on Belle at the farm. They argued heatedly about something. She had him arrested again, for trespass.

Lamphere was a man who could take it. He paid a fine for trespass and he remained in the neighborhood. It is even thought that he called on Belle again. He also continued to make various veiled threats about her, and once mentioned to Farmer William Slater that "Helgelein won't bother me no more. We fixed him for keeps."

Trouble also assailed Belle from another quarter. She got a letter from Mr. Asle Helgelein, a substantial citizen of Mansfield, South Dakota, who wanted to know what had become of his brother Andrew. Belle wrote in reply that Andrew had gone away, doubtless on a visit to his native Norway. To this whimsey Asle Helgelein answered that he was positive his brother had done no such thing.

Now we get a real sample of how Belle met a challenge of this sort. She sat right down and wrote Asle that she wished he would come to La Porte to aid her in a search for Andrew. She intimated, too, that searches of this kind cost money. If Asle replied to this invitation it is not of record.

For once in her life Belle Gunness was worried. Or so she seemed to M. E. Leliter, prominent attorney of La Porte, to whom the woman came on April 27, 1908. She told him she was mortally in fear of Ray Lamphere, the ex-hired man. He had threatened to kill her, she said. He had promised to burn her house around her ears. In view of these things hanging over her she wanted to make her will. It is significant, perhaps, that she did not ask for police protection from Lamphere.

Attorney Leliter drew up a will and she signed it. It left her estate to her two children by the late Mr. Sorenson and her one child by the late Mr. Gunness. In case the children did not survive her, the estate was to go to a Norwegian children's home, a sort of orphanage, in Chicago.

Leaving Mr. Leliter's office, Belle proceeded to the La Porte bank—where she paid off a five-hundred-dollar note. Then she returned to the farm.

Early next morning farmers on the McClung Road saw the Gunness home in flames. It burned to the ground. Only the hired man, one Joe Maxon, escaped, and he said he barely made it. Noise of the flames licking at his room had awakened him, he said, and he jumped out his second-story window in his underwear. He vowed that just before jumping he had shouted loudly to wake Mrs. Gunness and the children but had received no reply. They had been in the house when he went to bed.

When the embers had cooled slightly, searchers found four bodies. Three were readily identified as those of Lucy and Myrtle Sorenson, Belle's daughters, and of Philip Gunness, her son. The other corpse was the headless body of a woman. All four were found on a mattress in the cellar. On top of them were the charred remains of the pride of Belle's parlor, the fine upright piano.

Sheriff Albert H. Smutzer was called. He viewed the scene and arrested Ray Lamphere, the farm hand who had been doing so much talking about Mrs. Gunness. Immediately upon his arrest and without so much as one question asked him, Lamphere asked one of his own. "Did Widow Gunness and the kids get out?" he inquired.

But Lamphere denied any knowledge of how the fire started, even when he was confronted by John Solyam, a neighbor's boy, who identified Lamphere as the man he had seen running from the Gunness place just before the flames were noticed. "You wouldn't look me in the eye and say that," Lamphere asserted.

"Yes, I will," the lad said, and continued, "You found me hiding behind the bushes and you told me you'd kill me if I didn't get out of there."

Lamphere was indicted for murder; and a charge of arson was left, as you might say, hanging over him, just in case the other charge wasn't sufficient. The victim named in the murder charge was of course Mrs. Gunness. But, and the doubts began piling up one on top of the other, *was* the headless body that of Mrs. Gunness?

Swan Nicholson, neighboring farmer who had known Mrs. Gunness over a period of six years, viewed the headless corpse and said, without qualification, no, it wasn't that of the hefty widow. It wasn't tall enough, it wasn't big enough, and, well, it just didn't look like her at all. C. Christofferson, another farmer who had often called at the mystery place to do plowing and other work, was as positive as Nicholson had been. No, he said, that body had never been Belle. And so said Mrs. Austin Cutler, an old acquaintance.

From Chicago came Mrs. Nellie Olander and Mr. Sigurd Olson, sister and brother of the Jennie Olson who had lived with Belle and had "gone to California" not long before. Mrs. Olander and Mr. Olson told authorities they had known Belle ever since they could remember and that the headless body was of someone else, not Belle.

A tragic visitor at this time was Antone Olson, father of the missing girl. He came from Chicago to view the charred bodies. Jennie's was not among them. Mr. Olson told police he had planned to visit the Gunness home on the following Sunday to see if Jennie was all right. He said he had dreamed a few nights before that the Gunness home had been burned to the ground and Jennie was in the fire. It had worried him.

Physicians measured the charred remains of the headless woman. Making proper allowances for the missing head and neck, they concluded that the corpse was that of a woman five feet three inches tall and weighing about one hundred and fifty pounds. Belle, as those who knew her agreed, had not been a hair under five feet seven and weighed at least one hundred and eighty-five pounds, possibly more. Swan Nicholson was quite definite. The Widow Gunness, he said with sober assurance, weighed two hundred pounds if she weighed an ounce.

Clerks in La Porte stores who had sold Mrs. Gunness various articles of wearing apparel were interviewed for their knowledge of clothing sizes. These figures were compared with estimates of acquaintances. Physicians had meanwhile made careful measurements of the corpse. The two sets of measurements, one real, the other estimated, indicated that the body found in the cellar must be that of someone other than Belle. This is how they compared:

	Victim (inches)	Mrs. Gunness (inches)
Biceps	9	17
Bust	36	46
Waist	26	37
Thigh	25	30
Hips	40	54
Calf	12½	14
Wrist	6	9

Despite these discrepancies and admitting they would like to have more definite proof, police authorities said the headless corpse was that of Belle Gunness. Three rings on the left hand were considered additional proof. One was set with diamonds and had no markings. A plain gold band was engraved "M.S. to J.S. Aug. 22 '94"; another gold band was marked "P.G. to J.S. 3-5-'95." It was reasonable to believe that these rings had to do with Belle's first marriage, to Mads Sorenson, and her second, to Peter Gunness. Because of the condition of the flesh it was impossible to say if these rings had been on these fingers for a long time.

Presently, as in all such cases of doubt, there came forward those witnesses who are apparently present, in swarming numbers, when any skulduggery has come to light. Half a dozen persons volunteered the information that they had seen Mrs. Gunness driving a woman to the farm on the night of the fire. Descriptions of this mysterious party varied from "slim" to "fairly stout." All agreed she had been "a dark woman."

What the harassed authorities needed was a head for the corpse, or at least a skull. Search of the barns and outbuildings and of the near-by swamp revealed nothing in the form of a head. The sheriff was prepared to call it a day—to let the whole confusing matter rest as it was and to go ahead with prosecution of the farm hand, Lamphere, for murder of Mrs. Gunness. Doubtless that is exactly what would have happened had it not been for the appearance on the scene of Asle Helgelein of Mansfield, South Dakota. This was the brother of Andrew, the man Belle had reported to Asle as on his happy way to Norway. Asle had not known of the Gunness fire until his arrival at La Porte. He had come simply to find his brother.

Asle went to Sheriff Smutzer with his suspicions that Andrew had somehow been done in by this woman he had come to marry. The sheriff didn't seem very interested, but Asle was persistent and the sheriff finally agreed to make another inspection of the premises. In the high-fenced yard, the gate to which had to be broken by police, were noted several soft depressions in the ground. Joe Maxon, Belle's last hired man, the one who barely had escaped from the burning house, told officers that Belle once had him wheel dirt into the yard to level the partly filled holes. Contained rubbish, Belle had said. At the urging of Asle Helgelein deputies took shovels and started digging.

The first layers under the soft earth were indeed rubbish— old cans, bottles, and so forth—but suddenly a digger let out an exclamation. He came up with a good fat gunny sack. In it was a body well hacked but still in fair condition, everything considered. Helgelein looked closely at the remains. "That's Andy," he said.

The deputies now dug with a right good will. Before sun-down that day, which was May 3, 1908, they had uncovered the remains of at least four more bodies. One of these was identified as that of Jennie Olson, the girl who "had gone to California." One of the others was of a tall man with a dark mustache. The two others were of children.

Next day the yard yielded four more bodies. On the third day only one body was found. That made a total of ten in the yard. If the four in the cellar were added, the grand total was fourteen—an impressive number for so small a farm.

When he was informed of the bodies found in the yard, Lamphere, the ex-hired man, screamed in his cell. "Bodies, murder, Helgelein!" was his curious cry. "My God, that woman! Now I know what was going on!"

Not all of the bodies could be identified, but positive identifi-cations were made of those of Jennie Olson, Andrew Helgelein, John Moo, and Ole Budsberg. For reasons that need not be gone into here, three other bodies were presently presumed to be those of one Olaf Lindblom and one Eric Gerhalt, both Norwegians who had come, separately, to visit Belle, and that of a hired man whose name was never known.

The remains of several *other* bodies were mere fragments—

fingers and other small bones for which comparative skulls and trunks were missing. As physicians attempted to sort the hundreds of spare parts, the heavy table and the vat in the Gunness cellar took on a possible new meaning that made strong men shudder. Had that vat been used for purposes other than the scalding of hogs? One couldn't know, but police and physicians now looked at the several cleavers found in the ashes with new interest.

With Belle's private boneyard apparently exhausted, police felt that the investigation was completed—finished. They hadn't reckoned with the growing public rumor about that headless corpse and its possible connection with the mystery woman seen with Belle in her buggy on the night of the fire. New witnesses came forward. They had seen this same dark woman get off the evening train from Chicago. Belle had met her at the La Porte depot. They had driven out the McClung road together, toward the farm.

Maybe so; but Joe Maxon, Belle's final hired man, had seen no strange woman that night, although he admitted it was possible one could have been in the house without his knowledge. "It sure was a queer place," he allowed in what was a fair attempt at an understatement.

No matter what Joe Maxon said, local opinion had it settled that the headless corpse was that of a woman the crafty Belle had imported to the farm for just such a purpose. Belle herself was safe elsewhere, somewhere. So the story grew and solidified.

Dr. Ira P. Norton, La Porte dentist, had been very busy at the time of the Gunness fire and had not then connected the fire with a former patient. With the Gunness farm and its odd harvest now on the front pages of the nation's press, Dr. Norton recalled that he had done some dental work for the late Mrs. Gunness. He told police he could easily identify his own work, which was a bridge of gold and porcelain.

Police doubted Dr. Norton would have anything to work on.

They said that fire hot enough to consume a head would also consume, or at least melt, both gold and porcelain. Not so, said Dr. Norton. The gold caps would not fuse under 1800 degrees Fahrenheit. The porcelain would not disintegrate at less than 2000 degrees. "That would call for a blowpipe flame," the dentist said.

The next problem was how to sift the ashes and debris of a large house and find a few small teeth—even if they existed, which the police seemed to doubt. Louis Schultz, a public-spirited citizen of La Porte, heard of the quandary and went to the officers with a suggestion. He was an old sourdough, he said, not long since returned from the Yukon, and if he had a little lumber and some encouragement he would build a regular gold-mine sluice box right there on Belle's place. With plenty of running water handy he would sluice every jeasley bit of stuff in the ruins of the house, and if there was any gold to be found in the claim he damned well would find it.

This Louis Schultz was plainly God-given. The sluice was built in Belle's front yard; water was piped from the barn; and old Klondike Louis, the ninety-eighter, went to work on the strangest mining job of his career, while thousands cheered.

The thousands who cheered Louis at his work came not only from La Porte and surrounding towns but from Chicago, where the daily papers were whooping up the biggest story of the year and one of the best horror stories of all time. Klondike Louis, indeed, was a sensation. With his sluice box roped off and scores of extra deputies needed to handle the huge crowds, he shoveled tons of debris and washed it down over the riffles before the largest audience a sourdough ever had. At that time newsreels were in infancy and seem not to have caught the epic event; but newspaper photographers were all over the place, catching Louis in pose after pose.

Bets were made on the outcome. Chicago bookies formed pools on the day and hour Louis would strike pay dirt in the

Belle Gunness Mine. Vendors of popcorn and tonic circulated in the crowd, which on its peak day was estimated to be six thousand persons. On May 19, after four days of hard work, Klondike Louis struck the vein. Washed out from the muck and debris of the house was a piece of dental bridgework containing two lower bicuspids capped with gold, and four porcelain teeth between them.

Dr. Norton looked closely. "My work, positively," he said. "Those are Mrs. Gunness' teeth."

3

In November, Ray Lamphere, the ex-farm hand, went on trial in La Porte for the murder of Mrs. Gunness. He was ably defended by Wirt Worden and was acquitted. Tried for arson, he was convicted. Obviously the jury did not believe Mrs. Gunness was dead. Lamphere was sent to prison at Michigan City, where he died in 1909.

Before his death Lamphere told a long and sometimes disconnected story of his affairs with Mrs. Gunness to a trusty at the prison by name of Harry Myers, and after Lamphere's death Myers retold it to prison officials. High lights of this account were that Belle did *not* die in the fire. Despite the evidence of the dental work, the body was that of a woman Belle had lured from Illinois on the promise of housework, then killed and beheaded to preclude identification. The head had been destroyed by use of quicklime, "in a hole dug in the swamp."

Lamphere painted a horrible picture of the female monster on the prowl. With the stand-in woman butchered, Belle went methodically to work on her own three children, killing them one after the other with practiced hand, then piled the four bodies onto the mattress after dressing the woman's in some old clothes that would readily be recognized as Belle's clothing.

In all, Lamphere said, Belle had lured forty-two men to her

house.[5] Only one had escaped, presumably the alert George Anderson of Tarkio, Missouri, who had awaked to find Belle standing over his bed peering into his face so intently.

From her dupes Belle had got amounts of cash varying from one thousand dollars to thirty-two thousand dollars each, Lamphere said. Usually she first drugged their coffee, then bashed in their heads while they were in a stupor. She then dissected the bodies on the big table in the cellar, tied the parts into neat bundles, and buried them in the locked yard. On occasion she varied the montony by putting the bodies into the hog-scalding vat and adding generous amounts of quicklime

Lamphere admitted to Myers that he had helped Belle bury "several bodies" but denied he ever had a part in the killing. Jennie Olson had been killed because "she knew too much." It was the same with Belle's own children. The other unidentified children had been put in Belle's care by mothers or fathers of broken homes.

As for the late Peter Gunness, alleged victim of the bounding sausage grinder, Belle had killed him with an ax.[6]

Not all of the dying Lamphere's story made sense. No doubt it was also grossly exaggerated. Some of it was sheer fantasy. And he was oddly silent regarding his own relations with Mrs. Gunness. But on the subject of the headless corpse he was positive; it was not Belle. She was safely away.

And that is the opinion today of many oldsters around La Porte, who believe that Belle, who left only a small amount in

---

[5] I was immensely relieved to come across this figure "forty-two" in the record. There is something magic about forty-two in connection with apocryphal accounts of murders in series. Folklore has it, for instance, that Harry Orchard killed forty-two men; that Billy Gohl of Grays Harbor, Washington, killed forty-two; that Lydia Sherman of Connecticut accounted for a similar number.

[6] This part of Lamphere's story was given weight when a youngster of La Porte recalled having heard little Myrtle Sorenson, Belle's daughter, remark that "Mama brained Papa with an ax. Don't tell a soul."

her bank account, had killed the unknown woman, fired the
house, and left for other parts.

On a somewhat different plane Belle lives on just as Ambrose
Bierce, the old journalist, did for many years in spite of his
probable death in Mexico in 1916. As recently as 1931 Belle
was "seen" in a Mississippi town. In the same year the body
of a woman found in Los Angeles was thought to be hers. It
wasn't. For more than twenty years the sheriff's office at La
Porte received an average of two queries a month about Belle—
Belle the Hoosier Monster, the Queen of the Abattoir, the
Female Bluebeard. During the past decade the queries have
been fewer, but they continue.

Belle Gunness, in fact, seems assured of an enduring place
in the folklore of the region. I base this guess on the fact that
she is the subject of at least one ballad, and when a person
or an event gets into song it is not likely to be forgotten as
soon as one not in a ballad. The literary or musical merit of
the ballad has nothing at all to do with its lasting qualities, as
witness the doggerel about Jesse James, Jim Fisk, Floyd Collins, and other folk heroes.

The ballad about Belle I heard sung to the air of "Love, O
Careless Love," and the verses I have been able to unearth
are as follows:

> Belle Gunness lived in In-di-an;
> She always, always had a man;
> Ten at least went in her door—
> And were never, never seen no more.
>
> Now, all these men were Norska folk
> Who came to Belle from Minn-e-sote;
> They liked their coffee, and their gin:
> They got it—plus a mickey finn.
>
> And now with cleaver poised so sure
> Belle neatly cut their jug-u-lur [sic];
> She put them in a bath of lime,
> And left them there for quite some time.

There's red upon the Hoosier moon
For Belle was strong and full of doom;
And think of all them Norska men
Who'll never see St. Paul again.

One of the last direct links between Belle Gunness and the present day is an old, old woman confined in the Longcliff Hospital for the Insane at Logansport, Indiana. She has been a patient there for a good many years and is one of the characters of the institution. She worked at Belle's place for several months and is not adverse to talking about it. The favorite question asked this old woman is "What did Belle Gunness do with all those men?" And the invariable reply, accompanied by a truly horrible leer, is "She fed 'em to the hawgs."

On the subject of Belle being alive or dead the old crone is noncommittal. "Who knows?" she says.

If Belle still lives, as many believe, she is eighty-two years old in 1941. That's getting on, as they say; but should I happen on a farmhouse in some back-country place and the proprietor is a husky old woman who kills her own hogs, I'll be on my way—no matter the road or the weather.

CHAPTER EIGHT

PROFESSOR LEURIO AND DR. RULLOFF

IN MIDSUMMER OF 1842 a rather odd-looking young man appeared in Dryden, New York, and got a job as a common laborer on a canal there. He was big, strong, and bearded, which wasn't odd in a young man of a century ago. It was his head. His head was the largest ever seen in Dryden—bigger than Daniel Webster's, somebody said—and he was extremely broad between the eyes—eyes, by the way, which reflected an intelligence not usually associated with pick and shovel.

This young man gave the name of Edward Rulloff. He said nothing of his past life, but little by little, as he became acquainted in the small village, it got around that he was a highly educated person. Spoke several languages, was versed in law and in medicine, and knew the Latin names of all the flora and fauna in Tompkins County. Moreover, he wrote a gorgeous, flowing, copperplate hand in a day when penmanship was much esteemed. Dryden folk may have wondered why such an educated youth was working with a shovel, and wondered again what great university had fostered his learning. He never said why or which.

In Dryden was a small private school which happened to

be in need of a teacher for the fall and winter terms. Edward Rulloff got the job. Before September was gone, pupils at the school were telling their parents what a wonderfully interesting teacher Mr. Rulloff was. He was so different from teachers they had known. The new professor might begin a class in English. Before the hour, which seemed to the youngsters like ten minutes, was gone, he had touched on the Greek and Latin roots of words, traced the divergent American and British meanings of common nouns and adjectives, and destroyed, by implication, the myth of the Tower of Babel. He showed the origins of the alphabet and compared it with Chinese, with prehistoric picture writing. Using simple but dramatic terms and blackboard designs, he demonstrated the ancient roots of words.

It was all very new and wonderful to children whose knowledge of language—if it could be called knowledge—had been drilled into them by the barbarous mechanical method of parsing.

When Professor Rulloff took a class in physiology, it, too, was a new adventure for his lucky pupils. The names of bones became secondary. The human body became a romantic machine, operated by certain universal laws subject to mutations because of climate, occupations, and long heredity. He took his class on long walks during which he cited scores of plants, trees, and herbs, which he said contained all the so-called medicines the human body ever could need as correctives.

In one of Professor Rulloff's classes was Harriet Schutt, sixteen, fresh as a daisy, daughter of a large and respectable family of long standing in Dryden. She became fascinated with the big young man with the great head and the wonderful eyes, and the professor must have been taken by the youthful, black-haired beauty of his pupil. The couple were seen much together, and in autumn of 1843 let it be known they planned to marry.

In spite of Rulloff's popularity and high standing as a learned man in the community, William Schutt, Harriet's brother, protested the marriage. So did Brother Edward. Both felt that the family had a right to know something of the professor's past. Edward told the professor as much. Rulloff considered it an insult. He talked very high and mighty and remarked, no doubt with a mean sneer, that his obvious learning should be warrant of fine character, a *non sequitur* that has only too often gone unchallenged.

It is known, however, that Rulloff's big talk did not satisfy the Schutt brothers. They still muttered, even openly fought the marriage of their sister. Harriet paid no heed. On December 31, 1843, the couple were united.

The husband now dropped his teaching. He became Doctor Rulloff, botanical physician, who cured most if not all human ills by the use of simples—medicinal herbs. This art of the herbalist was of course as old as man, but in the nineteenth century professional medicine had made such progress that the use of the old simples had long since been considered outmoded, unelegant, and was practiced mostly by ancient crones of the witch-doctor type. But now, in 1843, in the unpredictable herd manner of Americans, a great wave of "natural healing" was just getting under way, and Doctor Rulloff, botanical physician, was on the wave.

Mrs. Rulloff wasn't long in learning that her husband had another side to his character than that of the fascinating and kindly teacher and physician. He was arrogant. He was moody. He had a bad temper. On one occasion, when she was pounding pepper for him in a mortar, he grabbed the heavy pestle and struck her over the head. Again, he cursed her roundly. No doubt ashamed to admit to her family, so soon, that the marriage wasn't happy, Mrs. Rulloff said nothing just then.

Within the year the couple moved to Lansing, not far from the southern end of Lake Cayuga.

In Lansing, Dr. Rulloff's practice grew fast. Medical laws were far from strict, in mid last century, and his right to the title of doctor seemed never to have been questioned. He performed several cures on local folk that were held to be remarkable. As his fame spread throughout the country he was one day called even to Ithaca, largest town in the region, to administer to the ailing baby of Brother-in-law William Schutt, who apparently had accepted the doctor at face value. The baby soon died, and so did its mother. "Both were beyond all help," Doctor Rulloff told his wife.

Mrs. Rulloff gave birth to a child in April of 1845, but its father did not seem to care a great deal for the baby. These days he was so filled with his work that he had little time for domestic ties. He also was rather brutal to his wife on several occasions; but these things were known only to Mrs. Rulloff and her mother, who came to visit at the time the child was born. At this period Mrs. Rulloff did complain of the treatment her husband accorded her, and one of her brothers warned the doctor to mend his ways.

On June 23 Rulloff called on a neighbor, a Mr. Robertson. He said he was going on a trip that might require his absence overnight. Would Miss Robertson, the neighbor's daughter, stay with Mrs. Rulloff until his return? Some Indians were in the community, he explained, and Mrs. Rulloff was frightened. Miss Robertson went over to the doctor's place and remained that day.

The doctor returned at about nine o'clock in the evening.[1] With him he brought two Indian women. He took them into the house and had his wife meet them, and then they were given presents and went away. The doctor discoursed on the

---

[1] How Dr. Rulloff spent that twenty-third day of June was never known. I think he went to Lake Cayuga on a scientific exploration—to determine where the water was deepest, or at least deep enough.

nature and habits of Indians, Miss Robertson recalled later, and especially of their language, which he said he knew very well. The only other incident that Miss Robertson recalled of that night was that the doctor wanted to give a dose of some medicine to the Rulloff baby, but Mrs. Rulloff, no doubt remembering what had happened to Brother Will's family, would not permit it. Miss Robertson went home.

Next morning neighbors noted that the blinds of the Rulloff home were closed. There was no sign of life about the place. Shortly before noon, however, the doctor appeared at the Robertson home. He wanted to borrow Robertson's horse and wagon. An uncle of his wife had called late the night before, he said, and had taken wife and child on a visit to Motts Corners, a village between Lake Cayuga and Lake Seneca. To make room for them, the uncle had left a large box of household goods at the Rulloff house. Now Rulloff wanted to take the box to the uncle's place and to bring back his wife and child.

Neighbor Robertson was happy to lend his horse and wagon. Half an hour later Robertson looked toward the Rulloff house and saw the doctor struggling with a big, long box, trying to get it into the wagon. Robertson went over and gave a hand. The box was quite heavy, he noted, as they lifted it into the wagon body. Somewhat later, when there was reason to recall the matter, Mr. Robertson referred to the box as "a big chest." Dr. Rulloff drove away, ostensibly for Motts Corners.

But Dr. Rulloff did not drive to Motts Corners, on that day or ever. Things pieced together at a later date indicated that he drove to and through Ithaca and on to an inlet of Lake Cayuga, where he busied himself briefly and then started back for home. On the way he picked up a group of school children and gave them a lift of a mile or so.

Rulloff arrived back at his Lansing home on the night of June 25, some thirty hours after he left. Robertson, who couldn't have been an overly busy man, saw the doctor drive into the Rulloff yard. He was a little surprised to note that the doctor still had the big chest with him, and he watched while the doctor, unaided and with apparent ease, lifted the chest from the wagon and carried it into the house. The doctor then returned the horse and wagon, thanking his neighbor—who noted that the horse was dry and sleek, showing no effects from the alleged trip from distant Motts Corners.

Late in the next afternoon Dr. Rulloff came over to the Robertson home again. He was alone and carried a large bundle, made, of all things, of his wife's shawl, over his shoulder. He seemed in fine spirits. He stopped, said Mr. Robertson later, and "called out cheerily," "Good-by, Robertson; don't be alarmed if we don't come back for two or three weeks. I and my wife are going on a visit between the lakes." By which was understood the district between Cayuga and Seneca lakes. He seemed in especially breezy humor, and added—"with a pleasant laugh"—"Don't let anyone carry away our house while we are gone." And he trudged away, whistling.

Dr. Rulloff and wife did not visit any known place between the lakes. The doctor himself went to Ithaca and visited with his wife's relatives, the Schutts, who were not satisfied with his story that wife and child were "visiting at Mr. N. Dupuy's in Madison, Ohio." They didn't think it seemed reasonable that Mrs. Rulloff would have gone so far from home without notifying her brothers and sisters. The doctor expressed himself as hurt, then as irritated, at the obvious disbelief. He asked for pen and paper; then he sat down and wrote, in one of the most ornamental hands ever seen, a long and endearing letter to his wife, which he addressed to her at Madison, Ohio, and mailed it.

The letter allayed suspicion for a day or so. But then Rulloff disappeared. While the Schutt boys were looking for him, a friend told Ephraim Schutt he had seen Doctor Rulloff on his way to Auburn. Packing a valise hurriedly, Ephraim Schutt went to Auburn, where he found his brother-in-law seated in a train about to leave for Buffalo and points West.

"What ho!" exclaimed Schutt. If Rulloff was surprised he did not show it. Mighty happy to see Ephraim, he said. He was on his way to Madison to visit his wife and he asked Schutt to accompany him and thus learn how unfounded his suspicions had been.

The two men went to Buffalo, where they had to change cars. They stayed overnight, and in the morning started walking to the depot together. There was a huge crowd in the depot. Schutt got aboard the train for Madison, but Rulloff didn't. He seemed to have got lost in the station throng. Schutt's suspicions were increased. He went on to small Madison, learned that no one there knew or had ever heard of "Mr. N. Dupuy" nor even of Dr. and Mrs. Rulloff; and now, thoroughly alarmed, he went on to Cleveland and notified police.

Edward Rulloff, as related, was a man of marked appearance, one who didn't look like just any man in the street. Cleveland police readily discovered him in a Cleveland hotel. They placed him under arrest. Rulloff talked so well and so convincingly that police would have let him go, with an apology, had not Schutt insisted the man was doubtless a murderer and was wanted in Tompkins County, New York. In the free-and-easy manner of the day, Schutt was sworn in as a deputy and took his manacled prisoner back to Ithaca to face a charge of having murdered Harriet Schutt Rulloff.

In considering the evidence, or lack of it, the Tompkins County prosecutor thought it too slim for the murder charge. No corpus delicti could be shown, although Lake Cayuga had been dragged once, twice, with the idea that the two missing Rulloffs might be on its bottom. So Rulloff was indicted and promptly convicted on a charge of abduction. In January of 1846 he was sent to Auburn prison for ten years.

He served the ten years, too. In prison he was the wonder

of all, convicts and guards alike. His energy and his learning seemed boundless. Put to work in the prison carpet factory, he designed patterns that were intricate and thought to be highly artistic. He kept his cell filled with books and spent his free hours, of which he had many, studying and writing. Often he taught a prison school class, to which he discoursed on the origins of language—a subject to which he was constantly giving much thought and on which he was forming strong opinions.

In prison he was good-natured most of the time, but had occasional fits of temper. He was released in January of 1856, only to be tapped on the shoulder by the Tompkins County sheriff. "We want you for the murder of your wife," that worthy explained. Rulloff was staggered only for a moment. Then he smiled. "Take me to the jail immediately, sheriff," he said. "I must get to work preparing for my trial."

During the decade Rulloff had been in prison, Tompkins County had spent "thousands of dollars" dragging Lake Cayuga to no avail. But it had been learned that at about the same time as the disappearance of Mrs. Rulloff and child an unknown man had sold the corpses of a woman and child to Geneva Medical College. The woman's corpse had long black hair, much like that of Mrs. Rulloff. There had been no marks of violence on either body, and they had been purchased by the college "without hesitation." But both corpses had long since ceased to be available for evidence. The prosecutor, however, had pieced together bits of evidence concerning that mysterious trip Rulloff had made with the big chest. It was all circumstantial; but it might do, especially in a district where all possible jurors had come to believe the doctor guilty of dark deeds.

Rulloff prepared for his trial and asked for a hearing, during which he sneered at the prosecutor's lack of knowledge of law. "You cannot," the doctor shouted accusingly, "try me *again* for the unfortunate disappearance of my wife. Even a backwoods shyster ought to know that much." The authorities decided the prisoner was right; they couldn't try him twice for the same crime. They had another idea: they charged him with the murder of his baby daughter, Dorothy, who had not been brought into the case before. All Tompkins County was pleased, though far from surprised, when a jury brought in a verdict of guilty in the first degree. Rulloff was sentenced to be hanged.

Conducting his own case from the start, Rulloff knew all the tricks. He now petitioned for and obtained a stay of judgment pending appeal to the state court of appeals, which appeal he composed in right smart legal language and sent to that august body.

Held in jail without bail, Rulloff ingratiated himself with the family of Deputy Sheriff Jacob Jarvis. A son, Albert, eighteen, was permitted to spend much time with the prisoner, who taught the boy both Latin and French. Months passed while the high court went slowly down its docket to reach the Rulloff appeal. They had not reached it when, on the dark rainy night of May 5, 1857, a team of horses and a buggy drove up to the Tompkins County jail. A moment later Rulloff slipped quietly out of his cell and into the buggy, which, with young Albert Jarvis at the reins, drove quickly away into the country.

A fairly adequate description of Edward Rulloff at this period was given in the reward posters for his arrest, which soon appeared throughout New York and neighboring states:

. . . is 5 feet 8 inches tall, stout built, short thick neck; large head; a man of quick, precise motions; stoops forward when he walks; speaks French, German and other languages; weight 180 pounds; broad between eyes; dark brown hair; dark blue or hazel eyes; broad full face: probably some calluses on ankles caused by shackles.

The escape had been sensational. Rulloff seemed to have vanished along with young Jarvis.

2

Two months or so after Rulloff's escape, a Professor James Nelson turned up at the office of the Reverend Doctor Barker, president of Allegheny College, Meadville, Pennsylvania. He had a remarkable head and was extremely broad between the eyes. This was of course nobody but Rulloff. As Professor Nelson he impressed President Barker with his vast learning. Allegheny's faculty was filled at the time; but Dr. Barker was happy to give a fellow savant a letter to an academy in the South, then in need of a teacher.

This letter was a highly flattering document which stated, among other things, that Dr. Barker had examined Professor Nelson in Greek, Latin, Hebrew, French, and German and had found him to be "one of the best linguists I have ever met."

Rulloff might have gone South and taken the teaching position suggested by Dr. Barker's letter except for one thing. He needed cash to travel and he had none. As usual with Rulloff he set about to get what he needed.

In Meadville he learned of one A. B. Richmond, a local "inventor and scientist," and made a call at Richmond's home. Here he noted a fine collection of marine shells, which he examined with interest. "This one," said Professor Nelson–Rulloff, picking up a specimen, "is not *Spondylus spinosus*, as you have marked it, but *Argonauti argo*." Scientist Richmond was impressed. He checked the specimen and found the visitor was correct.

Richmond was further delighted to find his caller an expert mineralogist as well as a conchologist of rare parts. On a second visit Nelson–Rulloff displayed a remarkable knowledge of insects, of which Mr. Richmond had a large collection.[2] Richmond was charmed. He took his new scientist friend into his

---

[2] I should like to have seen the home of Mr. Richmond. In it, if the record is to be trusted, were large collections of insects, shells, minerals both precious and otherwise, butterflies, birds.

confidence. He had invented a machine, he said, and he wanted
a working model made in order to secure a patent.[3] Rulloff
looked over the drawings and said he could make the model.
Richmond told him to go ahead.

During construction of the working model of the invention
an incident happened which did not seem significant until later.
Rulloff asked for an emery wheel to polish certain parts of
the model, and to Richmond he explained in detail the exact
sort of wheel he wanted. Richmond must have known a good
deal about emery wheels, for when Rulloff had finished his
description Richmond said, "Why, Professor Nelson, that is
the sort of wheel they use to polish cutlery in the Auburn penitentiary. Were you ever there?"

Professor Nelson's eyes blazed strangely for a moment.
"What do you mean?" he cried, then, seeing that Richmond's
remark was only a pleasantry, he laughed and remarked that
he had seen the type of wheel while on a visit to the prison.

Meadville of the time must have been full of inventors. Professor Nelson–Rulloff agreed to purchase one-half interest in
Richmond's device, and also an interest in another patent be-
longing to George Stewart of Meadville. While completing
work on Richmond's model, he asked Richmond and Stewart
if they would accept, in lieu of cash, five very valuable watches.
They replied yes. The professor then remarked that the watches
were in his brother's keeping in Warren County, only a short
way from Meadville; he would go there to get them and return
the following day.

Professor Nelson never returned to Meadville, and for a few
days both inventors Stewart and Richmond were at a loss to
explain the matter. Not for long, though. The Meadville paper
presently carried a news item reporting that a jewelry store

---

[3] It has been impossible to learn what sort of machine it was. It may even
have been of the perpetual-motion type, for in mid last century the country
was fairly crawling with machines that required no power and would run
forever.

in Warren County had been entered during the night and several watches stolen. This might have passed, but not a second news story: the stolen watches had been found hidden under a pile of lumber and they had been wrapped in a poster which the departed Professor Nelson had printed to advertise the new inventions of Messrs. Stewart and Richmond.

The poster led police to the two inventors. They told their story about the vanishing professor. Stewart was an amateur photographer. He had taken a picture of Professor Nelson at work. Police of Warren County looked at the photograph and thought they recognized nobody but Edward Rulloff, the celebrated criminal who had escaped from jail at Ithaca. But Rulloff was not to be found.

For a time Rulloff hid in New York state, and he wasn't having much fun doing it. He was forced to sleep in barns, under culverts, in the bushes of pastures. The chase had been close, the weather bitterly cold. Some two months later he showed up in Jamestown, New York, in rather bad shape. He was tired and worn and he had frozen one foot. He went into a Jamestown drugstore, displayed his knowledge of the United States Pharmacopoeia, and talked the druggist into letting him compound his own prescription for frostbite. In spite of this application the big toe on his left foot did not heal. He amputated it himself.

Going next to a hotel in Jamestown, Rulloff came face to face with a convict he had known well during his ten years in Auburn prison but who was now working as hostler at the hotel. Rulloff acted with characteristic promptness. He poked a gun into his old friend's ribs and promised to kill him should he mention Rulloff's identity. The fellow not only promised silence but convinced the usually skeptical Rulloff that he meant it; and the latter confided he was leaving town at once to go to Ohio, where he would teach school in a small town which he named.

In the very hotel where Rulloff was staying was one of the

reward posters for his capture. He could scarcely have checked out when his ex-convict friend went to Sheriff John Dennin of Chautauqua County with the information that the much-wanted man was on his way to Ohio. Sheriff Dennin took the trail. He found Rulloff already settled and running a writing school "in a small town in the interior of Ohio."

It would appear that Sheriff Dennin was given to too much talking about his professional work. In the hearing of a local farmer he bragged that he had located the noted criminal Rulloff and that he was going forthwith to Columbus, state capital, to get an extradition order from the Ohio governor. And Dennin did go to Columbus.

While Dennin was away, the farmer decided to cut in on the reward himself. He went to his local constable with word that the writing-school professor was worth a good piece of money if taken and delivered to Jamestown, New York. The constable arrested Rulloff and then, with the informant farmer and three other men, started with their prisoner for the nearest railroad station.

The account of just how it happened is not at all clear, but the record shows that in spite of his five captors Rulloff got out of the wagon and started to go away from there. He still had a gun in his pocket; and when his so-called captors started after him he began shooting, wounding one man. But he was retaken and then conveyed to Ithaca, not Jamestown, where the constable and his crew presumably received the reward.

Rulloff was now in familiar surroundings again, in the clink at Ithaca. It will be recalled that when he escaped from Ithaca jail he was awaiting a decision from the New York court of appeals. The decision was now ready and it held unanimously that Rulloff could not rightfully be convicted of killing his daughter when no body had ever been found. This decision was handed down in December of 1858.

When the high court's ruling became known, a mob of Ithaca citizens was quickly and enthusiastically formed with

the avowed purpose of taking Rulloff from jail and stringing
him to the nearest telegraph pole. Police spirited the prisoner
to the Auburn penitentiary for his own safety, and the prosecution looked around for some other charge that could be successfully prosecuted.

'Way back in 1845, during Rulloff's period as a botanical
physician, it was remembered, he had been called to treat the
wife and baby of William Schutt, his brother-in-law. Both
mother and child had died. That was almost fourteen years in
the past. The bodies were now exhumed, and a Professor Ogden
Doremus swore that both showed traces of copper poison.

The prosecution, however, did not think they had sufficient
evidence to put the man on trial. He was turned over to authorities of Warren County, Pennsylvania, for the affair of
the stolen watches. Nor did Warren County think it had a
case, either. After languishing in jail for many months the
man was discharged without trial.

Now there comes another obscure period in the life of
Edward Rulloff. He probably was connected with a bank robbery in New Hampshire and with a store robbery in Connecticut. The trail is dim, and the man had many aliases. But in
November of 1861 the trail became clear again. On the twen-
tieth of that month he was received at Sing Sing prison under
the name of James H. Kerron, having been sent up for two
years and six months from Dutchess County on a charge of
burglary.

In Sing Sing, Rulloff acted as bookkeeper in the prison
cabinet shop; and one who saw them described the pages as
looking like engraved copperplate. This same unnamed person talked with the prisoner, finding him "gentleness itself"
with a "most winsome manner." Winsome or not, he was held
for his full sentence—which expired in 1864.

In prison Rulloff had made friends with a fellow convict,
one William T. Dexter, sent up for a burglary job on the
Bowery. The two men were released at about the same time.

Now Albert Jarvis, son of the deputy sheriff at Ithaca, turned up again. He was the boy who had aided Rulloff to escape from Ithaca jail, back in 1857. These three men formed a sort of partnership for the purposes of larceny, burglary, and whatever else came up in the way of ready money.

The three men lived with the Dexter family, on Graham Street in Brooklyn, to whom Rulloff was known as Professor E. C. Howard. Rulloff acted as guide and counselor to the Dexter family and, indeed, appears to have run the family much as he pleased, using the house as his own, directing the purchase of food, advising on the legal aspects of rent collecting (the Dexters seem to have owned some houses or tenements), and impressing one and all as the profoundest thinker and scholar of modern times.

3

Now began the heyday of Rulloff's long career. The years from 1864 to 1870 were unquestionably the greatest he was to know, and also the most disappointing. He spent them in three general characterizations and in three general headquarters. At the Dexter home in Brooklyn he was Professor E. C. Howard, teacher of languages. He was the same Professor Howard over in Hoboken, New Jersey, where he had an office and conducted classes in English. At 170 Third Avenue, Manhattan, he was Professor Edward Leurio, *the* eminent philologist, master of twenty-eight languages and dialects, currently at work on a study that would shake the speech habits of the entire world. At the Third Avenue address he had a room in the house of a highly respectable family. His third characterization was that of Rulloff, the old, crafty criminal, who directed the forays of Bill Dexter and Albert Jarvis, his brother ex-convicts, over whom he seems to have had absolute power.

The man was pretty darned good in all three parts. On two days a week Professor Howard journeyed to his Hoboken office, where he taught the mysteries of English to polyglot immigrants. Sundays he usually spent at the Dexter home in Brooklyn, advising the household on everything. Much of the rest of the time he was Professor Leurio, at work in his Third Avenue study—which was piled high with books, manuscripts, and all the gear of a great scholar.

In his odd moments Rulloff directed the activities of his two thieves, Dexter and Jarvis. It was his custom to "case up" a job, as criminals say—to look over the premises, learn the habits of the occupants, and generally plan the strategy of the robbery or burglary or whatever seemed to be the best method.

One excellent haul, later traced to the trio, was the robbery of a silk-trimmings factory on Thirty-fifth Street, New York City. Only the best silks were stolen, for Rulloff's vast learning encompassed even the comparative values of taffeta, Chinese silk, the various brocades, and so forth. This particular robbery netted the thieves some two thousand dollars, but a night watchman was so badly beaten that he died. Rulloff advised his cronies to lie low for a time.

It was slowly made to penetrate the dim minds of his dupes that Professor Leurio was at work on his magnum opus and that they, Dexter and Jarvis, were to be of inestimable value to Progress by keeping the professor in funds. They were told that this magnum opus was a universal language that doubtless would be adopted by all countries and races, would bring understanding between nations, and would no doubt result in a peaceful and happy world. Wars, hates, even mild nationalistic antipathies, would vanish. Commerce would increase. Science and the arts would be enlightened by the easy exchange of ideas. Why, said Professor Leurio, a man would be able to go around the world, and to its poles, talking with all and sundry when Leurio's Universal Method was adopted.

Working furiously at his Third Avenue study, including much of the night, Rulloff was like a madman. The piles of

PROFESSOR LEURIO AND DR. RULLOFF   161

manuscript mounted one upon the other. The floor of his room was covered with papers and books. His landlady chided him because he would not stop to take sufficient food. Time and again she found him in the morning asleep in his chair, a pen in hand, the gas burning.

Other days he spent many hours in the Eclectic Library on Irving Place, where the attendants knew him as an odd, dynamic character whose mind was obviously crammed with much knowledge concerning words and their derivations—which was all he seemed interested in. He told the librarians, too, that he was preparing a paper on the scope of his big work, his Universal Method, which he planned to present at the next meeting of the American Philological Association.

Meanwhile Dexter and Jarvis kept doggedly at their robberies. How Rulloff managed to hold two criminals at work, risking their liberty if not their lives, to keep him in funds in order to complete a work on language must be left to the imagination. It is known that Dexter, at least, told a friend of Professor Leurio that he and Jarvis were supplying the professor with money. He seemed to take pride in the fact that his criminal activities were to result in a new universal language. Rulloff must have managed the men well, for not once in seven years were they arrested. All their hauls were not good, however, and at least on one occasion they stooped to the theft of a few bushels of potatoes.

Rulloff never squandered any of the criminal gains in riotous living. Whatever he spent went for rent, a very little food, and much paper and ink.

In July of 1869 the American Philological Association held its annual meetings in Poughkeepsie, New York. Professor Edward Leurio, dressed in a new frock coat and with a big silk hat, was present. He was permitted to present his great project to the assembled membership; and at the end of his talk he asked that the association take steps to sponsor publication of his study, which ran to hundreds of pages of beautifully written script. A committee was appointed to pass on the proposal, and reported that the work "did not come within the scope of this Association."

Professor Leurio was enraged. He displayed a moment of fierce temper to the assembled savants, then went away. Back in New York City he told Jarvis and Dexter that the lunkheads in charge of the philological group had no imagination and knew nothing of languages, anyway. He, himself, would publish the great work and give it to the world. It would take a good deal of money, he admitted, but he felt it could be raised with a little close application.

Months passed while Professor Leurio attempted to complete his Universal Method, and while Rulloff attempted to find profitable places to rob. Just how he happened to choose the town of Binghamton, over in south central New York state, can only be guessed; possibly his burglar friends got wind of a shipment of silks and learned its destination. In any case, the place selected was Halbert Brothers' silk shop on Court Street in Binghamton. On the night of August 21, 1870, two men broke into this store, which was undergoing alterations at the time, and aroused two clerks named Fred Mirrick and Gilbert Burrows, who were sleeping in the place.

Waking from deep slumber, Mirrick and Burrows saw two strange men piling rolls of silk on a counter. The clerks rushed the intruders and were getting the upper hand when a shot rang out in the room. The struggles of the four men ceased for a moment while a heavy, black-bearded man walked toward them, a smoking revolver in his hand. Burrows remembered afterward what a striking apparition the man seemed. A tall silk hat sat on his head—a huge head—and from under the rim two deep eyes blazed. This personage was wearing a frock coat, and his whole manner was commanding.

The two clerks thought at first that the third man might be a detective, come just in time to help. But the man was of course Rulloff, who had been watching the outside of the store

while his men got the silks. He now motioned his men to one
side. Then he lifted his gun very calmly and shot Clerk Mirrick
through the forehead. Just as calmly he took aim at Clerk Burrows and shot him, too.

Mirrick was dead, Burrows only badly wounded. The silk-
hatted man and his cronies left without the silks. Burrows
staggered out of the store, bleeding profusely, and got to the
home of Chief of Police Flynn, three blocks away.

The would-be robbers made a clean getaway, but in their
hurry they left several small articles in the store and a pair
of shoes. The shoes were patent-leather Oxfords and an interesting thing about them was that the left one had a notable
depression at the place where the big toe would fit, unless it
happened there was no big toe.

In the street near the store, looking as if it had been thrown
in a hurry, was a flowered carpetbag. In the bag was nothing
at all except a column-long clipping from some newspaper.
It dealt with the foreign and domestic policies of the Prussian
government, something that policemen of the time did not sit
up all night talking about.

Neither the shoes nor the bag seemed immediately important.

Binghamton was thoroughly aroused at the murder. Deputies were sent into the surrounding country. They arrested
everybody who could not give an account of himself. Two days
later the bodies of two men were found in the Chenango River,
a few miles out of town. They had been beaten, possibly killed,
before being thrown into the water. Burrows, the surviving
clerk, identified them as the two burglars.

In a pocket of one of the thugs was an identification card:
"William T. Dexter," with a Brooklyn address. In the other
thug's pocket was a key ring with an identification tag carrying the name of Albert Jarvis, Ithaca, New York.

A day later a posse of deputies met a large-bodied man with
a back beard, a large head, and width between the eyes. It was
Rulloff, but they didn't know it. The fellow explained his pres-

ence along the railroad tracks by saying he had been thrown off a train because he had lost his ticket. He had been going, he said, to Ithaca, where he was, of all things, to give a lecture. Apparently he talked the police into a daze, for they allowed him to get a moving freight train between himself and them. When the train had passed, he wasn't there any more.

Chief Flynn was angry at his men. He sent out other posses, and one of these found the same bearded man hiding in a barn on a farm less than half a mile from the railroad. They took him to Binghamton jail, where he said his name was Charles Augustus and where he spoke in a high tone of suing the police for false arrest. They would rue the day, he said sternly.

Here is perhaps the best example of the talkative powers of Edward Rulloff. Found hiding in a barn, his clothing dirty, his face and hands unwashed, by every apparent reason a perfect suspect, he talked so well that Binghamton police were satisfied they were holding not only an innocent man but a very important personage. The police, in fact, were in the very act of turning him loose when Judge Bolcom, formerly of Ithaca, happened into the room. He caught sight of "Charles Augustus" just in time and let out a roar. "Grab that man!" he shouted. "That's Rulloff!"

Fast talking and bluster were of no avail with Judge Bolcom. The judge knew his man and had long pondered the fate of Mrs. Rulloff and child. To the judge's assurance was added the fact of the Oxford shoes found in the silk store after the murder of Mirrick—the shoes with the notable depression where the big left toe fitted, if there was a big left toe. At the insistence of Judge Bolcom police forced the suspect to take off his shoes. The big left toe was missing.

Clerk Burrows was brought to the police station. He immediately recognized the man as the killer. Rulloff was put in a cell while police followed up the evidence found on the two drowned, or murdered, robbers.

At the Brooklyn address found in Dexter's pocket police

learned that Rulloff was Professor Howard, a "doctor, lawyer, and very great scholar" who was writing a big book. He often called at the Dexter home, Mrs. Dexter, the dead thug's mother, said, but he also lived part of the time with a Professor Leurio at 170 Third Avenue in New York City. At the latter address the officers gained entrance to Professor Leurio's room, and on the desk they found a copy of the New York *Times* from which one full column had been cut. The clipping found in the carpetbag in Binghamton fitted neatly.

4

Rulloff went on trial at Binghamton on January 5, 1871. The charge was murder of the silk-store clerk, Mirrick. This time the prosecutor had a good solid corpus delicti handy. A jury found the savant guilty. He was sentenced to be hanged May 5.

Again, and this time with the aid of counsel, Rulloff obtained a stay of judgment and addressed the court of appeals for a new trial. While awaiting the result he busied himself with his universal method of language and, due to an excellent press, became almost overnight something of a national sensation.

Binghamton papers published extracts from the method, including many of the five thousand examples which were "to establish the TRUE principles of the formation of language." Horace Greeley, editor of the New York *Tribune*, sent an emissary to Rulloff with galley proofs of a new translation of *Faust* by Bayard Taylor, an able man with languages himself. Scholar Rulloff looked over the proofs with no little interest, and gave the reporter an extensive interview in which he found both good and critical things to say of Taylor's version.

The big city papers now took up the case of the "Learned Murderer," and articles concerning his amazing field of knowledge were published. Letters to the editor appeared by the score. One writer proposed that he, himself, whom he described as a failure in life, be permitted to substitute in serving the hangman's noose and that the great Rulloff be not only spared but aided in publishing his revolutionary study on a universal language. Petitions were soon in circulation for the pardon of one of the coldest-blooded killers of his generation.[4]

Governor Hoffman of New York was appealed to. He did not pardon Rulloff, but he did appoint a sanity commission to examine the condemned man. The commission found that the prisoner was in sound physical and mental health. There was nothing to do but to hang him.

During the period when the sanity commission was debating the case, Professor George W. Sawyer spent an afternoon with Rulloff in his cell and later wrote what is probably the shrewdest estimate of Rulloff the scholar.

Dr. Sawyer found that the prisoner's knowledge of Greek words was indeed remarkable and that the facility with which he used such words for the purpose of founding his universal language was nothing short of startling. His method, at first glance and without critical reflection, seemed amazingly simple and original.

But [said Dr. Sawyer] his knowledge seemed to be fragmentary and ill-assorted. Endowed with a strong intellect and quick inventive faculty, this strange man seems to have early in life determined to use words as counters, literally speaking. As children use blocks to build houses in any form, according to fancy, so Rulloff seems to have determined in the exercise of his will to make a universal language, for no one principle of which he should be indebted to anyone else. For that reason, instead of pursuing farther an acquaintance with classical literature, he rests satisfied with the comparatively slender acquisitions of early life, and, with a large stock of words retained in memory, he coasts about to find a theory that shall comprise them all.

---

[4] Knowing that Americans will sign petitions for almost anything, I tried vainly to find a copy of one demanding the eminent crook's pardon. But I have no doubt that several such petitions were in circulation and that hundreds signed them who had no more knowledge of Rulloff's character than they had of Greek roots.

Then dusting off his own classical learning in the manner of most professors, Dr. Sawyer concludes:

Thus, upon the Procrustes bed of this theory all words are to be laid, and cut short or made long according to the requirements of a fanciful method.

During his last days Rulloff confessed to his counsel that he had killed his wife and child back in 1845. Beat them to death with an iron pipe, he said; then wrapped their bodies with "untempered steel wire that never could become unfastened," attached a heavy mortar to the body of his wife, a flatiron to that of his child, and put them into the big chest. He drove Neighbor Robertson's mare and wagon to Lake Cayuga; stole a rowboat, in which he took the bodies out into the lake and threw them overboard. They were never recovered.

In his last hours he also admitted—or rather bragged—of having given poison to the wife and child of his brother-in-law, William Schutt. "I wanted him to suffer for his opposition to my marriage to his sister," Rulloff said, which was one way of paying off a snub.

It will be remembered that nothing had been known of Rulloff's early life—his life before he appeared at Dryden, New York, as a canal laborer in 1842. But now, almost thirty years after, when he had attained international notoriety as the "Educated Murderer," facts of his obscure early years came to light.

He was born Edward Howard Rulloffson, in 1819, in the backwoods settlement of Hammond River, not far from St. John, New Brunswick, Canada. His parents were described as being "respectable people of Dutch ancestry." Young Rulloffson did not attend school until he was twelve, but at home his mother had given him "a wide education in many subjects." From the age of four he had read everything he could lay hands on.

After some formal schooling he had worked in a St. John store until it was destroyed by fire, then as clerk in a lawyer's office. At this period St. John citizens suffered from a series of burglaries, one of which was in the home of the lawyer for whom young Rulloffson worked. A day or two later the lawyer was somewhat surprised to see his clerk wearing a suit of clothes he recognized as having been stolen from his house. The young man did not deny the theft. He was sent to the New Brunswick prison in 1839, aged twenty, and served two years.

On his discharge from prison he disappeared and was never seen again in the province. What he did between his release and his arrival at Dryden in 1842 is not known, but it is safe to say he was up to no good.

Rulloff spent his last night, says one old account, in alternately boasting of his achievements in the world of knowledge and in the "utterances of revolting blasphemies and obscenities." He also "profanely repulsed all religious aid." On the seventeenth of May in 1871 he was properly hanged in front of the jail at Binghamton.

One could wish that before the trap was sprung he had left some message, preferably in the language of his Universal Method, for the guidance of future philologists. But his last words were "vulgar and profane mouthings, horrible to hear."

CHAPTER NINE

THE CRIME IN THE VALE OF TEMPE

THE SUDDEN APPEARANCE of a worthless young Jukes in the midst of an old and excellent family is so rare, and usually so inexplicable by any known scientific reason, that the black sheep becomes of greater interest than if he were the issue of some casual amour of nameless and probably criminal morons.

In New England, where George Abbott was born, families counted for a good deal and his family, though not distinguished, was as good as they came and dated back almost if not quite to The Beginning, which was, of course, in 1620 on the Rock at Plymouth. His paternal grandfather was Eliphalet Abbott, the proud and, by rural Yankee standards, the wealthy proprietor of Abbotts Mills in Fairlee, Vermont, next town to Thetford, wherein was the Abbott homestead with broad acres along the Connecticut River. The Abbott farm was in that part of town called North Thetford.

On his mother's side George Abbott came from a long line of Wilmots—also of North Thetford, where both Abbotts and Wilmots had lived for generations. "Good old Green Mountain stock" was the term, and there wasn't any better term along the Vermont side of the upper Connecticut.

George Abbott, however, was born in Salem, Massachusetts, where his father was a successful businessman, in one of the fine ancient houses of McIntire influence, if not of actual design, which were common there in 1857. His mother died three days after he was born and he was adopted by his uncle and aunt, Mr. and Mrs. Israel Abbott of Salem. The boy was given a careful bringing-up and was sent to Brown School, a private institution, until the age of ten, when he removed with uncle and aunt to North Thetford, to live on the old homestead.

A schoolmate recalls that young Abbott made a favorable impression when he arrived, "attired in a handsome blue suit with brass buttons," in the town where both Abbotts and Wilmots had "so long sustained an honored name." Young Abbott wasn't quite eleven when he began his long and eminently successful career to prove that at least one Abbott was well worth hanging.

The boy's first derelictions were stealing from pupils and teachers at the North Thetford school. He was bright enough and learned easily, but he found it impossible to keep his hands off the pens, pencils, jackknives, and other small articles of his school mates. And one account of his school days points out, with an implied curse in the direction of the late Erastus Flavius Beadle, that young Abbott was given to the reading of dime novels. When one learns that a bit later the boy also chewed tobacco, the explanation of his entire life becomes clearer.

Within a year the lad had begun stealing more valuable articles, things like clocks and jewelry, which he hid in a cave dug in the Vermont bank of the Connecticut River. At the age of fourteen he accomplished something of a record, for the kiddie class, by stealing a good-sized cast-iron stove. For this he was arrested and brought before the justice of the peace.

The lad's father was called from distant Salem, and he and Uncle Israel managed to settle the case out of court. Young

Abbott showed what he thought of such soft doings a few months later when he shot and killed the dog of the man who had had him arrested over the stove, and even threatened the man himself. He seems not to have been arrested for this exuberance.

Working on the Abbott farm at this time was a hired man named Pete Duplissy, one of a family that had often appeared in the Vermont records of petty larceny, sneak thievery, and other prowlings—a family of no goods described graphically by a Thetford worthy of the time as a "mess of egg-sucking, doughnut-robbing, cigaroot-smoking scallawags." Late in 1874 Pete Duplissy and young Abbott, then seventeen, were arrested for entering what was described as the dwelling house of Samuel H. Hale in Orford, New Hampshire, but what must have looked like a rural Tiffany's, and for stealing there "40 silver watches, value $400; 20 gold bosom pins, value $25; and silver watch cases to value of $200." Another indictment charged the two youths with entering the home of Thomas Fifield of Orford and of stealing "$84 in cash, 2 gal. whisky value $10, 3 gal. gin value $12, 1 gal. brandy $6," which indicated Squire Fifield to have been well bolstered against both the inclemencies of the rigorous climate and the bites of *Crotalus horridus*.[1] Still another charge brought at this time was that Abbott and Duplissy had stolen the following articles from the shop of H. H. Conant, Orford harness maker: two revolvers, one hundred keys, one buggy whip, one dollar in cash—all valuable equipment for night prowlers.

At Plymouth on November 5, 1874, young Abbott was sent to the New Hampshire penitentiary at Concord for four years. On learning of his son's disgrace his father committed suicide in Salem by hanging but left his estate to George, when he

---

[1] New Hampshire proudly claims that no wild rattlesnake has ever been seen within its borders; but Squire Fifield lived on the Vermont line and Vermont to this day offers a bounty on rattlers, which, however, are much scarcer than in the 1870s.

should become of age, with Samuel Cally, mayor of Salem, as administrator.

When George Abbott was released from Concord prison in 1878, he was legally of age; and he went immediately to Salem, where he received his father's estate—reported variously as being between three and five thousand dollars, a lot of money for a young man who read dime novels and smoked cigarettes.

Just how Abbott disposed of all this cash in a year's time must be left to the imagination. Even B. H. Corning, who wrote a classic monograph on the man entitled *Corning's Life of Abbott-Almy, as Looked Up by Him*, could not find out. Author Corning covers these twelve months in the life of his hero merely by saying ominously that "he lived a fast life in various places until his money was spent."

There is no doubt that the money was spent. In the summer of 1879 Abbott showed up at Uncle Israel's farm in North Thetford penniless and went to work pitching hay. When haying was over he went away without telling his uncle where he was going.

It wasn't long before the usually quiet and safe rural region on both sides of the Connecticut from White River Junction, Vermont, to Woodsville, New Hampshire, was terrorized by a night prowler, or prowlers, who committed daring burglaries and was never seen. Homes, schools, stores—everything but a post office—were entered and goods and personal belongings stolen. Abbott was of course suspected, but where was he? The sheriffs of Lebanon and Hartford, of Hanover and Norwich, of Lyme and Thetford, of Orford and Fairlee, all tried to find out but didn't. Young Mark Ware, a farmboy of Thetford, made the discovery.

On election day, 1880, when James A. Garfield and Chester Alan Arthur—the latter allegedly a Vermonter—were being elected to the highest offices in the land, young Ware, who wasn't old enough to vote, spent the day roaming Thetford mountain. In an almost inaccessible place which commanded a

wonderful view of the Connecticut River Valley he discovered
a small cave filled with loot and containing other evidences of
habitation, including a stove *and a small bull's-eye dark lantern* such as often could be seen in the pictures in Mr. Beadle's
dime novels and which, as even the bucolic young Ware must
have known, was never carried by anyone except burglars and
detectives.[2]

Ware looked the cave over with the excitement any boy
would have found in the circumstances. He noted that the
entrance was well hidden from view below by trees. He took
his bearings well and then struck out for the village, where
he reported his discovery. Next day a posse armed with rifles
and shotguns went to Thetford mountain. It was agreed, says
one entertaining account, that no shot should be fired unless
Abbott was sighted. A little later two posse members ran across
Abbott himself but did not have a chance to fire. Abbott, rifle
over his arm and looking like business, suddenly appeared and
asked what they wanted way up there. They replied they were
squirrel hunting. It would seem fanciful, but this account has
it that Abbott thereupon asked the hunters if they were good
shots. They suggested that all three shoot at a mark to decide
the question. Abbott fired first, and presently a dozen armed
men were hurrying to the spot.

Abbott was surprised, but he wasn't giving himself up without a try. He started to shoot and to run. A posse bullet in his
leg and two more in his body brought him to earth. He sur-
rendered and was toted to the village on an improvised
stretcher.

Given medical attention and thought to be in a dangerous
if not a critical condition, Abbott was put in charge of Sheriff
Solon Berry in a private home. For several hours Berry sat

[2] This same lantern is now the property of Mr. Roger Johnson of Spring-
field, Massachusetts, New England's noted expert on caves. It is a coal-oil
affair with a sliding shutter to close off the light and a cone-shaped top with
vents for smoke and gas.

by the bed, while his prisoner moaned with pain and then relapsed into what he thought was a deep sleep. The sheriff, as sheriffs will, left the room for a moment to see a man about a couple of dogs, and on his return five minutes later the prisoner's bed was empty. Abbott, naked except for a night-shirt, had grabbed a quilt from the bed, opened a window, and gone away.[3]

This, you will recall, was November in Vermont. The wounded man was found by a posse next day, hiding under a railroad culvert, practically frozen. He was put in the Chelsea, Vermont, jail. At the spring term of court he was sentenced on a burglary charge to fifteen years in the Vermont prison at Windsor, being admitted on June 23, 1881.

Abbott became Convict 2527. On his commitment he was twenty-three years old, five feet eight inches, one hundred and fifty pounds; with hazel eyes, dark hair, a scar over the right eye. He admitted to no religious preference or gainful occupation. He used tobacco, but in the matter of alcohol was listed as "temperate."

Windsor prison in 1881 was not exactly the sort of place to make a mollycoddle of a man. Erected in 1809, it had improved somewhat, but not too much, since the years John Reynolds was there and wrote of his experience as an inmate: "Many a time have I made large balls by scraping the frost with my hands from the stone walls of my cell." So cold were Reynolds' hands that "I had to tax my ingenuity to turn over the pages of my Bible." But Windsor was in 1881 still an old-fashioned prison and its wardens kept old-fashioned discipline. Escapes were almost unheard of.

---

[3] George Abbott may have had a low taste for prose, but he liked good poetry. In Abbott's clothes Sheriff Berry found a notebook with the following lines inscribed:

> He either fears his fate too much,
> Or his deserts are small,
> Who will not put it to the touch,
> And win or lose it all.

A fifteen-year stretch looked like a long time to George Abbott. He laid his plans carefully to accomplish what only one other man had been able to do in three-quarters of a century—to get over the big Windsor wall.

After some months Convict Abbott was put to work in the prison engine room, a job he continued to hold until his departure. In the meantime he saved every piece of string and cord, no matter how small, he could lay his hands on. In his job in the engine and boiler rooms he often had occasion to work with pipe, and whenever chance offered he hid a short piece of the iron tubing. Working with infinite care and patience throughout months and years, he braided his thousands of bits of string into a stout, serviceable rope. Into loops of the rope at proper intervals he inserted a length of pipe, until the finished job represented a pretty good ladder. How he managed to hide this contraption during its long stages of manufacture isn't known to this day.

On the evening of September 30, 1887, the ladder was ready, and hidden in a good, handy place. Convict-engineer Abbott rang the seven-forty-five signal (he had to ring it every quarter hour) to show the warden he was at his post. The bell in the warden's office rang on the minute. The eight-o'clock bell never sounded. During the intervening fifteen minutes Abbott ran across the prison yard, scaled the wall, and let himself down on the other side with his homemade ladder.

It was a clean getaway. Windsor prison never saw George Abbott again.

2

Along with Windsor prison the escaped convict left his real name behind him. Henceforth and until the day of his death he was Frank C. Almy, the name by which he is remembered. During his first three years of freedom he ranged through many states. There are gaps in his life story at this period, but it is known that he worked as an oysterman in Baltimore, as a steel-mill employee in Birmingham and in Youngstown, as a riveter in Delaware. Prison had at least got him into the habit of working. He worked on a farm near Fort Smith, Arkansas, and in a factory in Jamestown, Pennsylvania. In Texas he was a ranch hand, and in Georgia he worked a few weeks as a stationary engineer.

But the West, apparently, was too much for him. In June of 1889 he showed up in Peabody, Massachusetts, destitute of clothing except for a few rags, and worked a while for a Farmer Wilkins. He left Wilkins in November, then labored briefly for Moses Clark of 27 North Franklin Street, Lynn. In late December he got a job as engineer at Brown's Glue Works, Marblehead, where he remained until the following May. During this time he boarded with a Mrs. Caroline Morse, by whom he appears to have been heartily disliked. And why not? Mrs. Morse, who is to be thanked for giving the best description of Almy's habits at this period, said that for one thing Almy had a "ferocious appetite." Seems he stored away enormous quantities of food, at breakfast, dinner, and supper, and had the table manners of a Berkshire hog. Moreover, he "had a peculiar lowery look while eating"—which, one gathers, was no way to look while consuming the excellent fare provided by Mrs. Morse.

Her boarder also smoked Blackstone cigars, which stamped him as a Yankee; but he was none of your shy, retiring Yankees. He was, Mrs. Morse avers, "familiar on slight acquaintance"—so familiar, in fact, that Mrs. Morse had to "put a stop to his kissing my daughter Alice," then fourteen years old. But Almy never roamed at night. He remained in the boardinghouse every last evening, his landlady said, talking little, and never about himself, but doing a deal of reading. Mrs. Morse came to know his favorite books, which he got from the public library in Abbot Hall. Almy's taste hadn't changed much since childhood. His favorites in the Marblehead library were *She, King Solomon's Mines,* and *The Three Guardsmen.*

On March 1, 1890, Mrs. Morse lost her gluttonous boarder. Almy went to work for A. W. Howe, a market gardener in near-by Danvers; here he often boasted to another hired hand, one Freeland Lovelace, of his extraordinary exploits in the field of amour. He left Howe's employ on the Fourth of July.

You could never tell where Frank Almy would light next. This time he went to Whitefield, New Hampshire, where he worked for part of a week in Brown's sawmill. On July 11 he applied for a job as hired man at the farm of Andrew Warden, on the Lyme road, a bit more than a mile from Dartmouth Hall in the college town of Hanover.

Living at the farm were Mr. and Mrs. Warden and their two daughters, Christie, aged twenty-four, and Fanny, sixteen. Christie was a good-looking girl of the medium-blonde type, of "fine, rounded form and discreet manners." She was active in the Grafton Star Grange, Patrons of Husbandry, for which she acted as secretary; and she also did much clerical work for Professor C. E. Petee, master of Grafton Star Grange and dean of the New Hampshire College of Agriculture and the Mechanic Arts.[4]

Young Fanny Warden, who must have been a shrewd judge of human character, took an immediate dislike to the new hired man—a dislike that grew into a quiet, cold, implacable hate as lasting as the granite rocks in the Warden pasture. It was different with Christie. She was attracted to the handsome and much-traveled stranger, not knowing of course that his travels had been made in the kind of cars that have their gross and net capacities stamped on their barn-red exteriors. And Frank Almy, the two-time loser and escaped felon, Vermont's most celebrated criminal in more than a decade—Almy found this sweet rustic belle all that he could desire.

---

[4] Founded in Hanover in 1866, this school was moved to Durham in 1893 and is now the University of New Hampshire.

The courtship proceeded closely along the orthodox lines of rustic courtships of the place and period. Christie worked buttonholes in Frank's shirts. Frank wiped dishes while Chris washed. They wrung clothes together, and gathered flowers. As summer turned to autumn, the couple strung popcorn to decorate Grafton Star Grange hall for the annual harvest supper. They went to husking bees together in Norwich, just across the Ledyard bridge from Hanover. The Wardens were members of College Congregational Church, and every Sunday the hired man and Chris attended services. For a church supper Chris baked the kind of cake Frank liked. When winter came, as it never fails to do in New Hampshire, Chris and Frank went on sleigh rides and on straw rides to whist parties.

Chris even did her best to raise Frank's taste in literature. From the Grange library she brought home the massive *Last Days of Pompeii*, which they read together. At Christmastime he gave her a nice handkerchief; she gave him a tie in a case. More significant to the course of the affair, perhaps, was that Frank found an old glove of Christie's in the Warden attic and this he kept with him at all times, day and night. He also carried a bunch of hair combings from the girl's head.

What seems incomprehensible today is the fact that George Abbott, under the name of Frank Almy, could work and live and love and appear socially in and around Hanover for a continuous period of nine months and not be recognized for who and what he was. Hanover is some fifteen miles from North Thetford, where Abbott's sensational arrest and escape had taken place. The criminal doings of Abbott were still a topic for discussion in the neighborhood, and his feat of escaping from Windsor prison was much talked about. One is forced to the conclusion that neither Vermonters nor New Hampshire folk got around a great deal in 1890.

The record indicates that in spite of Chris' liking for the Warden's hired man she did not lose her head. She wanted to know more about the man who had asked her to marry. In one of several letters made public later, Christie had written: "Frank, you came to us a mystery and remain one yet. We know nothing of your past life, except what you have been pleased to tell." Chris went on to say that she, too, was "lonely, like yourself."

In another letter from Chris to Frank she indicates that he told her a little something of his past life, or had at least admitted he was not as pure as he might be. She held out some hope to him and also gave him a mild dose of metaphysics, along with some sound advice as to how to behave if he wanted to win her. This letter became locally famous after it was printed in the daily press. It shows a fading Calvinism, some Yankee smugness, no little common sense, and a passing acquaintance with the high-toned and literary love-letter styles of the period.[5] Wrote Christie in part:

Dear Friend: I don't know as you expect an answer to your letters, and perhaps you do not require one, but to be honest with you and true to myself, I think you should know how I feel toward you. You already know, for I have told you, the sort of man I wish to love. . . . You have set yourself in defiance of God and man. I believe you have suffered the misery that must follow. You surely would not wish me, whom you love, to share that misery.

Since living with us you have not gained my highest regard or respect, nor that of my relatives and friends. Your conduct at the card table has given me more insight into the dark side of your character, of which you have spoken, than any other one thing. . . . I would never think of marrying a man to reform him. The reformation must come first. I am free to confess that should a man with a clear record desire my love, he would stand a much better chance than yourself. But there are none such that I know of. . . . Frank, I shall test the strength of your love. Can you open your heart to all good influences, practice a rigid self-control, and wait patiently? If it is ever so, I believe you

---

[5] At this time the Hanover *Gazette* and many other New England country papers were serializing, usually on their front pages, columns of drool by one Robert Grant, the "famous author" of something entitled *The Confessions of a Frivolous Girl*. The chapters were interspersed with advertisements for Dana's Sarsaparilla, which cured everything except, obviously, an addiction to saccharine fiction. Christie's letters indubitably show the effects of Mr. Grant's prose.

must win in the end, for you have many fine qualities that I admire, and I cannot help liking you, with all your faults. . . . I fear I am not worthy of such a love, but I cannot be satisfied unless the man I love is able to help me to become better—for I am weak—rather than to drag me down.

This letter certainly indicates that Chris and Frank were having serious discussions of love and marriage.

Almy had agreed to work for Farmer Warden until the first of April, 1891. He did so and he hoped to remain longer. But Mr. Warden, whose decision may have been strengthened by the seething hatred of young Fanny, told Almy his services were no longer required. It seems Almy had displayed a mean temper on several occasions. Then, too, Mr. Warden may have had a vague uneasiness regarding the man. But the fellow left the farm and the town of Hanover with his real identity still unsuspected. Christie was in tears the day he left. Fanny was jubilant.

From Hanover, Almy went to Salem, Massachusetts, where he picked up a suitcase of clothes he had previously left at a boardinghouse. He next appeared in Dorchester, near Boston, where he went to work in the woodworking shop of Edward Lynch and boarded at Mrs. Michael Quinn's, 1264 Dorchester Avenue, where he showed Mrs. Quinn a photograph of a pretty young woman who he said was named Christie Warden. He was in love with the girl, he said. "If I don't have her," he told his landlady, "then no other fellow will, either." He left Mrs. Quinn's on June 8.

On June 13 Almy bought a ticket in Boston for White River Junction, Vermont, four miles from Hanover. Arriving at Hanover that evening, he walked up the railroad tracks to Norwich, crossed the bridge, and continued to the Warden farm. All was quiet. Circling the house, he went through the field and into the barn. A little after two o'clock in the morning he was snugly hidden in a haymow of the Warden barn, not more than sixty feet from the sleeping house.

3

For the next thirty-two days Almy remained in the barn, emerging only at night to forage for food at neighboring farms and in the villages of Hanover and Lebanon—a practice at which he was adept through long experience. Twice he made attempts to see Christie at night: once when he actually entered the Warden house, went upstairs and into Christie's bedroom—to find the hated Fanny there, asleep—and again when he entered the home of Professor Petee, in Hanover village, thinking Christie was there. Instead he found a Miss Amelia Thompson, who awoke to find a strange man by her bed. In a gruff voice the intruder threatened her life if she made outcry, then went away.

On a second nocturnal visit to the Warden home Almy did not attempt to find Chris but contented himself with going into the parlor, where he turned over the sheet music on the piano and ran his fingers softly over the keys Chris had played on so often. He spent the days hidden in the barn writing love verses to Christie and fondling her old glove he had carried so long. On one of his night excursions he cut the initials "C & F," surrounded by the conventional heart, in the bark of a beech tree.

On July 17 the hidden man, listening from his post only a few yards from the house, heard the Wardens planning to go to a Grange meeting that evening. He was elated. His hopes beat high. Now, he thought, he should have an opportunity to talk to Chris alone; to ask her to flee with him, perhaps to Texas. He kept his eyes glued to his observation post, which was a large knothole.

Just as twilight began to fall he saw Chris come out of the house, dressed in dainty white, and alone. Now was his chance. He started to leave the barn but just then saw Mrs. Warden, Fanny, and another woman—who was Mrs. Louisa Goodell—join Christie. Almy withdrew, unseen, into the barn and watched the three women walk away in the direction of the Grange hall.

Night came on, and a wonderful night it was. A great yellow
moon beat down on as pretty a countryside as the moon ever
saw. The trim white houses gleamed with luster amid the green
fields and hills, and lights winked here and there across the Connecticut River Valley. Grafton Star Grange closed its meeting
a little after nine o'clock. Mrs. Warden, her two daughters, and
Mrs. Goodell began the mile-long walk to the Warden home.

Some fifteen minutes later the four women came to the pretty
field in the shaded hollow known locally and classically as the
Vale of Tempe, a beautiful spot through which a small brook
murmured softly. A cedar fence separated the small field from
the road, and in the fence was a set of bars—a farmer's gate—
and near the gate was a great, fine Balm of Gilead tree, now in
midsummer filling the Vale of Tempe with a strong, heady fra-
grance. As the women entered the big tree's deep shadow a man
suddenly appeared. He carried a revolver in his right hand and
did not attempt to conceal his identity.

"Mrs. Warden," he said, "you know me. I'm Frank Almy."
The women were too dumfounded to speak. "I only want to talk
to Christie," the man continued. "The rest of you run along."
Then he turned to the older Warden girl. "Christie," he said,
"I have come a thousand miles to meet you." He grabbed the
girl by an arm. Young Fanny grabbed Chris by the other arm,
and the three struggled a moment. Almy stuck the gun in Fanny's face. "Fan, I hate you," he said, and probably meant it.
"Unless you let go, I'll kill you." With a wrench he pulled
Chris from Fanny and flung her through the fence bars. Following Chris, he took her by the feet and began dragging her
over the ground.

Fanny climbed through the fence. Almy's gun blazed in the
dark and a bullet whistled close to the girl's ear. But Fan kept
on. Again he fired, and Fanny threw herself to the ground and
heard the bullet go by overhead. Mrs. Warden and Mrs. Goodell
were running down the road, shouting for help.

A few moments later—and nobody seems to have known how

long— the sound of a scuffle came from the darkness of the hollow, then a pitiful cry. It was Christie. "Help, Fan!" she cried. "He is tearing all my clothes off."

Fanny, crouching and wondering what to do, heard running footsteps on the road. She hurried back to the gate. Emmet Marshall, a passing farmer, had been attracted by the women's cries. Fanny explained quickly what was happening, and she and Marshall got through the bars and started up the hollow. Just then came the sound of a shot, then a despairing cry and another shot. As Marshall and Fanny hesitated, they saw the figure of Almy dash across the hollow and run into the deep cover of a maple grove.

Fanny and Marshall found poor Chris lying on her left side, her head in a pool of blood that was still growing. She had ceased to breathe. Marshall hurried to the village and returned with Dr. C. P. Frost. The doctor found the dead girl half-naked, dressed only in her stockings and bits of her waist and underclothing. Her pretty white dress, her petticoats, and pieces of underclothing were scattered around the scene. Her hat and shawl were found on the way to the fence bars.

Doctor Frost surmised, from his first impressions, that the murder had been accompanied by rape. At a later and thorough examination of the body, held in the Warden home, the doctor could not be sure. The girl had been shot first, he concluded, through the head. The second shot had been so placed as to destroy any evidence of rape, if rape there had been.

Before midnight the great bell on Dartmouth Hall began to toll, and Hanover village learned of the crime in the Vale of Tempe. Townfolk, professors, and students at summer classes scurried around to get guns for the man hunt which began immediately. Before daylight two hundred men were beating the woods and searching barns and other outbuildings in the neighborhood. Posses ranged both banks of the Connecticut and looked under bridges and culverts. No trace of Almy was found.

Next day the town of Hanover offered a reward for arrest of

the killer. The state added a sum to the reward. Sheriffs formed searching parties in the many towns up and down the valley. Not even a sign of Almy was found. An unusual thing in any hunt of this sort was that the search for Almy did not even turn up any of those countless imaginative persons who are forever seeing mysterious parties just disappearing into a woods, or flitting through a pasture, or driving a black horse and a covered buggy down a road at a fast clip. As day followed day and then grew into weeks, the excitement faded. Nobody, so far as one can learn, had yet connected the fugitive Frank Almy with the fugitive George Abbott, respectively wanted by the states of New Hampshire and Vermont.

Thirty-one days passed thus. During all this time Almy was nowhere but in the Warden barn, the same hiding place he had used for a month before the murder and whence he had fled direct from the Vale of Tempe. With a hay knife he cut tunnels in the mows of dry clover and timothy through which he could crawl. His chief observation post was where it had been before—inside the corner of the barn nearest the house, sixty feet away.

With his eye glued to the knothole, and with one could wonder what thoughts, he watched while the black hearse drove up to the house and then drove away with what had been Christie Warden, the weeping family following.

On other days he watched while posses of armed men—men looking for *him!*—passed up and down the Lyme road. He listened when C. O. Hurlbert and Silas Brigham, Grafton County sheriffs, came to talk about the case with the Wardens. And at night he foraged for food. At night, too, he spent part of his time at Christie's grave in the near-by cemetery. He ranged the night fields and woods for wildflowers to put on the grave. Once he dug a tiny spruce tree in the Vale of Tempe and planted it near the grave. Often he sat at the grave all night until lighting skies warned him to his hide-out in the hay.

Late on the afternoon of August 18, a full month after the

murder, Mrs. Warden went to the barn to look for some missing chickens. She discovered a small opening in the foundation of the barn which had casually been covered with a piece of board. She took away the board and looked. In the hole were an empty jelly tumbler and ten or twelve empty cans which had contained salmon, oysters, sardines, and fruit. There was also an empty beer bottle.

Mrs. Warden returned to the house in a reflective mood, and told her husband about what she had found. With neighbors F. W. Davidson and N. A. Frost, Mr. Warden did some further looking around the barn. They found another cache of empty cans and bottles, along with a businesslike club—"nicely whittled," as Yankee Davidson typically noticed—and quite freshly made. Next day they went to the village and notified Deputy H. C. Brown.

Brown conferred with leading citizens, and it was proposed that the Warden barn should be watched. Sheriff Brown and Professor G. H. Whitcher agreed to stand post that night.

The sky was cloudless and another bright moon shining. Taking a long route through the fields in order to keep out of sight of the barn, the two men made their way to a point in the cornfield which afforded a complete view of house and barn and other buildings and sat down to wait. Nothing occurred until one-twenty next morning, when they saw a man come out from behind the barn. He seemed to know where he was going. He started in a direct line, walking fast, for the small apple orchard near the house. The hidden watchers held their breath, for it seemed the man was coming to their hide-out. But he stopped under a heavily laden apple tree not fifteen feet from Brown and Whitcher. They couldn't tell for sure if the man was Almy or not but saw he was barefoot, ragged, and very thin. He had a bag with him which he filled with apples, meanwhile eating like one half-starved. Then he put the bag over his shoulder and went back whence he came, passing around the east end of the barn and so out of sight.

Without waking the Warden family Brown and Whitcher hurried to Hanover village and quickly gathered a force of forty-odd men, some of them armed. After considerable discussion the group divided into two parties. One posse went up Wheelock Street, thence across the fields to the Warden place to form a semicircle around that side of the barn. The other posse went out Lyme road and formed a barrier around the other side of the barn. Then they sat down to wait for daylight.

Around six o'clock volunteers approached the barn, arms at the ready, and entered. All was still, except for crickets at work in the mows and the lowing of a cow in the stable. Men climbed into the hay and trod it, ramming pitchforks down. They searched the stables, the henhouse, and every part of the structure.

Meanwhile somebody had thought the occasion demanded more help, and the big bell on Dartmouth Hall sounded a general alarm. Church bells also were rung in Norwich and Lebanon. By eight o'clock several hundred men had arrived at the Warden farm, among them Sheriffs Stevens of Lancaster and Clark of Lebanon. At a council of war it was decided that Almy —if Almy it was—was still in the barn. Many favored setting the barn afire, but leading spirits thought another search should be made.

Volunteers stepped forward and the advance began. The interior of the barn seemed as lifeless as it had been earlier. Charles C. Hewett, a summer student at the agricultural and mechanical college, was treading one of the mows, a long pitch-fork in his hand, a gun in his pocket. Every few steps he would stop and prod the fork into the hay as far as it would go; the last time he prodded, a gun flashed from the hay and a bullet skimmed along the fork handle and took a small piece of hide off his knuckles. Two more bullets followed the first. Hewett dropped his fork and squatted low as he drew his gun. He also gave voice to one of the finest pieces of understatement on record in the old Granite State.

"I guess," Charles Hewett shouted, "I guess that man Almy's in this barn."

So Almy was. As Hewett watched he saw the hay in one spot rise up like a wave and the body of a man appear. Hewett fired. The man seemed to stagger, then fall back. Hewett fired again and again until his gun was empty. Just then Almy rose up and shot, the bullet barely making a crease along the ridge of Hewett's nose. Hewett ducked behind a beam, seeking to reload. But he didn't have time. Almy was creeping up on him, his revolver cocked, when Hewett dived off the beam and through a hole in the barn floor, a shot following him.

This was action a plenty. Azro Turner, of Norwich, was standing on a ladder during the shooting. Now Almy sighted Turner and began firing, striking Turner in the shoulder and causing him to drop to the barn floor.

When the smoke had cleared, Almy was still in the haymow and the barn was clear of the posse.

Outside, the original posse had grown to six or seven hundred persons—some said a thousand. It wasn't more than once in a century or so that staid Hanover had a man hunt of this sort. It was more like something out of Beadle's paper-backed novels.

Again a call for volunteers was made, and some forty men, more wary now, entered the barn. They were greeted by a shout. It was Almy, still hidden in the top mow. He said he would give himself up if assured he would not be lynched.[6] Authorities promised he would be treated like any other fugitive and be given a fair trial.

For a few minutes Almy seemed to be debating the subject. He tossed a bundle of papers down to the floor, saying that "in that you'll find the written cause for the crime I committed." It

---

6 This fear of lynch law must have been the result of Almy's travels in the West and South. Neither in New Hampshire nor in Vermont has there ever been a lynching, white or black.

proved to be letters from Christie Warden and some of Almy's own statements regarding the murder. In about ten minutes Almy came down, very slowly, for he had been wounded just below the left hip and was also bleeding from his scalp.

Taken in a buggy to Wheelock's Hotel in Hanover village, Almy's wounds were treated and he was kept in bed under guard.[7] Just who identified him as George Abbott is not clear; but before he was able to walk, old acquaintances, friends, and even relatives from Thetford, Fairlee, and Orford had made his identity clear. The press, which by now was in a dither over the Wild West aspects of life in Hanover, New Hampshire, made note of the fact that Almy and Abbott were one and the same, although both press and public continued to think of him as Almy.

As Almy–Abbott's past came to light, the authorities of Grafton County felt they had no jail strong enough to hold the man who had escaped from Vermont's Windsor prison. The prisoner was taken to the big city of Manchester, and at every station the train was nearly mobbed by people curious to get a look at the noted murderer.[8]

After a stay in Manchester jail Almy was taken to Woodsville to be indicted by a grand jury. The court assigned him counsel in the persons of Alvin Burleigh and Joseph Story. The trial was held at Plymouth and, had the courthouse been large enough, would have been attended by two, perhaps five, thousand persons. Plymouth had never seen such a crowd before. Almy pleaded guilty, and was permitted to tell his story to the jury. He seems to have expected nothing short of hang-

---

[7] George U. L. Leavitt, deputy from Lebanon and today in 1941 still a deputy at seventy-five, was Almy's guard that night. He tells me Almy gave as his "reason" for killing the girl the fact that Mrs. Warden had forbidden Christie ever to see him again.

[8] Harlan C. Pearson, the well-known columnist of the *Patriot & Monitor,* Concord, New Hampshire, remembers this period vividly. A youngster in 1891, Pearson had the great privilege of driving newspaper reporters hither and yon in fast rigs to cover what Pearson still thinks was New Hampshire's most sensational murder case.

ing; but in his rambling account he obviously endeavored to make out a case of extenuating circumstances, inferring that Christie Warden had promised to marry him—a statement not borne out by any of Christie's letters that were made public.

Although a few lightheaded females of the type well known to murder courts everywhere were set to weeping in sympathy for the handsome murderer, he seems to have had few well-wishers in the crowd.[9]

Fanny Warden gave evidence at the trial and was not backward in displaying the loathing she had always felt for the man. As for Almy, one reporter present noted that when Fanny was on the stand "Almy's cruel eyes glistened like a serpent's."

The jury agreed with the prisoner that he was guilty, and after a long delay, during which a new trial was denied, Almy–Abbott was nicely hanged at Concord prison on May 16, 1892, by Sheriff Hurlbert and the warden, "being assisted in the performance of their duties by Deputies Arthur E. Davis, Woodsville, Charles R. Colburn, Littleton, W. S. Leonard, Rumney, and W. B. Richardson, Canaan."

The Vale of Tempe at Hanover, theretofore known only to college students as the woody glen where D. Webster, Dartmouth '01, used to go to be alone while perfecting his eloquence and as a good place to have class pictures taken, now took on added stature as the scene of a "romantic and fiendish crime."

Some inquiring reporter visited the Vale in November of 1891, three months after the murder. He found that "every twig of the clump of willows where Miss Warden was killed has been cut off, and carried away. The trees are now bare poles." Other happy morons had stripped the bark off every tree "in this dreadful hollow" and written their names on the inner bark. The observant reporter perceived that "the spelling and

---

9 Cushman Parsons of Colebrook, then a lad in Holderness School at Plymouth, managed to attend part of the trial. He heard Almy explain that although he intentionally killed Christie by a shot through the head the second shot was accidental. The subject has often been debated around cracker barrels.

chirography tell that education and ignorance alike have
yielded to the fascinations of the fatal spot."

Of late years the Vale of Tempe has been serving neither
orators nor murderers, but is used in winter as a ski run.
Among Dartmouth men of recent vintage there is no knowledge of the Almy–Warden affair; but natives have a sizable
stock of folklore concerning it, and parts of a ballad are remembered.[10] Men in late middle life particularly recall that for
many months after Almy's capture young boys feared to go
into barns, even long-familiar barns, lest some deadly contemporary of Almy's lurk on the shadowy beams.[11]

---

[10] This ballad is worthless because it is *consciously* "humorous," something
that should never occur in a song about a tragedy. It was sung to the currently popular air of "Ta-ra-ra Boom-de-ay." The last verse reads:

> So they hanged him by the neck,
> On the gallows, yes, by heck!
> So he rests beneath the sod,
> For Almy's gone to meet his God.

[11] Gray Hannaford, now of Lisbon, New Hampshire, says that for months
after the Almy capture he never pitched a forkful of hay out of the Hannaford mows in Northumberland without expecting to bring up a sinister-looking
man with a gun in each hand and sudden death in his eye.

CHAPTER TEN

WHO CALLED ON SARAH MESERVEY?

VERY FEW OF THE thousands of tourists who motor north along the Maine coast every summer visit Tenants Harbor. Few ever heard of it; for it is more than sixty years since the sleepy little hamlet roused itself to produce one of the Pine Tree State's greatest mysteries and then relapsed happily into the quiet it had known since 1814, when a British man-of-war landed men to capture near-by Fort St. George's.

To drive to Tenants Harbor you turn south at Thomaston, where Maine's especially grim prison stands on Limestone Hill, and run down a peninsula of pretty coves and inlets. Ten miles down this salt-sprayed neck of land is Tenants Harbor, a tiny cluster of weathered homes and a store. Not far from Tenants a footpath leads through small fir trees to the jagged shore where the Spouting Horn booms intermittently as tide and wind combine to rush the ocean into a narrow, rocky passage and throw water forty feet into the air. The Horn is on Harts Neck, named for an old shore family long before Captain Nathan F. Hart got his name into the newspapers.

In 1877 many of the menfolk of Tenants were mariners of one kind or another; and in October of that year Captain

Luther Meservey kissed his Sarah good-by and shipped in a schooner, the *Bickmore*, for a four-month cruise, by no means a long voyage in a community where old men still talked of the China trade.

The Luther Meserveys lived near the far end of the village, next to the meeting house. Beyond was Mark Wall's house and barn, and beyond that, by exactly seven hundred and sixty feet, was the home of Captain Nathan F. Hart.

Sarah Meservey was a tall, spare, fearless woman of about thirty-seven years who in sixteen years of married life with Captain Luther had become well accustomed to spending months alone. She was said to have been an extremely careful woman about money, which, in any New England town, must have meant something approaching parsimony; and she was also considered rather uncommunicative, hardly an oddity in a Yankee village.

Two months passed with Captain Luther at sea; and with Sarah at home, seen at least once every day when she went to the post office for mail. On Saturday the twenty-second of December, at an hour generally and pleasantly described by witnesses as "early lamp-lighting," Sarah Meservey went, as was her custom, to the post office in the village, some five minutes' walk. She tarried there a few moments, learning that Mark Wall had taken her mail, then started for home up the snowy road, overhung with salt mist, and on the way was met and spoken to by Clara Wall, fourteen, and also by Mrs. Sophia Wall.

When Sarah Meservey returned from the post office that night, she did not go on the few steps to the Walls' to get her mail but turned into her own dooryard, went into the house, and closed the door.

Next morning, which was Sunday, a young son of Mark Wall was sent to the Meservey home with the mail his father had brought for Mrs. Meservey. Although he hammered long on the door, and right smartly, the lad got no reply. He noticed that the blinds, contrary to custom, were down, and then he went back home.

This Sunday was the twenty-third of December. No one saw Mrs. Sarah Meservey that day nor the next. She did not go to the handsome tableaux which townfolk presented in Centennial Hall on Christmas night. She was never seen at the post office again, nor elsewhere, for that matter, alive.

Time went on even in Tenants Harbor, which in 1878 must have been horribly unique among small places; for during the next thirty-eight days no effort was made to know the whereabouts of Sarah Meservey. One may wonder, vainly, if nobody remarked her absence at the post office or on the road into the village. Here was a hamlet possibly of seventy or eighty persons all told, all well known to each other, all of families long established in the community. Did no one notice that the paths leading through the snow to both front and side doors of the Meservey home became faint, then completely obliterated by new snow? Did not Pastor Richardson, whose house was eighty-five feet from the Meserveys', notice Sarah's absence from meeting? Did not any of the Harts, the Walls, the Bickmores —all close neighbors on this brief stretch of road—note the closed blinds?

One cannot know today; but nothing in the record indicates that the least curiosity was shown until January 29, five weeks after Sarah was last seen. By this time the letters, catalogues, and patent-medicine almanacs for the Luther Meserveys had accumulated into a prodigious pile in the tiny post office.

Who first had the idea that the matter of Sarah's absence ought to be looked into is in doubt, for both civic pride and mortal fear entered the affair once the investigation had been completed. It seems certain, however, that the subject was brought to the attention of Whitney Long, first selectman and therefore officially the most important man in the village, by Captain Albion Meservey, cousin of the absent Captain Luther.

Selectman Long hadn't yet heard of Mrs. Meservey's disappearance, but he was perfectly agreeable to an official visit to the Meservey home. With Captain Albion and Fred Hart assisting, Selectman Long made the call. The three men entered the yard, sheer white and level with undisturbed snow. All shades were down. All windows were coated thick with frost. Getting no answer to a rapping, the men found a rear window open and crawled in.

Inside, the house seemed to have that completely deserted feeling—a sort of infinite silence one thinks of as without beginning, without end. It was cold, too. The kitchen seemed to be in some confusion. A glance into a small bedroom off the kitchen showed that the bed was unmade, something not often seen after seven o'clock of a morning in Tenants Harbor. But it was a larger bedroom on the ground floor that caused the three presumably strong men to shudder. Furniture was upset and broken. Parts of a broken mirror were scattered over the floor, and so was blood—much blood, splashed on the walls and baseboards and splattered on floor, rug, and chairs. Practically in the middle of all this upheaval and wrapped tightly in a quilt was the body of Sarah Meservey.

It is said that the three investigators were "surprised" to find Mrs. Meservey in such condition. One could wonder, if, in a house whose temperature hovered around zero and whose blinds had been drawn for five weeks, they expected to find Mrs. Meservey sitting comfortably in a rocker, knitting and reading the latest issue of the Rockland *Opinion*. But there she was on the floor, quite dead.

The condition of Mrs. Meservey and her house, so First Selectman Whitney Long thought after some deliberation, called for the attention of High Sheriff A. T. Low of Rockland. He was notified, and came next day with a physician and the coroner. These officials found that a white woolen scarf, called a cloud, had been wrapped so tightly around Sarah's neck that death had been due to strangulation.

The woman had suffered several bruises and cuts during

what had obviously been a gallant struggle, but so much blood was noted that it was believed the killer, too, had been injured. The woman's arms had been brought up above and behind her head and tied at the wrists, in good seaman's knots such as were used in tying reef points, with a length of cod line—suggesting something done before and not after the woman was killed. She was fully clothed even to coat and overshoes, which led the officials to believe she had just returned from the village and had been attacked on entering the house. Except for the un-locked window, all doors and windows were fastened.

Bloodstains were found in other parts of the house; bloody finger marks—they weren't called prints then—were on the kitchen wall, and in the sink was a basin of discolored ice. On a bedroom floor was a paper collar, torn and bloody. On the floor of the kitchen was a piece of brown paper, on one side of which was a date scrawled in pencil: "Monday Eveng 24." On the other side was: "i cam as A Woman She was out and i [wait] till She Come back not for mony but i kiled her." The word "wait" is here substituted for an indecipherable scrawl.

Of greater interest in an isolated community where habits were strong and seldom changed was the particular type of half a dozen burned matches found on the floor of the kitchen and bedrooms. These matches were known as English, being very long and slim and quite rare in Tenants Harbor—even in Maine. Sarah Meservey had used not English but Parlor matches, cylindrical instead of square and tipped with brightly colored phosphorus. Almost but not quite everybody else in Tenants Harbor used nothing but Portland Star matches, which had a very small head of a light red, almost an orange, color and were square.[1]

---

[1] For longer than I know, or can find out, Portland Star matches were standard equipment in Maine, New Hampshire, and eastern Vermont. They came in cards, were broken off one by one as used, and burned for the first few seconds with a hellish blue flame. The stench was uncommonly pungent and bad. But in my youth people who used other than Portland Stars were thought to be just a little queer—harmless, perhaps, but odd.

Inspection of the house, upstairs and down, indicated that somebody had been looking into bureau drawers and cupboards and closets, perhaps in search of money—of which, it seems, the Meserveys were known to have "at least $150 in old silver" and from two to three hundred dollars "in other money." This knowledge of ready cash on the part of the community would seem to throw doubt on Sarah Meservey's alleged reputation of being uncommunicative.

The physician reported that the crime of rape had not been committed. The sheriff took charge of the scrawled note and the matches. Until Captain Luther Meservey returned from the sea it would be impossible to say if the house had been robbed.

After viewing the scene Sheriff Low formulated the theory that Mrs. Meservey had been attacked directly as she entered the house, possibly by a person surprised in ransacking the place, and that she had put up a valiant fight. Neither the use of cod line to tie the woman's hands nor the complicated knots could mean much in Tenants Harbor, where so many men followed the sea. But were the hands tied before death, and if so why? The more one thought of the matter the deeper the mystery seemed.

Now nobody in Tenants Harbor was old enough to recall a murder mystery in the community. Affairs like this might happen in big cities like Bangor and Portland, but they were known only through newspapers and were faraway events as vague and remote as an assassination of a grand duke in Russia. Strangers were seldom seen in Tenants Harbor and no one, just then, could recall any strangers in December, when Mrs. Meservey was last seen alive. So now a terrible sort of horror, unknown to larger communities, settled upon the tiny hamlet where everybody knew everybody, where Meserveys were related, either by blood or by marriage, to half the population.

Sheriff Low received plenty of help and advice, doubtless more than he wanted, in his search for clues. Particularly active

were Levi Hart and Captain Albion Meservey, the latter, as
said, a cousin of the dead woman's husband. But little progress
had been made when Captain Luther Meservey put in at Bath
harbor on February 16; he was just buying some gifts for his
wife when notified he had been a widower since December. The
captain hurried to Tenants but could not bring himself to
enter the house at once. A bit later he did enter, at urging of
the sheriff, and found in a drawer the "sum of two hundred
dollars." Whether any other cash was found, and even how
much money was missing, is not stated in the record.

Three days after Captain Luther Meservey's return home,
Mrs. Levi Hart of that village received an anonymous letter,
written in pencil, dated February 10 but postmarked February
16 at Philadelphia. The letter came in a well-creased envelope,
suggesting that it might have been sent to Philadelphia in another envelope and there remailed. Said the note:

To Mrs Livi Hart
   i thought i would drop you A line to tell your husband to be careful
how he conducted things about Tenants Harbor cause if he dont he
and a good many others of the men will get An ounce ball put threw
them for tell them that it is no use trying to catch this chap for he will
not be caught—so be careful who you take up in st. George you shall
hear from me again in three months. D M

The "st. George" refers to a near-by village, Saint George,
which is also the name of the town in which Tenants Harbor is
situated.

From the letter's dates and the time elapsed, as well as from
the creasing of the envelope, Sheriff Low believed it had been
written by someone in Tenants Harbor and sent to someone in
Philadelphia—perhaps with an accompanying note explaining
that it contained a valentine and asking that it be remailed.
The writing looked much like that in the even more illiterate
note found on the floor not far from Mrs. Meservey's body.

Receipt of the anonymous letter, known to everyone in the

village within a few hours, not only created a sensation second
only to that of the murder itself but also caused villagers to
look at one another with increased suspicion. Could it be that
behind some face known for years, possibly for a generation,
there lurked the knowledge of the murder and the letter? Tenants Harbor had a period of troubled sleep such as usually was
known only to mariners' wives who had gone to bed reading
"The Wreck of the Hesperus."

It soon became common knowledge that Sheriff Low had
asked four men to submit samples of their writing in which "i
kiled her" occurred. And on March 8 one of these men was arrested and lodged in jail. He was Captain Nathan F. Hart,
next neighbor but one to the Luther Meserveys, described as
forty-nine years of age but looking much younger, stout, thick-
set, with a blue-black beard (said to have been dyed) but no
mustache. A reporter from the Rockland *Opinion* thought that
Captain Hart's face was "pleasing." The captain took his arrest philosophically but appeared very despondent.

It would seem that a number of things entered into Captain
Hart's arrest. The Harts both had been married and divorced
previous to their marriage, and Simeon Sylvester, Mrs. Hart's
son, rather suddenly—or so it seemed—had more money than
usual. He explained this happy condition by luck at cards. An
unidentified newspaper of the time remarked loosely, without
giving any contributing reasons, that "up to the time of his recent conversion Hart had been known as a pretty hard character." Hart and his wife, it appears, had but recently "ex-
perienced religion," and some said this miracle had taken place
after Mrs. Meservey's murder. The sheriff and his advisers
also thought they saw a similarity in Hart's writing and the
writing of the anonymous letter and the brown-paper note.

The business of the matches found on the Meservey floor was
brought up, too. They were said to be of the same sort used by
the Nathan Harts and by nobody else in Tenants Harbor.

The grand jury of Knox County found a true bill against

Captain Hart and in their deliberations seem to have been greatly impressed by an expert brought in by the sheriff. This man who testified so tellingly before the grand jury was Professor Alvin R. Dunton of Camden, Maine, "Author of the Duntonian System of Penmanship, and the Oldest Expert on Hand-Writing in the United States." Not only because of the part he was to play in the case but also because he was a man of unusual parts and character, this remarkable personage deserves more than mere mention.

When he appeared before the grand jury in the Hart–Meservey case, Alvin R. Dunton was only sixty-six years old; but he had the head, the beard, and the general demeanor of a true patriarch. A huge man, with noble brow and eyes, his great white whiskers flowed wild and untrammeled from ear to ear and well down over his waistcoat. His command of language was termed amazing and his diction had the easy flow, the rises and falls, and the great moments of a Webster, or at least of a James G. Blaine. Of an old Maine family, his grandfather was Abner Dunton, "of giant stature and great strength," who was drowned in Lake Megunticook in 1787 when the ice broke under him.[2]

Professor Dunton appeared before the grand jury as expert for the prosecution. Holding pages of a ship's logbook which were said to be in the hand of Captain Nathan Hart, Professor Dunton testified there could be no doubt: the hand that wrote the brown-paper note and the anonymous letter were one and the same with the hand "that wrote these pages of the log book."

Captain Nathan Hart was placed in prison to await trial. Before this began, another anonymous letter made its appearance. The first letter, it will be remembered, came to Mrs. Levi Hart and stated, among other things, "you shall hear from me

---

[2] Folklore of the region has it that men who came to get his body gazed in awe at the destruction this gigantic old man had wrecked. In his efforts to free himself he had broken up better than half an acre of ice.

again in three months." But the second letter was addressed not to Mrs. Hart but to Mrs. Mahala Sweetland, an old resident of Tenants Harbor. Like the first it was written in pencil; but this time it was postmarked Providence, Rhode Island. Except for one passage, which was said to be "obscene as well as vulgar" and was never published, the letter is given in full below. It is important to keep in mind that, regardless of where or when it may have been written, on May 16, the day it was mailed in Providence, Nathan Hart was in jail and had been in jail for two months.

Said this second letter:

Providence, May 16, 1878

Take time and read this before you give it up.

Sarah Meservey Murder

Mrs Sweetland. As you ar a woman that i knew would stand reading this letter [six words illegible] i used to live in St. George once and knew a good many people—i havent been there much for 20 years but i had reason to visit there last winter as you no doubt [word illegible] i intended to wright to Chas sums or deacon long levi Hart of some of them men that I never liked but as i wanted all to know the truth i thought you would be a good one for that. i shall wright more this time than i did before as i think it will be my last for at least 10 yrs—and as a man of my word i will wright another as the last one dient satisfy the people—i think this will satisfy them that they haven't got the man with in there reach that did the deed—and i am going to tell them some of what i have done and of what i am going to do—i am 1 of the hardest hearted of human men of the human white race living and if god lets me live 10 years longer i will be satisfied to die then—i am a man from 25 to 75 years old once i was a good man when i had a father and a mother but they have both been taken from me one was murdered and the other almost the same it turned my prays that i was used to praying for i had good Christian folks but it turned my prays to revengefull one so i started out went to sea and from then i learned to swear, steal and to kill—i have been Capt and Mate and i have done some ofl hard things but i am bout done goine to sea now—all i want is revenge on people that has harmed me and is going to i dont blame people for wanting to get me if they can but they have got to work don't forget that friends—now i will tell you why i happened a longe

St. George last winter—long time Ago I was stopped in St. G and i
went to S. Meservey a little and not knowing mutch about her i tried
some of my natrouls Cappers on her and the result was a slap in the
face and told to get or she would take the shirt bosom from me and i
got but i told her that she would see the time that i would do as i liked
and that is why I have waited this only to see if she had ever told eny
body A thing A bout it but i am pretty safe on that part And you gave
me good time to make every other thing safe by letting her lay in the
house so long—i went to the house to fulfill my promise to get the
money to kill her and set the house on fire but i had more work to do
than i expected—was in a schooner at the time i happened there in
some part of [illegible] At dusk and at 7 o'clock I met her face to face
in her Cook room and before she had time to scream i give her a gentel
tap on the starboard brow and she fell to the floor senseless i tied her
hand and legs picked her up and laid her on the bed in the room where
you found her—then i lit the lamp turned it low locked the door put
the Curtains down to kill the light and in a few minutes she came to
her cencis i asked her if she remembered me and remembered what i
once wanted and she fetched a scream and i cought her by the throat
but she schreamed so hard that i had to strike her in the head again
and then she fainted then i laid her as i wanted to and accomplished
my desire. She had on double clothing and with some trouble i but-
toned them up again she soon came to a gain and then what little blood
and swolen face she had she count scream but could whisper She asked
me for some water the first thing and i found her some water bathed
her face cleared her throat so she could talk quite plain but she was
pretty smart for she was fooling me on her strength i then asked her
for her money and she said i will give you all will you let me live and
of course I told her yes. She told me where it was where no persons
would think of looking it was in a place in the house that was fastened
up so that it had to be opened with an ax So i left her on the bed to go
find the place all as she had explained it to me but let me say threw
my carelessness i left her on the bed with her hands tied before her
while looking after something to pry open the place for there wasnt
an ax or any other tool in the house I herd a noise up in the cook room
i went up her loose and out standing up tring to open the door i will
say here she must have chawed the line in too and had more strength
than i supposed she could have but i caught her dragged her back into
the room shut the door and there is where the squabble commenced
i undertook to tie her again but she was too strong She fought like a
tiger she would Break the cod line as fast as i would get it back on

her hands then we was in the dark and I would keep her under me of course she would take to screaming and if all the people hant been deaf or bout dead they would have herd her 1-2 mile i would then threaten to shoot her if she didnt stop but she seemed to know my mind for i didnt entend to kill her till i got the money so that dient scare her eny and i had to haul all the clothes of the bed to pile over her head to kill her voice for i never saw sutch a voice in my life * * * * * * * * * * * * * * * * but i counkqued her at last but I dont think I should if in a noughts the things tha' came to that had happened to be her cloud i tried to choke her with the cod line but i count for as fast as i would get it around her neck she would get her hands between her neck and line and break it and i count make her give up eny how i tried—i told her once if she dient stop her nois that i would stab her to the hart and if she had eny thing to say or to leve be hind she had better say it She told me where there was some more money if it would let her live. She said it was luther's money and where it was but if i only got what she told me she had i would leve until he had and she called me by name and says kiss luther for me and lay me on my bed in the room next to the road so i told her i would send him a kiss that i took from her bloody lips So tell him here is the kiss (*) but to lay her on the bed that she desired to be laid on i count for she was gaining strength all the time and i knew that she would scream so·they would hear her eny body that past by—but if one 6 or 12 had come to helped her i should have showed them good play before they would have captured me for I had what i knocked her down with—i ounce ball shooter 2—7 shorts pistols and a dirk knife but it was getting late and i had to be getting a board so not to rais suspicion where i was gone to for i expected to hear from my works by the next day so she was growing stronger all the time so i got hold of her cloud and concluded to choke her to deth instid of stabbing her i had to stop her nois but i was as long as 1-2 hour before i could get it around her neck and then i dient get it altogether round her neck but i got it so at last that i got a couple turns round her neck and arms and i got one quare pull and one square knought a gain you bet and she dient't breathe more than two times and i got up i had no matches nor could i find eny and i was a nasty mess my coat vest and shirts was soaked in blood by her hands hanging around me and my pants was wet threw to my skin draws and all— and i had cut my overshoes all to peaces on a looking glass that was setting i one part of the room and i had lost my gloves and hat but it was 11 o'clock and i had to be going i got up and felt around the room for bout 10 minutes then i went out washed myself some and took the

stick from of the top of the cook room window went out and got as fast
as i could get with out hat gloves or Eny thing but before the next
morning i had got all washed up and burnt up my bloody clothes got
the buttons sunk them in 18 fathoms of water and had 3 hours good
sound sleep but i expected to hear a out cry of my work and that is
why i left that not saying that i went there as a woman for i thought
that you mite think that it was the rawley woman the old lady but
things went on smoothly nothing was mistrusted of me doing eny
thing for i looked out and not let her scratch or bite me and i never
lost a teaspoon ful of blood and i never see so much blood come from
eny body in my life and i have put the dirk knife to more tha 1 persons hart i should think there was a large buckett-ful and all from
her hed from 1 scar on the starboard brow and the rest out of her
mouth and noes—well as soon as we got in i left as i heard nothing
of the affair and i got for St. George as soon as i could get there after
my hat and money i stopped one night to make sure nothing had been
suspected and the 15 night from the time i first entered i went to the
house at 11 o'clock went into the barn and got the ax and pried the
window open it was swelled down hard i went in lit the lamp that i set
on the table and went into the room where she was found my things
went down and got my $1100.0,0 that was nicely packed in a little box
went back where she was give her a kick in the ribs and told her i had
got all i wanted of her and if she wanted eny thing more i was ready
to give it to her i gave her a sweet smile and left her went out of the
window Concluded not to burn the house and what other little money
there was in the house—the first i herd of her being found or to find
out mutch was to Bristol abroad of the schooner levie hart that a jones
fellow told me all he knew a bout it the next i herd they had 2 or 3
boys up for trial well let me tell you if a pretty large boy had under-
taken to done what i did you would have found him where you found
her if she aint taken care of him and came and told her self for i would
rather take my chance with levi hart or Steve hart open handed than
to fight one like her again but i guess i wont tell you eny more a bout
her un less you want to know very bad and if you do offer a handsome
reward and i will tell you and i will get the money and you will never
find me dont forget that fools if the State County or town has got millions of $ to spend on my case let them start for i am willing to die
after i fixe a dozen or so as i want and intend to—livie hart for one in
less than 1826-1-4 days this is his destiny i shall be in St George—if
i can i shall steal his horse and gig and if i cant i can furnish one my
self i have been in Philadelphia i have been in New York in portland

Boston and other places where there has been St. Georges—and found out what people intend to do with me—i shall tie him heels upward so his hed will smell dust drive at a moderate rate once around the squair hitch the horse to a tree leave him for somebody to find in the morning and to those who wants to cut me to peaces i shall find them out and cut their tongue out and let them live as long as they will and so i say to all the folks in St George who helps and believes Condemns a innocent person for i know when you have the rong one for i personally and god only knows who did that deed of murder do there is Capt John bickmores property i long to get to work there and i went up to the New house and had a mind to get it on fire but i thought it would be insured on so they wont lost mutch but dont forget they have a maiden daughter and a good many others that some of these days will pay the det all the det they owe for all i want to get is three more men like myself or like what you think hart is for if he can do what you suppose he has done for i herd he went into the house and looked at her and helped take her out of the house in the middle of a crowd—if he can do that he is one of the men i want for i could do that as easy as i can wink i herd if they got the wright man they was a going to put him in the toom with her i could have staid there one month and come out fat —So I say to all that they better make up to that man all that he loses and more to give him as good a schooner as you have got—for the rong you have done to him—And to you Mrs Sweatland for your daughter's safety show this letter to his wife before you give it up—then Copy it if you want and to send this to head qrs—for i sepose they will want to preserve it for a while the last time i was in philadelphia i stood as near the man that offered 500 and 1000 dollars reward for knowledge of that letter—that i could have put my knife to his hart without stepping once but i dient want as little a sum as that nor him as long as he doesnt try to harm me—and for sending that letter to philadelphia and to a man i think that knows for his interest not mine has and will hold his tongue but i will tell you as a man of my i dient send it from St George and i would give you this in short hand or enything if it had thought that you could have found it out—for i thought that you would make as bad a mistake as the expert did when he pronounced my writing som body's else he would find some difference between this and the other and my log books if he could see them i live in the state of New York if you would like to know and i have had some of the smart ditectives on my track as there was in New York City and had them along side of me and talked of the affair and bit my lips till the blood come from them to keep from laughing at the prospect of getting me—

well i have been three hours wrighting to you and more i will mail it this day and the present hour—So i say in closing dont forget that i am a man of my word i sepose you would like for me to give you a little course wrighting to let you know that i wrought the other so i will wright levi Hart.

There can be no doubt that this letter was written by someone who knew Tenants Harbor well. It may even tell what happened in the Meservey house that night Sarah returned from the post office; the condition of the body and that of the house itself were in keeping. It is filled with strange inconsistencies. Were they real or purposely fashioned? Twice it says that the "rong" man has been arrested, but it does not attempt to throw particular suspicion on any of the men mentioned.

The letter was turned over to Sheriff Low, who called Professor Dunton to examine it. The professor had been doing some investigating of his own. He had learned, since his appearance before the grand jury, that the five sheets of logbook entries alleged to have been written by Captain Nathan Hart had not been written by Hart at all but by Captain Albion Meservey. Now in perusing the Providence letter Professor Dunton felt certain that both it and the Philadelphia letter, as well as the brown-paper note, were written in the same hand that made the five logbook pages.

Professor Dunton did not leave certainty to his own skill. He had all the documents photographed and took them to Boston, where he submitted them to "two other experts"—L. S. Fairbanks and George A. Sawyer—who agreed that the hand that wrote the logbook pages had written the anonymous letters. Fortified with this bolster to his own findings, Professor Dunton returned to Maine with the determination to "right the wrong I unwittingly did" by the testimony at the grand-jury hearing. He was sure, he told both Sheriff Low and L. M. Staples, who was to prosecute Hart, that Captain Hart was an innocent man, the victim of a terrible series of circumstances plus an out-and-out frame-up.

2

Captain Hart's trial began on October 1, 1878, at Rockland, before Judge John Appleton. Captain Hart's eyes, a reporter noted, were "blue and frank, with a pleasant expression," but his mouth was "large, with colorless lips, wearing a smirk that gives them a crafty, treacherous cast." Which sort of left things right where they were.

Prosecutor Staples was assisted by L. A. Emery, attorney general of Maine. J. H. Montgomery and R. F. Dunton, not to be confused with the professor, were Captain Hart's counsel.

Prosecution informed the jury of its theory of the crime, which it said it would prove beyond any doubt. The theory:

Mrs. Meservey was killed in early evening of December 22, not the twenty-fourth, by a person who knew the Meservey house, knew that the woman was living alone and that at the moment she had gone for the mail. The murder was not a planned one, but was incidental to the main purpose of robbery and was committed after the robber was surprised in the act of searching the house for cash he knew was hidden there.

Prosecution told the jury it would be shown that the brown-paper note in the house—dated December 24—was not left there at the time of the murder but was put in later. That nobody but Nathan Hart put it there while on a supposed errand to Harts Neck, three miles distant. That Nathan Hart put it there because he knew he could not produce a good alibi for the night of the twenty-second, but that his very presence at Harts Neck on the twenty-fourth would serve to clear him if suspicion should arise. It was all very clever, prosecution averred—just a little too clever.

The jury was also told that it would be shown Hart seemed to know all about the knotted scarf and the cod line and told others about them before the body had been disturbed and the cause of death determined. Even worse, or so prosecution termed it, was that Hart had a dream, before the body even was found, in which he dreamt Sarah Meservey had been murdered.

As for the anonymous letter received after Hart's incarceration, it would be shown that the prisoner had enjoyed opportunity to write it himself and to have it smuggled out of the jail for mailing in Providence. The other letter, from Philadelphia, had been received while Hart was still free.

With its theory of the crime before the jury, prosecution set out to prove it—first by calling Clara Wall, fourteen, who testified she had met Mrs. Meservey between six and six-thirty on the night of December 22 and noted she was wearing her white cloud, carried a reticule, and wore magenta-colored mittens. Mrs. Sophia Wall also met Mrs. Meservey that night at "early lamp-lighting"—maybe five, maybe half past, maybe six.

Mark Wall, neighbor, testified that the shades of the Meservey home were usually up, but on the twenty-third they were down. He had asked Mrs. Albion Meservey where Sarah Meservey had gone and was told "on a visit to Thomaston." This statement, at such great variance with the terribly obvious fact, appears not to have been followed up by defense counsel.

Charles Crocker, put in charge of the house by Selectman Long after the body had been found, told of finding the brown-paper note on the floor between the stove and a window in the kitchen.

Dr. Woodside, present at the autopsy, was of the opinion that nobody knew the scarf or cloud was *tied* tightly around Sarah Meservey's neck until the day after the body was found.

Levi Hart, some sort of cousin to the prisoner, testified that he had taken an active part in the detective work. Four men were at first suspected, he said, one of whom was Simeon Sylvester, the card-playing stepson of the prisoner. But three of the suspects were eliminated for one reason or another. On the evening of the day that Levi Hart's wife received the anonymous letter, he had met Nathan Hart at a meeting of something called the Iron Clad Club. Although theretofore the two men had always been friendly, said Levi, on this occasion Nathan had not spoken to him. He had thought it queer.

Prosecution now sought to make a good deal of Nathan Hart's dream prior to discovery of the murder. He had spoken of the dream to a number of persons—including Mrs. Nelson Hall, who testified at length as to exactly when she heard about the dream. Other witnesses were put on the stand to show that Nathan Hart "knew about the cloud being tied around Mrs. Meservey's neck" before arrival of the coroner. Among these latter witnesses was one Vinal Wall, whom defense counsel impeached by hauling forth a bit of Wall's past in connection with theft of money.

Next witness was Captain Albion Meservey, related by marriage to both prisoner and victim, who returned from a voyage in the schooner *Irene E. Meservey* about a month before the murder. On past voyages the prisoner had been mate on this ship, said Captain Albion, and a very good and faithful mate. The present mate was Merrill C. Hart, a distant relative of the prisoner.

Most damning evidence in the eyes of many was that given by Warren Allen, who was in charge of the Meservey house from sunset to midnight on the day the body was found. Allen said the prisoner had come to him that evening and asked permission to enter the house. It had been refused. Prisoner had then asked, Allen testified, if he could come early in the morning "before anyone was stirring." Allen had told him no.

Prosecution now brought forth two handwriting experts in the forms of Albert S. Southworth and George A. Sawyer, both of Boston, the latter of whom had been visited by Professor Dunton. Dunton had believed that Sawyer was in agreement with his own findings, but now both Sawyer and Southworth gave opinion that all of the notes and certain portions of two logbooks, said to be entries made by Captain Hart, were in the same hand.

Meanwhile Professor Dunton sat in the courtroom and only

by great self-control managed to keep from breaking into the orderly procedure of the court. He was champing at the bit, this bearded old man of Gath, almost boiling over in his desire to get to his feet and demolish the evidence being built up against the prisoner—the man whose plight Dunton, rightly or wrongly, felt himself responsible for. But the professor had to wait while more witnesses appeared for the State.

Prosecution offered a deposition of one Warren Hart, admitted over objections of defense counsel. Some six months before the murder, this one of the numberless Harts testified, he was in the company of the prisoner and the prisoner's wife. The conversation, it seems, was on the subject of the extra-marital relations of men and women, apparently not unheard of in Tenants Harbor; and Mrs. Nathan Hart said to her husband that "you once got your face slapped and shirt bosom pulled out by a woman." [3] Mrs. Hart explained the reference in front of her husband by saying it was Sarah Meservey who had resisted Captain Hart's advances.

Next witness was Sheriff Morse, keeper of the jail, who was put on the stand to show that the prisoner had had opportunity to write the anonymous letter mailed in Providence and a chance to have it smuggled out of jail by his wife, who was with him a good deal during the first weeks of his incarceration.

Prosecution now stooped—and stooped seems to be not too harsh a word—to putting a fellow prisoner of Captain Hart's on the stand. He was one Wilbur Thomas. What he was convicted of is not shown, but he was in jail with Captain Hart and one night heard Hart, who must have been a great one for dreams, groaning and muttering in his sleep. Witness said he had distinguished words in the muttering: "Don't murder me!"

---

[3] It should perhaps be explained for benefit of a younger generation that in the seventies and for thirty-odd years thereafter, paper shirt bosoms, called dickies, were much in vogue. A seven-ply bosom could be torn off every day in the week, like a calendar, revealing in sequence an astonishing array of stripes, polka dots, flowers, and so forth. They were considered very nobby by many.

All this would appear to be pretty thin stuff, but it was admitted as competent evidence.

As its final witness prosecution put Allen Andrews, a brother of the murdered woman, on the stand. He told of meeting Captain Hart at the Meservey house on the day the body was found, and of asking the captain who had the house opened. "I did," he quoted Hart as saying. "I have been putting Albion Meservey up to having the god-damn tomb opened all winter." Asked why he called it a tomb, Hart was said to have replied, "I knew she was dead in there all the time."

Defense counsel opened with a statement that it would prove the prisoner had not written the Providence letter; in fact, it would be shown that the writing in this letter was *far more like that of one of the state's witnesses*. It also would be shown that the prisoner was at home all evening the night of the murder. The testimony of Convict Thomas, as well as that of Allen Andrews, would be refuted. First defense witness called was Miss Lydia Sylvester, stepdaughter of the accused.

Said Lydia, "I was at home on the evening of December 22. So was Captain Hart. I called him at four o'clock from the pasture. He came in. He gave Tommy some instruction in navigation. He had his tea. Afterward he lay on the lounge. Then he got up and cleaned some game. Then he lay on the lounge again and read." The witness said she did not go to bed until nine.

A villager, a Mr. Whitehouse, testified he was at Captain Hart's home on the evening of the twenty-second and the captain was at home. This was about eight-twenty, and after. Simeon Sylvester—who had once been under suspicion because of spending so much money—testified that he had found Captain Hart at home that evening between five and six o'clock. Mrs. Hart, wife of the accused, was permitted to say that her husband was home on the evening in question and that on the evening of the twenty-fourth he had gone to Harts Neck on an errand. Other witnesses were put on who sought to refute the evidence given as to exactly when Captain Hart had spoken of the white cloud tied around Mrs. Meservey's neck. And then Professor Alvin R. Dunton got his chance.

The handwriting expert for the defense took the stand looking much like the popular conception of the leading character in the Book of Moses. He had been an expert in the subject, he said, since 1837. Had taught penmanship in "many states and in foreign countries." He was author of the *Manual of Free-Hand Penmanship*, used by no less than the public-school system of Boston.

Professor Dunton told the jury he had studied the anonymous letters and two logbooks. The person who wrote the letters was the same who wrote the first five pages in logbook number one. "But," thundered he, "since I gave testimony for the State at the grand jury, I have discovered that Captain Hart did not write these five pages." Then, with what a newspaper reporter said was a "stream of eloquence," the professor went on to say that Albion Meservey wrote the first five pages in logbook number one—admitted it, in fact—and hence was without question the author of the anonymous letters and the brown-paper note.

It is quite possible that Professor Dunton, as experts will, got somewhat off the track of direct testimony and became enmeshed in his fascinating theories of natural and disguised handwriting. Such things can happen. Whatever the reason for it, counsel for defense broke in to ask the State to go ahead—to cross-examine the professor. "But I'm not through with my testimony," the witness declared with some heat. Before he sat down he managed to emphasize the fact that he had first been given to believe the first five pages in the number-one logbook were in the handwriting of the prisoner, and had later learned them to be in the hand of Albion Meservey.

Last to go on the stand was the accused himself. He made a very good witness—quiet, a little sad, always polite, and in complete command of himself. He was at home on the night of the twenty-second. On the night of the twenty-fourth he went

to Harts Neck to carry a gift to a granddaughter. He had told
Vinal Wall about the murder, but he had not mentioned about
the white cloud being tied around the victim's neck because he
had not then known about it. He never told anybody he had
been trying to get Albion Meservey to open the house all winter nor had he referred to it as a tomb, god-damned or otherwise. He had written no anonymous letters. There was something he wanted the jury to know, however: on the night he
was returning from Harts Neck he had met a man—a stranger
perhaps; but he couldn't be sure, for it was murky and the
man was holding his coat over his head. He had no idea who
the man was. The dreams about the murder had been *after* he
had seen the body of Mrs. Meservey. He denied any knowledge
of the murder.

In summing up for defense, counsel said that no motive had
been shown. If Hart were guilty, then his guilt patently impli-
cated his wife; and surely the jury, who knew her, could not
believe that Mrs. Hart was capable of such a thing. Moreover,
if Hart did tell Allen Andrews he had been trying to get Albion Meservey to open the house all winter, then why had not
Meservey heard of it? Andrews, said defense counsel, was obviously a liar of the worst sort. As to testimony of the State's
handwriting experts, such testimony was worthless; for handwriting could be disguised to trick anyone.[4] The defense's own
expert, Professor Dunton, had been put on the stand only, said
counsel, to show that experts could differ.

The State had the last go at the jury. It sought to show that
the testimony given by Captain Hart and his immediate family at the trial differed from that at the grand-jury hearing.
Allen Andrews' testimony about getting the house opened had
not been impeached. The prisoner's trip to Harts Neck on the
twenty-fourth was merely an alibi to fit in nicely with the

---

[4] If this remark was quoted correctly, I should like to have seen the expression on Professor Alvin R. Dunton's face.

brown-paper note dated the twenty-fourth, which was written by the prisoner.

Now, as to the anonymous letters, said the State, it was significant that the first letter appeared just when suspicion was beginning to fasten on the accused. The second letter went to Mrs. Sweetland because she was friendly to the accused. And no further letters appeared after the prisoner's wife was forbidden to visit him alone.

As to Professor Dunton, either he had known all along, as others did, who wrote which parts of the logbooks or he was an unconscionable dunce.

After a very explicit charge by the judge, the jury retired for some two hours. When they returned to the courtroom, early night had fallen and the gaslights burned brightly. The verdict was murder in the first degree.

Maine in 1878 did not have the death penalty. Captain Nathan Hart was sentenced to the state prison at Thomaston for life.

3

The Rockland *Opinion* of October 11, 1878, summed up the case and trial by saying that "the result of the trial is generally considered to be right. The belief in Hart's guilt is almost universal."

But if Tenants Harbor and the State of Maine thought for a moment they were done with the case, then they did not know the character of Professor Alvin R. Dunton. Still convinced that Captain Hart's plight was due in no small measure to his testimony before the grand jury, the whiskered patriarch, in whose veins flowed the resolute blood of the gigantic icebreaker of Megunticook, now bestirred himself mightily. Captain Hart had barely had time to get a prison haircut before Dunton fired the first gun in what was to be a thirteen-year campaign to clear Hart's name. This first gun was a letter to the Camden *Herald* in which Dunton set forth his belief that Albion Meser-

vey was the guilty one. Basing his theory on his expertness in
the field of handwriting identity, he laid on with a heavy hand.

Traveling at his own expense up and down the Maine coast,
and even to Boston, Providence, and Philadelphia, Dunton
sought out witnesses, talked with them, got some of them to
change or modify their testimony, and secured sworn statements. He kept up a terrific barrage of letters to the press of
Maine and Massachusetts. Every one of these letters doubtless
contained libelous matter; and when editors removed this or
that part of a letter and left blanks in place of the names of
persons, Dunton became convinced of a vast conspiracy to keep
an innocent man in prison. He sat down and wrote a book.

This book, now rather rare, was entitled *The True Story of
the Hart–Meservey Trial, In Which Light is Thrown Upon
Dark Deeds, Incompetency, and Perfidy; and Crime Fastened Upon Those Whose Position, if not Manhood, Should
Have Commanded Honest Dealing.* Heavily embossed on the
book's cover is the picture of a man, obviously meant to repre-
sent Captain Hart but lacking the blue-black beard, who is
peering sadly from behind a barred door, and a different title
from that on the title page of the book: *Nathan F. Hart, An
Innocent Man in a Felon's Cell.* It appeared in 1882 and was
published in Boston by the author. I doubt the book ever was
published that contained more actionable matter to the page.
The attack on County Attorney Staples, who prosecuted Hart,
is a fair sample. It has a chapter to itself entitled "The Devil
and Hell Outdone by Lindley Murray Staples," and one of the
mildest paragraphs concerns the alleged derelictions of Staples
as a public official. It reads:

He allowed grog-shops to flourish and multiply undisturbed. The
power was palsied in the corrupt hands of L. M. Staples to check these
polluted fountains of crime, beneath whose dark waters sink in disgrace, shame, and death, to the horrible depths of a drunkard's grave,
father and son, rich and poor, high and low, the strong man in his
weakness, the wise man in his folly.

When this book was being composed and published, Maine was in one of its age-old throes over prohibition; and booze, although consumed locally in vast quantities, was officially the work of Satan. Hence Author Dunton was leaving no bottle unturned in his effort to discredit Staples on all fronts, but the effort was unsuccessful.

In Dunton's book and many public letters, even defense counsel for Hart comes off badly; and one would believe that Prosecutor Staples was a fiend who had sat up nights plotting to undermine justice with the sole object of keeping an innocent man in prison. When he was sued for libel, and he seems to have been sued two or three times, Dunton replied with both prose and poetry. Here is a sample:

> The rotten branch a prop requires,
> And so do rascals, thieves, and liars.

When a number of persons spoke of getting up a petition to present to the governor of Maine for a pardon for Hart, Dunton wrote to the papers: "Hart does not want a pardon, as he has done nothing to receive a pardon for. I, for one, glory in the spirit he manifests."

In his book Dunton speaks of two more anonymous letters received in Tenants Harbor, both dealing with Hart's innocence. One came in 1880, the other in 1881. They were mailed in South Boston, and signed "Sarah Meservey Murder." Apparently no official attention was paid to them.

Although, as said, Dunton reiterated scores of times that Albion Meservey was the guilty one, Meservey himself gave an interview in which he said that both he and his wife believed Captain Hart wholly innocent. Albion Meservey went further. He said that at least two other persons besides Hart tried to get into the Sarah Meservey house while the body was being guarded, and that neither of them was called as witness at the trial. He also stated that at least one other person had seen a stranger, or at least a man with a coat held over his head, walk-

ing in the neighborhood on the night of December 24, just as
Captain Hart had related and that this witness was not called
at the trial.

During the years he fought for Hart's release, Professor
Dunton claimed to have found still others who had seen this
mysterious man on Harts Neck that night.

But Dunton's attacks finally aroused Albion Meservey to defend his own good name. He filed suit for libel, asking the conventional twenty thousand dollars in damages. A warrant for
Dunton's arrest was issued, but the expert got wind of it in
time and fled to Boston. Judgments later were awarded Meservey to the amount of almost two thousand dollars, but he seems
never to have been able to collect. And the professor continued
to libel not only Albion Meservey but also his pet hate, Attorney Staples, as well as Clara Wall, the witness, whom he
charged with a grave crime that had nothing to do with the
Hart case; Merrill C. Hart, mate on the *Irene E. Meservey;*
Mrs. Albion Meservey; Deacon Long of Tenants Harbor; and
lastly Sarah Meservey herself, about whom he printed a story
reflecting on her honesty, or lack of it, in money matters.

Professor Dunton's book could well be described, in the language he himself liked, as an almost complete and unmitigated
chaos of unrelated fact and scurrilous fiction. In it one seldom
can know *who* said this or that. Of its three hundred and nine
pages, only about fourteen are given to the trial; and even here
the author breaks in with remarks so often that one cannot
know whether it is the evidence one is reading or merely Author
Dunton talking. Its last five pages, all in fine print, are "testi-
monials" to the excellent character and abilities of Alvin R.
Dunton and they include words of high praise, indeed, from
William Gaston, an ex-governor of Massachusetts; Samuel
Adams, chief of police of Boston; R. M. Morse, Jr., district
attorney for Suffolk County, Massachusetts; and many other
prominent Bay State citizens.

Worthless as most of Dunton's book is, one finishes it—or at least I did—with the feeling that there is still something of a mystery about the murder of Sarah Meservey. He does, one must admit, make a strong case for his theory—a *fact* to Mr. Dunton—that Captain Hart did not write either the brown-paper note or the anonymous letters. It is impossible, too, to think of this old war horse as anything but honest, no matter how violent or even how wrong his convictions possibly may have been.

Captain Hart died in prison on October 9, 1883, aged fifty-four. At this time, so well had Professor Dunton worked, a newspaper had this to say: "A great many people believe Hart was innocent, and had he lived a very earnest effort would have been made at an early day for his vindication and release." One might wonder if Dunton's work was not "a very earnest effort."

The captain's funeral was held at Tenants Harbor and was attended by nearly everybody in the village. Professor Dunton came from distant Boston and managed to get in a few words of testimony that he still believed the man wholly innocent.

The funeral did not stop Dunton's efforts. But almost to a day, eight years after the funeral, the stanch old fighter, his whiskers longer and whiter but his spirit still strong, died in Camden, where he was born seventy-nine years before.

I realize that no one who was not present at a trial should ever judge its outcome, or justice—especially a trial in which circumstantial evidence played so great a part as it did in this one. I believe Captain Hart had a fair trial. I believe that residents of Tenants Harbor, none of whom apparently raised a hand to get Hart out of prison, were better judges of the man's character than any outlander could be.

But at least Albion Meservey and his wife believed Hart innocent to the time of his death and, for all I know, for the rest of their lives. I do not think that Hart's counsel exerted themselves to the extent they should. What one could wish to know, and never will, is the identity of those "two persons living in Tenants Harbor" who wanted to gain admission to the Meservey house before the body of the murdered woman was removed. And who was the mysterious character holding a coat over his head who was seen, not only by Captain Hart but by another and unnamed person, walking the wild shore that twenty-fourth night of December, 1877? I have seen a few odd characters walking the Maine shore, and some of them did not look like Santa Claus.

CHAPTER ELEVEN

FOLKLORE OF AMERICAN MURDER

AND SOME NOTES ON THE SCENES OF CRIMES, TOGETHER WITH ACKNOWLEDGMENTS AND BIBLIOGRAPHICAL DETAILS

IT IS DIFFICULT to know what elements in a crime serve to preserve its memory through several generations, often for a century or more, and dignify it into minor history. If the criminal, or victim, becomes the subject of a singable and sufficiently maudlin ballad—preferably ungrammatical—then his name will last a long time, as witness the cases of Jesse James and Billy the Kid. If the criminal, or at least the case, gains a literary following, it makes for lasting qualities, too, as the people of Fall River, Massachusetts, well know through the efforts of Alexander Woollcott, the late Edmund Pearson, and others who have written essays about Miss Elizabeth Borden of that city.

Motion pictures have supplanted the dime novel as the immortalizing agent, so far as the mass public is concerned, and are just about as accurate. I recall that, of a recent moving picture concerning her grandfather, Miss Jo James of Los Angeles was quoted as saying the sole resemblance between fact and the picture was that Jesse often did ride a horse. But Jesse James was not a murderer anyway, in the sense the term is usually employed. Jesse was a "bad man," and so was the adenoidal punk whose death should have brought lasting fame and a big monument to Sheriff Pat Garrett. Incidentally, and in spite of what most people believe, Miss Lisbeth Borden was no murderess, either. She was clearly acquitted of any crime, and lived quietly for another thirty years, going to her reward as recently as 1927.

I do not believe that what might be termed the lasting qualities of a criminal case become apparent for at least a quarter of a century. All of the cases in this book are that old, and many much older. At least nine of the ten seem to be pretty solidly settled into the tradition, the folklore, of the communities where they occurred. The odd one, that concerning the learned Dr. Rulloff, took in a little too much territory to get into local folklore.

In Portland, Oregon, where I first conceived this book some six years ago and began to collect material for it, many of the older generation thought I should include the story of Emma Merlottin, the beauteous lady of light morals who was found hacked to death in her Yamhill Street establishment early one morning, I believe, in 1888. The case is interesting, I'll admit, but chiefly because it was never solved. To this day old-timers in Portland mutter mysteriously about a "certain well known businessman" of the 1880s and will tell you that *he* knew who killed poor Emma and why.

Other oldsters said I should include the mystery concerning the murder of a man—one John Coneally—whose body was found in the cellar of an unfinished hotel and whose ghost has since been seen rather often by the hotel's colored waiters.

But unsolved mysteries, unless they have exceptional features, are a dime a dozen. Every community in the land has them, and the classic of this type is of course the unsolved kidnapping of Charlie Ross, still going strong after well over half a century.

The first case I did select from the Oregon country, that of Joshua Creffield, is, it seems to me, the most incredible of all the cases I have studied along the West Coast. I became acquainted with it through Tom Burns of Burnside, the old-time Socialist orator of Portland, who had heard Creffield perform. The late John Goltz, Portland city detective whom I knew well, also knew Creffield and considered him the greatest religious impostor Oregon had ever seen—and Oregon has seen many such. A friend, Harry Veness, attended Creffield's trial for adultery, and gave me a good description of the man; as did Major General George A. White, now commanding a division at Fort Lewis, Washington, but in 1906 *The Oregonian's* demon reporter who covered the entire affair. Even Joe, the Number One Japanese Boy redcap at Seattle's King Street Station, helped by fixing the spot where Esther Mitchell pulled her pearl handled revolver and fired. Ed Pascoe, now night clerk in Hotel Croft, Tacoma, who stood so close that blood splattered him, was of help in setting the scene.

It is in Oregon's Willamette Valley, however, that "Creffield and his Holy Rollers" are firmly embedded in tradition. The late Frank B. Irvine, long time editor of the *Oregon Journal* and before that editor of a Corvallis paper, often discussed Creffield and his works in the old Portland Press Club, regrettably now no more. From him I got many fine points not given prominence at the time. And during recent visits in Corvallis, several middle-aged people told me what living in Corvallis was like when Joshua was alive and possessed of all his great powers. The files of the *Corvallis Gazette-Times* and of *The Oregonian*, as well as the *Seattle Post-Intelligencer*, all furnish good running stories of the major events.

The folklore concerning Creffield and his band deals mostly with the prophet's unquestioned great virility, and is wholly

unprintable. Enough of it is going the rounds, even at this
late date, to make a stupendous footnote for Krafft-Ebing or
Havelock Ellis. It seems likely, thirty-five years afterward,
that Prophet Joshua's memory will live longer than that of
any other local miracle worker, including that of the Reverend
Billy Sunday, who lived long in the Beaver State.

Of Chapter Two

The case of Alma Nesbitt is scarcely remembered outside
Hood River and The Dalles, Oregon. I first heard of it when
I went to the former place, back in the 1920s, to write an
article about the celebrated Hood River Cragrats, the group
of hardy mountaineers who have made so many sensational
rescues of would-be climbers on the slopes of Oregon's highest
peak. Almost twenty years later I again visited the community,
this time in the genial company of Edward M. Miller, Sunday
editor of *The Oregonian.*

You know how it is when your mind gets going on an old
story that you once knew and thought you had forgotten.
Things start coming back, slowly and one thing at a time, then
faster while they gather volume like a tumbleweed, rolling on
and on, wafted by that mysterious wind out of the past which
we call memory, pressing into the mind so fast that at first
you cannot relate them one to another. But in time they form
a pattern.

It was that way with me and the weird case of the Lone Girl
Homesteader, as Miller and I drove the seventy miles east from
Portland to Hood River. Here was a case that still stirred the
minds of old men and women, the very stuff of which lasting
folklore is made. We recalled fragments we both had heard in
times past, of yellowed newspaper accounts, and agreed that
the affair was probably the classic crime of Oregon's great
open spaces.

The village of Hood River stands boldly on terraces over-
looking the broad and tumbling Columbia. Back of the village

the valley of the same name begins and runs to the very base
of Mount Hood. Near the head of the valley is Parkdale district, where the Lone Girl Homesteader lived.

Since about 1900 Hood River valley has been more or less
famous as a place of fine fruit. It raises and ships apples and
strawberries to much of the world, and its apple brandy is
potent and noted. The valley has also been known for its
gentlemen farmers who began coming here shortly after the
turn of the century. They were so many and so gentlemanly
that small Hood River, away in the back-country, used to
have a University Club, with Harvard, Brown, Yale, Cornell
and other Eastern colleges represented. Many artists came to
paint, too, and some remain. But this immigration of talent
and culture had barely begun in the days of the Great Homestead Murders. Alma Nesbitt had been a genuine pioneer in
the upper valley.

In Hood River village we found Bert Stranahan at home.
While Mrs. Stranahan brewed us excellent coffee, her husband, seventy and as straight as a hickory, told us of that day
thirty-six years before when the Mysterious Stranger came
to town. When he was done he showed us the road to Parkdale.
"You'd better run up there and see the country," he said. "It
isn't just the way it used to be, but the scenery is the same
as it was when Alma pitched her claim there."

We drove eighteen miles through endless orchards up Hood
River valley to Parkdale hamlet, with its school and store, then
to what had been the (probable) scene of the crime. What
appeared to be a dude ranch was in process of getting under
way. This land is situated near the very head of the valley and
fair against the base of the big mountain. On one hand we
looked for miles down the gorgeous valley, and on the other
there was the tremendous fact of the mountain itself, filling
all that side of the world.

The air was high, balmy and sweet, and the scene made one
understand why artists came here, to live ever after in this

spot. Could a man live here, with all this to look at, and keep murder in his heart? Not in apple-blossom time, anyway. But in March . . .

In the folklore of this case I did not find, contrary to usual tradition in cases of circumstantial evidence, any doubt that the right man had been hanged. But the valley teems with embellishments. I was told that George Nesbitt was led to the spot where his mother and sister probably were killed and cremated, by an angel in a dream. But I am suspicious of all angels and all dreams. They appear too often but are never heard of until after the event.

On occasion, I was told, a ghost has been seen in Parkdale, and at least twice two wraith-like figures were glimpsed moving up the valley road from Hood River. Chiefly, however, the folklore deals with crimes Norman Williams is said to have committed before ever he came to Hood River. Once, so local rumor has it, he tired of his current wife and tossed her into a deep well. Again, somewhere in Iowa, he disposed of a rival for a girl's favors, but how this was accomplished is not clear. Other crimes charged to him are even vaguer, but implicitly believed.

From Hood River I went to The Dalles, seat of Wasco County, to see Judge Fred W. Wilson, gentleman, scholar, and historian, and also the chief reason for the hanging of Norman Williams. In the intervening years Judge Wilson has heard many a strange case from the bench, but none, he says, in which the meshing of evidence was so tight and so fortunate. The Judge permitted me to spend hours with the transcript of the trial; and on this, and with comments from the Judge, from Mr. Stranahan and others, I fashioned my version of the affair.

OF CHAPTER THREE

The lore connected with Harry Orchard would seem practically without end. Before I set seriously to work on this case

I had been assured by lumberjacks, by hardrock miners, even by staid businessmen, that Harry Orchard was responsible for the deaths of forty-two persons. Often this figure was more, never less, but forty-two seems the favorite number in relation to Orchard's lethal accomplishments. Then, the men who *knew* Orchard—"Harry an' me was just like that"—are as numberless as those who "once sparred four rounds with John L. Sullivan" and, in turn, are like unto the drops of the sea.

I knew that most of the principals in the famous Idaho case were dead. William Borah had just died a United States Senator. Big Bill Haywood, whom I had heard speak, was long since dead in Russia. Clarence Darrow, whom I had known, was gone. So were the Messrs. Moyer and Pettibone. But I knew that Harry Orchard remained, an inmate of the Idaho penitentiary almost as long as I could remember. So, from The Dalles I went to Pendleton, Oregon's Roundup City, and took a United Air Lines plane. As we approached Boise, Idaho's capital city, I could look down on the piles of brick and stone that I knew made up the prison, tucked snugly away in a brief spot of green at the base of yellow-brown hills, bare and stark even in summer.

Boise was sweltering in a dry heat, but there was nothing dry about Boise hospitality. Friends already had made arrangements with the warden, P. C. Meredith, for me to talk to Idaho's most celebrated convict.

A blistering sun beat down into the penitentiary yard as the warden and I walked across it to the little shack next to the chicken and turkey pens inside the Big Wall. Not a breath of air was stirring, and the blazing sunlight made everything sharp, life-size. It was Sunday and the prison quiet was intense. We went into the comparable gloom of the shack and were welcomed by Harry Orchard.

I saw a stocky, healthy man, really seventy-four years of age but looking and talking and moving like one of sixty, perhaps less. His florid and tanned face had a pleasant smile.

His hair is light and thinning. He is about five feet seven inches tall and has broad shoulders. There is no trace of prison softness about him. The number on the back of his coveralls is 1406, and since he acquired that number almost six thousand more men and women have entered the establishment . . . In thirty-five years even a state with a sparse population like Idaho can produce a sizable number of convicts.

Orchard's greeting was pleasant and easy. He had been sitting in an old rocker when we came, reading some Adventist literature, and at first our talk turned to William Miller, the Vermonter who is generally credited with being the Prophet of that church and with whose history I had some acquaintance. Orchard was happy to know that I no longer drank liquor but he regretted that I used tobacco.

On the wall was a well-filled bookshelf, a homemade affair, containing mostly religious and "inspirational" works—*The Book of Life, The Hope of the World, Prisons and Prayer, Education and the Will*, a biography of General William Booth, and another titled *Theodore Roosevelt, First American.* Orchard said that in his spare time from the prison chickens and turkeys, of which he has charge, he was bringing down to date his own story, in autobiographical form, and he showed me a pile of neat manuscript he keeps under his pillow. (A letter from Mr. Orchard in February, 1941, tells me that he will have his manuscript ready by late summer and that the book will doubtless be titled *A Sequel to the Confessions and Autobiography of Harry Orchard.* "It will deal in the main," he writes, "with the subject of reformation, not from without alone but from within as well, for I think the two are inseparable . . . If it were not for the transforming power of the Gospel of Jesus Christ, the world would have never known my story.")

We sat in the shack and talked. "I like chickens and turkeys," Orchard said, "and I hope to get outside this place for a few years before I die. I'd like to make some experiments in cross-breeding chickens which aren't possible here in the prison.

"Until I became interested in chickens I hadn't thought a great deal of getting a pardon or a parole. Last time I applied was in 1921. That's almost twenty years ago. When I first came to the prison I helped in getting the clothing shop started, then worked in it. That was abolished. So later was the prison shoe shop, where I also worked. Then I made brushes, good brushes, but I had to quit when it became impossible to get the right kind of bristles, which come from Russia and nowhere else. So, now it's hens and turkeys. I keep busy all the time."

We sat and talked out the long hot afternoon, while the air was filled with the drone of summer insects and with an occasional baying from the prison bloodhounds in the nearby kennels. I watched to see if the hounds' mournful baying had any effect on the old Rocky Mountain Dynamite Man, who had often smeared his shoes with oil or turpentine to preclude tracking. None was visible. He talked freely of his past life and crimes, detachedly except when Big Bill Haywood's name was mentioned. Then Harry Orchard's eyes glowed like two black coals. If he showed any animosity, or at least any emotion that day, it was only when he spoke of Big Bill. "No friend of the working class," he said.

I was acquainted with Orchard's story long before I met the man. And here he was. Could this healthy, kindly-spoken person with the likable smile and the easy address be the greatest killer in America's long list of notable killers? Beside Harry Orchard, I knew, Billy the Kid had been but mildly lethal, the machine-gunners of Chicago's Prohibition heyday, merely irritating. Even that queen of the abattoir, Belle Gunness, seemed a bit futile compared to Orchard. Here in the flesh was old Death & Destruction himself, the one and only Rocky Mountain Dynamiter. I found him a most able and interesting conversationalist.

The Orchard tradition is strongest in Colorado and Idaho, and especially and naturally so in Boise. Dick D'Easum of the *Statesman* there, who with Bruce Kelley, Harry Shellworth and P. C. Meredith gave me so much help in meeting the right people, attempted to put me onto another story, or stories, in place of the Rocky Mountain Dynamite Man. Mr. D'Easum maintains that southern Idaho, in an older day, had the most interesting crimes in the United States, and his dossier is formidable support for his contention; but Orchard's spectacular record, it seemed to me, needed dusting off.

James Stevens, the well known author, now of Seattle, was a schoolboy in Weiser, Idaho, in 1905. His most profound memory of that period is of his teacher informing the school one snowy morning, and in a hushed voice, there would be no classes that day because ex-Governor Steunenberg had been assassinated. And there followed a time, as Mr. Stevens remembers well, when even tough Idaho ranchers lived in fear of further bombings and eyed every stranger closely to see if perchance a length of fuse were hanging out of his pocket.

Orchard has appeared in an immense amount of fragmentary literature, chiefly in newspapers and magazines. He seems to have achieved the impossible by being rated an enemy of both Labor and Capital; and why Joe Hill(strom), the Wobbly poet and singer, never fetched a few verses about Orchard, is a mystery. The man's own book, *The Confessions and Autobiography of Harry Orchard*, copyrighted in 1907 by Doubleday, Page and published by Metropolitan Church Association, is extremely rare. Through the courtesy of the Boise Public Library and the University of Washington Library I was permitted to use a copy of this work, which I had read before but was never able to buy. Those interested in the background of the case will find more or less first-hand accounts in the following works: Siringo, C. A., *A Cowboy Detective*, Hammond, Indiana, 1913; and *Riata and Spurs*, by the same author, Boston, 1927; Hutton, May A., *The Coeur d'Alenes*,

or a *Tale of the Modern Inquisition in Idaho*, Denver, 1900;
Coeur d'Alene labor troubles, 56th Congress, 1st Session,
House Report 1999, 1900. The most misleading account of
the affair I have ever read is contained in *The Pinkertons*, by
Richard Wilmer Rowan, Boston, 1931.

When I had finished my interview with Orchard and talked
with citizens of Boise who knew something of the case and
trial, I read the *Statesman's* day-to-day account in the files of
the Boise Public Library, and prepared to go on to the scene
of the next crime. Before I left, however, two incidents occurred
to show that Idaho still retains some of its pioneer flavor.
Within twenty miles of Boise a squatter shot and killed two
United States marshals who had been sent to remove him, and
he was taken only when burned to death in his cabin, fired by
incendiary bullets of possemen. And in Boise itself, a lumberjack, down from the pine hills to get his teeth fixed, was
arrested on a disorderly charge—but what a charge! He was
given, it seems, to chewing up and swallowing the beer glasses
he had just emptied. "When I'm drinkin'," he told the court,
"there ain't nothing I like better than a good solid meal of
beer mugs." Boise has a city ordinance expressly forbidding
the eating of beer glasses.

Doubling back on my trail, I went to Seattle where I turned
a sample of the handwriting of Albert E. Horsley (Harry
Orchard) over to a graphology expert. The professor of
graphology reported as follows on the mind, spirit, nature and
talents of the professor of dynamite:

"Active, adaptable, creative, imaginative, observant, psy-
chic, resourceful . . . Aggressive, independent, jovial, noncommittal, strong-willed, witty . . . with the possible weaknesses
of dislike for detail; impulsiveness, moodiness, too frank, too
emotional . . . but adapted to athletics, commercial art, dra-
matics, medicine, music, public speaking." And the professor
of graphology added a note of warning: ". . . and his health
should be guarded."

Reflecting that Albert E. Horsley's health had seemed guarded and very good, I took the Milwaukee's fine Olympian to Minneapolis.

OF CHAPTER FOUR

First I ever heard of pretty Kitty Ging came from Ben Hur Lampman, newspaperman of Portland, Oregon, but in 1894 a youngster in Wisconsin. "It seems to me now," said Mr. Lampman, "that the only subject of conversation in Wisconsin and Minnesota at that time and for two or three years afterward was the affair of Kitty Ging and Harry Hayward. Not even the Hinckley Fire made so much talk."

Through the efforts of George T. Springer of Minneapolis I talked with certain oldtime newspapermen and retired businessmen, who for reasons of their own shall be anonymous, and with others, all of whom had seen and some had talked to Hayward, and one who had known Kitty Ging. Merle Potter and Tom Dillon of the *Minneapolis Tribune* were especially helpful in putting me in touch with the persons who knew most. I had to take but few notes because in Mr. Springer's private library was a copy of the remarkable book by Oscar F. G. Day. The title is worth quoting in full: *The Ging Murder and the Great Hayward Trial, The Official Stenographic Report, Containing Every Word of the Wonderful Trial From Its Opening to Sentence of Death; the Rulings of the Court; Speeches by Frank M. Nye, W. W. Erwin, Albert H. Hall and John Day Smith; the Court's Charge Etc., Etc.* It was put together in 1895 and published by the Minnesota Tribune Company of Minneapolis. Although this book, as said, is hard to come upon, the case itself made such an impact on at least two generations of Minnesotans that it still has a solid place in local tradition, due, I am sure, to the fancy trimmings it acquired by word of mouth, by old-fashioned handing-down from father to son, and yes, from mother to daughter.

One can still hear in Minneapolis that the semi-literate Hayward was a high-toned man, a college graduate, a polished fellow, although the stenographic report of the trial shows him to have had odd ideas of correct English. Then, too, he was handsome; and this he may well have been, for in spite of a walrus mustache, and considerable retouching of at least his tie and collar, the photograph of him in Mr. Day's immortal book presents a good-looking dude, especially in contrast to the opposite page from which leer the witless features of poor Claus Blixt.

This making of a suave man of the world out of a criminal who owns, or rents, a dress suit, is a favorite practice with Americans. Hardly a city or town that has not marveled when a man in evening clothes, even though rented or stolen, has killed his sweetie, robbed a drunk, or blown a safe. Ipso facto he becomes a gentleman, probably a millionaire, and doubtless a scholar, certainly a man of the world. That's what the press made out of the crude, semi-literate bum, Hayward, when it was learned he had been seen in the Grand Opera House in a suit of evening clothes.

The old saw about "clothes do not make the man" is never better refuted than when an American criminal is caught red-handed wearing evening clothes. Today, almost half a century after the Ging–Hayward affair, Minneapolis remembers distinctly that Hayward was a polished man, a sort of Van Bibber gone wrong, a Svengali bent on swag from insurance instead of from song. If in addition to the rented suit he wore that night, Hayward had added an opera cloak and a cane, I am sure that Minneapolis today would tell one that Hayward was a member of a fine old New York family of Dutch colonial stock, and doubtless a patron of the arts and a member of Phi Beta Kappa.

In Minneapolis, oddly enough, I failed to find there was ever a song about the tragedy of Kitty Ging; but later, when I talked to A. R. McColley, a former Minnesotan now living

in far Washington state, he immediately began to recite the
words to *The Fatal Ride*, which was popular in his youth.
From his aunt, Mrs. May Jones of Mankato, Minnesota, I got
the sad lyric complete:

THE FATAL RIDE

Minneapolis was excited,
For many miles around,
A terrible crime committed
A mile or so from town.
'Twas on a cold and winter eve,
The moon had passed away,
The road was dark and lonely,
When found dead where she lay.

When for pleasure she went riding,
Little did she know her fate,
That took place on that lonely road,
By the way near Calhoun Lake;
She was shot while in the buggy
And beaten, 'tis hard to speak,
Until her life has vanished
Then cast into the street.

Oh, how could he have done that deed,
So terrible to do?
Or how could he have killed a girl
With a heart so kind and true?
It was a cold and bloody deed;
It was a terrible sin,
To take the life of one so true
As she had been to him.

REFRAIN

Then tell the tale of a criminal,
Kit was his promised bride.
Another fate to answer;
Another fatal ride.

That song is in the best tradition, and style, of homemade poesy, an excellent sample of what happens when local bards celebrate an event close to home.

Of Chapter Five

We left Minnesota at Taylors Falls, and crossed the fabulous St. Croix River not far from Angle Rock, that flinty old boulder cursed by generations of river drivers. The Rock is still haunted by the scores of ghosts of rivermen who lost their lives in breaking log jams, here in these stony canyons where the St. Croix runs faster than the milltail of hell. It was dangerous water.

We rolled north for hours through Wisconsin farming country where only the names served to remind us that this was once the very heart of the white pine belt, names known to every old lumberjack, names like Cumberland, Barronett, Spooner, and Hayward. And from Hayward on to Winter, the tiny one-street hamlet where thirty years ago eleven saloons did their best to allay the thirst of the thirstiest men on earth, and failed.

In Winter's one beer parlor I talked to Bill Rankin, tough and weathered from half a century in the woods, and with others like Bill who had come to Winter in days when the air was filled with pine, when loafers sat on freshly cut stumps, if they sat at all, and when a man smoking a cigarette was driven down the trail like one with leprosy. Yes, Bill said, he could show us the way to Cameron Dam, but we couldn't roll in there on no rubber tires. We should have to walk the last few miles.

Some eight miles out of Winter we turned off the highway onto what had been a logging railroad's grade. It was tough going, for the frozen ground had thawed in spots, and every few rods wicked spikes stuck up from rotting old ties. "Last feller come along here," Bill remarked cheerfully, "them spikes took every tire off his car." Pretty soon we came to the Thornapple River, and here we stopped. The old bridge was a heap of jackstraw logs in the water.

Crossing the stream by leaps from stone to log, we came up on the other side. Bill took his bearings only for a moment, then hit south by west at a good clip. Through acres and acres of thornapple brush he led the way, with the multi-spiked branches clutching at us, tearing our clothes. Then, across a wild grass meadow and into a bog frozen not quite hard enough, into which we sank over our shoes at every step. The day was sharp and bright, but this was desolate country on any old day. Scrubby thornapple, the tall wild grass, and dry reeds— that was all. I could count all the pine trees we saw on the fingers of two hands. Repeated forest fires had killed all the natural second-growth timber.

Two miles further we emerged from the bog on the edge of a large field, long since gone to wild grass. Below us the small river bent in a curve, and the water was deep and dead. But it wasn't Cameron Dam that made the deadwater. The few remains of that celebrated structure reared up from the shore. Beaver had moved in below it, now that all the shooting was over, and had dammed the Thornapple River within a few yards of where man once had dammed it. I wondered idly if the present dam was not the result of some ancient folk memory of the animals, dating from long before the first white man, handed down from beaver to beaver through generations of the patient little creatures, waiting while man came, stayed awhile, then went away, leaving the river to be reclaimed by those who could not live without it.

Anyway, here was Cameron Dam, given back to the original dam builders of this and all other rivers. And the big wild field, this was the John Dietz farm—the fort, the stronghold, the place where today one could, as on any other old battle-field, still plow spent bullets from the ground. Nor had the forest reclaimed its own, in the usual manner of forests. All was bare, wind-swept, desolate. On the far side of the stream were two pines, fifty years old perhaps, and the only living things still here that had witnessed the events which had put these few acres into headlines across the continent. Below the dam I could see the winding river glinting here and there on its meandering way through an interminable swamp, on its way to the Chippewa, then the Mississippi.

The Dietz house and barn were gone, but I could easily trace their outlines in the wild grass. Scuffing, I kicked up the back of a castiron stove, a length of rusted pipe, and two pieces of an iron bed. Back of the house was a deep hole, the old root cellar. I sat on the cellar rim and looked at the scene. It struck me that I had never viewed a place that seemed more remote, more forgotten, more passed-by, than these melancholy acres of swamp and barrens of the late and redoubtable John F. Dietz.

The Battle of Cameron Dam was well into folklore, much of it contrary to fact, almost before the powder smoke along the Thornapple had blown away. Many newspapers sent reporters to cover the battle who wrote stories that today would be eyed coldly by most any city editor. The press must be getting better, for at least two-thirds of the stuff printed at the time not only was as inaccurate as reporting well could be, but had a bias no self-respecting editor would permit outside the editorial columns in these later years. John F. Dietz was pictured as a sort of Embattled Farmer who had been set upon and persecuted without end by a fiendishly cruel lumber company. The more than twelve hundred pages of court testimony I read in the Sawyer County courthouse at Hayward give one an entirely different idea, or they did me, and Dietz' own testimony was largely responsible. Added to this were the measured opinions of dozens of persons living in the community at the time who had no particular friendliness either for Dietz or for the lumber concern.

I realize, of course, that the newspaper reading public would not care to read about an embittered farmer, no matter how

honest in his beliefs, suffering obviously from a truly colossal
persecution complex. Nor would such a case appeal to a reporter as very lively copy. Hence, Dietz became in many
papers a man fighting lone handed against all the evils of
aggressive capitalism. In part of the foreign language press this
attitude took as rabid a stand as it did in the *Appeal to Reason*,
the Socialist weekly, then very powerful. Published in Minneapolis in 1912 by Waldemar Friedts Forlag was a paper-
covered book titled *John F. Deitz* (sic). It is in Norwegian,
and a translation I read showed where much of the "folklore"
current among Scandinavian lumberjacks has come from. As
a history even approximating the facts this book is worthless;
but its author was patently not even casually interested in
facts. The book is a crude Marxian tract, decorated here and
there with what are obviously apocryphal incidents in the life
of its hero.

The *Wisconsin State Guide*, compiled by the Writers
Project of the WPA and published in 1941, does not help matters much. Reading it one would believe that the Cameron Dam
battle occurred at Cameron, instead of at Winter, some sixty-
five miles distant, where it did happen. And this account is in
little accord with the facts of the eminently clear record, which
is to be found in the court record and in *136 Northwestern
Reporter*.

Of Chapter Six

I had scarcely got off the Grand Trunk at Flint, Michigan,
before I was reminded of the chief business of that city. On the
way to my hotel the taxi driver turned half way around. "I
suppose," he said, "you came to drive a new car home?"

It was a question, but the tone of voice indicated it was a
mere pleasantry and that the reply would of course be affirmative. I have never owned a car, and a car, new or otherwise,
was the last thing I would be thinking about, even in Flint,
Michigan. I was thinking of Bad Axe, my destination, rumi-

nating with deep satisfaction on the marvelous backwoods flavor of its name, glorying in the rough and ready settlers who had found a broken single-bitted ax near a stump and named their settlement forthwith. It was in the grand tradition of the American frontier, this naming a new place for a thing, a condition, or an event. I thought of Spotted Robe, of Hungry Creek, and of Thief River Falls, all good but none in my estimation quite so rich as Bad Axe.

The taxi driver's abrupt question slowly entered my consciousness, and I was genuinely shocked—shocked that a man on his way to Bad Axe should be asked if he were going *to buy a new car!* I was startled into speech. "What did you say?" I asked. He repeated his obscene question. "No," I replied, "I didn't come to get a new car. I came here for an old corpse." "Oh!" he said, with reverence for the dead in his voice, then relapsed into silence. I went back to conjuring about Bad Axe.

After breakfast with Colin McDonald, of Flint's lively *Daily Journal,* we with Mrs. McDonald headed north into Huron County, on the very tip of what in Michigan is called the Thumb. We drove first to Ubly, a sleepy hamlet, then still north to Bad Axe, county seat, a pretty village with an orthodox main street, a courthouse, jail and village green. Nothing remained to show that Bad Axe was once a lumber town, but on the green was a relic of its greatest industry. This is a gigantic grindstone, the largest I ever saw, and on it an inscription: "In Memory of Grindstone Industry 1835–1935." Grindstones from Huron County sharpened the axes that felled Michigan's timber and ground the scythes that cut pioneer wheat in points west. Today, I was told, Bad Axe is an important trading center for the farming country round about, and, like most towns on the Thumb, is something of a summer resort.

A respectable amount of lore has been built up around the strange and tragic affair of Dr. MacGregor and the Sparling family. Some of it would be in poor taste to print, but much is proper and runs true to pattern. The late Dr. MacGregor, who was either a murderer or the pitiful victim of horrible coincidence in the matter of circumstances, has been pictured by some in the district as a true miracle worker in the field of medicine. "A very wonderful doctor," the stranger will hear. This school of thought believes the doctor was persecuted by unnamed parties because he sent many of his patients to a hospital in Canada, instead of patronizing local institutions. In the same community, too, it is possible to hear that Dr. MacGregor was a master of the black arts of poison, a villain fit for a Poe. "Used to try out his concoctions on animals first," is one story.

When it comes to the reason behind the governor of Michigan's extraordinary pardon of Dr. MacGregor, I could learn of no ulterior motive. Was it political? I think not. Possibly I might have learned—if anybody knows—had I not been a stranger. But I have many good friends in the state, and none of them knows, so far as I am aware, of any reason for the pardon other than that given by Governor Ferris himself— "absolute innocence."

This odd case came to my knowledge through Colin Mc-Donald. He also told of another weird affair on the Thumb, that concerning the Brent family of the charmingly named Grind Stone City, which included a fine old haunted house and no little skulduggery. But authentic material on this case proved difficult to find, whereas the *Huron County Tribune* of Bad Axe contains expert reporting on the trial of Dr. Mac-Gregor. Still living in Bad Axe, too, is Judge Xenophon A. Boomhower, who prosecuted the case, who was most courteous and helpful. So far as I know the Sparling–MacGregor case never brought forth a pamphlet. A brief critical article concerning its legal aspects appears in *Convicting the Innocent*, by Edwin M. Borchard, New Haven, 1932.

For reasons I don't pretend to know, Michigan has had so

many interesting crimes that it was not easy to choose. William Webb, Flint librarian, and Dr. W. H. Marshall of that city, both of whom have a large stock of Michigan history and folk-lore in their retentive minds, nearly persuaded me to one or more crimes in the Flint neighborhood; and George Newark, my old lumberjack friend of Harbor Springs, had several promising cases in the western part of the state.

Of Chapter Seven

Unhealthy as the Sparling farm had been, I was assured that a certain farm in Indiana was in its day the most lethal forty acres of ground in all the Republic. This assurance had been given me more than once by a Hoosier friend, Julius Meyn, who swore on a volume of the *Collected Poems* of James Whitcomb Riley that sweetness and light were not all that Indiana has produced. I met Mr. Meyn in Chicago.

Both snow and rain were in the air as we left the Loop and ran down the sandy flatlands to Hammond, Indiana. Smoke hung in a pall over the South Shore, for the air was heavy and Steel was busy as it hadn't been busy in years. In South Chicago, by the river, a Bessemer converter flared into blow, sending high its red and orange and violet sparks until they were lost in the smoke. Cinders rattled on the top of our car.

Hammond was busy, too. So were East Chicago, Indiana Harbor, Gary—all great names in Steel. Busy and grimy, with small volcanoes of molten metal erupting here and there from the endless yards and buildings. A street clock said it was eleven in the morning, but the automobile lights were on, and needed.

Slowly we emerged from the murk of the Cinder Shore, level as a pool table, and into the rolling farm country of low hills. This was Indiana, and fields on both sides of the road held scattered shocks of brown-yellow corn, weary from the weather, limp and dejected. At this time of year the fields would scarcely have attracted the song-writing team of Dresser & Dreiser. Some of the most uninteresting farm architecture in America edged the drear fields. A huge signboard, purely historical by then, asked the wayfarer to Vote for Willkie. Hedges of thornapple marked farm boundaries. A slate sky hung low.

It would have been a cheerless ride alone, or in less excellent company than I had. But my companions were Hoosiers, both native and adopted, with a fund of Indiana folklore ranging from La Porte to Evansville and in period from Robert Dale Owen to John Dillinger. We drove to La Porte and out a back road to the ground once celebrated as the farm of the Female Bluebeard. The sky turned darker than ever, and it hung low over as bleak and dismal a swamp as one could wish for. A perfect setting. This was the place to which so many men came, their eyes alight with love, and from which so few ever departed. The five of us sat on a fence and mused on the scene, and each of the four Hoosiers recalled some rumor or other he had heard of Mrs. Gunness. "In her day," Thelma Jones summed up, "Mrs. Gunness was as well known in her line as Mr. Riley was in his."

And it is true. Of all the many Bluebeards of both sexes the United States has produced, none I believe has been the subject of more comment, or the source of more folklore, than Mrs. Gunness whom, as we learned in and around La Porte, many persist in thinking to be alive today in 1941 and enjoying a hearty old age, no doubt still doing her own butchering. As was the case for decades with John Wilkes Booth and Jesse James, Belle Gunness lives on in that misty, unmapped half-world that Americans have made and lovingly preserve for certain of their folk villains. Indeed, I fully expected to see Belle pop up at Chicago's Century of Progress world's fair in 1933, complete with cleavers and a supply of quicklime; just as "Jesse James," complete with affidavits as to his identity, put in an appearance at a recent fair in Fort Worth, Texas.

Throughout northern Indiana and Illinois people tell that

Belle's victims numbered forty-two, for some occult reason a favorite number in old wives' tales. It is said, too, despite the record, that Belle always married her victims after being certain they were well insured. School boys and girls in the La Porte district of thirty years ago often heard terrifying sounds issuing from the swamp near Belle's place, including cries for help, but whether with a Scandinavian accent or not, I could not learn. Many middle-aged folk today believe the swamp is haunted.

But of all the lore concerning Belle, the most typical is a tale that she was "always kind to children and dumb animals." This sort of thing is a hoary old favorite with Americans. Captain Kidd was kind to children and dumb animals. So were the ghastly Bender family of Kansas. John Dillinger was kind to his mother. Harry Tracy was very good hearted. Miss Elizabeth Borden loved cats. So it goes. In regard to Mrs. Gunness it should be remembered that her well fenced boneyard held the remains of at least two children. But the tales of her kindness, one feels sure, will never down.

Theories, which have by now solidified into unshakable "facts," have it that Belle employed a perfect production line in her killing which never varied. The steps: 1) drugged coffee, 2) a good stout blow with an ax, 3) removal to the cellar, whose door was "always well oiled so it wouldn't squeak," 4) a neat job of dissection, and 5) immersion in the lime vat, or burial in the yard, the gate to which was "always well oiled so it wouldn't squeak," or—and this version is very popular—feeding the corpse to the pigs.

I could not discover that Belle had ever been the subject of a serious monograph, or even of a popular pamphlet. Vincent Starrett, the writer, an able student of crimes, told me that Belle doubtless had received more newspaper space in Chicago than any other female he could name off-hand, including Little Egypt; and in the files of the *Chicago Tribune* I found a good and gory running account of the denouement of the case. This

paper resurrects the story every few years. At the Chicago
Public Library Mr. Hewitt and Mrs. Sutton were no time at
all furnishing me with the many dates on which Mrs. Gunness
was treated by the "World's Greatest Newspaper."

OF CHAPTER EIGHT

As I pointed out earlier, there seems to be no particular
tradition regarding Edward Rulloff, the so-called educated
murderer. In Binghamton, New York, where he was hanged,
the sons and daughters of persons who attended Rulloff's last
agonies remember their fathers' telling them he was "intel-
lectually one of the marvels of the time." That his arrest and
trial was what could be termed a national sensation there can
be little doubt. *The New York Tribune* of the period devoted
many columns of fine print to him, and shortly after he was
hanged a pamphlet *The Man of Two Lives* had a wide sale.
It was through the kindness of Norman L. Dodge, erudite
editor of *The Month at Goodspeed's Book Shop*, Boston, that
I was permitted to use a copy of this now rare pamphlet, and
also a studious article on Rulloff reprinted from the *American
Journal of Insanity*.

OF CHAPTER NINE

In contrast to the lack of lore about Rulloff are the apparently endless tales of that other double-headed criminal, the
man born in Massachusetts as George Abbott, imprisoned in
Vermont under the same name, and hanged in New Hampshire
as Frank Almy. I was brought up, you might say, with knowledge, or rather tales, about this man, for I went to school for a
period in Lebanon and West Lebanon, both near the scene of
the crime; and in Vermont I often heard old Charles Morrison,
who knew Windsor prison pretty well himself, discuss his
fellow convict Abbott. All grown folks in my boyhood had
stories to tell of Abbott–Almy and Christie Warden.

As late as 1940, when I mentioned the name of Frank Almy in a talk at the New Hampshire Book Fair, I was inundated by middle-aged and elderly folk, all with some vivid memory of the case. "What a handsome man he was!" many women remarked, and one seemed to recall that when he was hanged his head was pulled from his body. This yanking off a head at a hanging is a favorite that recurs again and again in hand-me-down tales about criminals. A variation which incidentally appears to be more fact than fiction concerns the death on the gallows at Windsor, Vermont, of Mrs. Mary Rogers, an eminent Green Mountain murderess of the early part of this century. Her hanging, it is said, was so bungled that her neck was not broken. She slowly strangled to death, with appropriate gurgling noises, which, when one eyes her record closely, leaves one quite composed.

So imbued was I since childhood with the alleged romantic bearing and adventures of Abbott–Almy that I found this story the most difficult of all to write; I had to unlearn so much before I could accept the unvarnished facts concerning this bucolic thug. For instance, I grew up with the idea that Abbott–Almy was a sort of neolithic (dates meant nothing to boys) Jesse James who lived, probably for years and years, in a cave two miles long in some Vermont mountain, meanwhile directing with skillful hand the activities of a large band of robbers and cutthroats who terrorized much of the known world, even to the other side of Lake Champlain and the Hoosac Tunnel. Windsor prison, on which I had gazed in awe, had been strong enough to hold old Charles Morrison for duration of *his* sentence, I knew, but for Abbott–Almy its great walls had been as butter.

The first man hunt for the escaped convict, I gathered, was accompanied by five thousand armed men and at least two thousand bloodhounds. And the bloodhounds I had in mind were all Great Danes and mastiffs, for I had never seen the sad, kindly bloodhound, but had often attended a performance by one of Stetson's Original Uncle Tom's Cabin companies—a Number Six company, probably—which used the big fierce dogs, and never bloodhounds.

This same Abbott, when he became Almy, so I was sure from what I had heard of local folklore, accomplished his disguise with arts scarcely less magnificent than those credited to Dr. Jekyll. His "romance" with the beautiful Christie Warden was somewhat vague as to detail, but it was very wonderful. And Christie Warden, I was certain, was more beautiful than the ingénue with Price Webber's Dramatic Stock Company who saved the hero from being cut into boards in the great sawmill scene in *Blue Jeans*—which is to say she was the most beautiful girl on earth. Christie was also a very good girl, doubtless as pure as my Sunday school teacher around whose head was often seen a gaseous object approximating a halo.

Dartmouth men who had graduated in the 1890s were filled with stories about the second and final man hunt for Almy. That last battle in the barn, as I was often told by wearers of the Green, was an epic comparable to Harry Tracy's Last Stand in the wheatfields of eastern Washington, perhaps even to that of the Jameses and Youngers at Northfield, Minnesota. In Vermont and New Hampshire, at least, Frank Almy was as fearsome to youngsters as old Jesse Pomeroy, the long-lived sadist, was to boys and girls in Massachusetts.

It was somewhat of a blow when I learned, as I did through the aid of the New Hampshire Historical Society, that Abbott–Almy had been—of all things—a hired man on a farm and not a very good hired man at that. This was almost too much for a farm boy. But Major Hammond and Miss Fulford of the Society insisted that I learn all the horrible facts, and they proceeded to stack the facts higher than Haman in the newspaper file room.

The Society has a good copy of the very rare *The Life, Trial and Confessions of Frank C. Almy*, by John Lane, published at Laconia, but when I do not know. The *Concord Monitor* of the period was alert and highly competent in covering the affair. The *Hanover Gazette* often became excited, but its news accounts took for granted too much knowledge on the part of the reader, a fault of most country papers, then and now. The *Union* of Manchester had several good first-hand accounts, and a partial summary. In many, and perhaps in all New Hampshire papers of the time were news items of incidents relating to the affair. One chapter in Clay Perry's excellent book on caves, *Underground New England* (Brattleboro, Vermont, 1939), deals with Almy.

In the Grafton County courthouse at Woodsville I had the unstinting aid of Mrs. Anna Proctor who dug into court records for facts newspapers seem to have ignored. Mrs. Proctor also uncovered that sterling biographical fragment titled *B. H. Corning's Life of Abbott–Almy as Looked Up By Him*, which is my favorite title for a biography.

It is to be regretted that the one song about Almy that became popular has the smirk of the conscious comedian in it. It was the same with the song about Miss Elizabeth Borden. This is no manner in which to treat popular villains. Had Almy performed his deeds in the South, and especially in the Southwest, you may be sure a sound ballad of some length—doubtless of forty-two verses—would have made its appearance promptly, possibly before the subject had been cut down from the gallows. This paucity of ballads about folk heroes and villains in the North must stem from some vitamin deficiency. Great disasters in the North have often inspired ballads. Offhand I can recall one about a railroad wreck—in Ohio, I think —whose last lines were "an awful human carnage, a dreadful wreck of cars"; another about the collapse of a textile factory in Lawrence, Massachusetts; still another about a mine disaster in Pennsylvania.

It is true that Belle Gunness, Norman Williams, and pos-

sibly a few other criminals in the North have been subjects of
balladry, but the South and the West seldom fail to let *any*
villain pass without a good, long-winded maudlin song.

The handing down of tradition is as strong in Maine as it is
elsewhere in New England, and in 1917, when I first heard of
the Hart–Meservey case, it was not yet forty years in the past.
In my regiment of field artillery, composed about equally of
Maine and New Hampshire lads, were a number of men from
Knox County, Maine, scene of the crime. All of them were
under forty, under thirty even, but they spoke of the murder
of Sarah Meservey as if it had been the day before yesterday.
They knew men and women who had played prominent parts
in the affair, and some were related to the victim or the murderer or both.

The boys of Knox County, for the most part, held that
Captain Hart had guilty knowledge, may even have been the
actual murderer. But—and this is an important and recurring
"but" in the best tradition—they also believed that Captain
Hart *did* see a stranger with a coat over his head, walking the
wild shore that December night. Speculation as to this Unknown's identity, so far as I remember, never settled on anybody. This stranger, this mysterious party out for a stroll
in winter and holding a coat over his head—which is not at
all the way most Maine coast folk walk the shore—this Unknown is almost a symbol in folk tales of American crimes.

Who, now, was that mystery woman, "dressed in black,"
whom Belle Gunness met at the La Porte railroad station? *Was*
she a stand-in for Belle? Who was that "tall, thin woman in a
long coat" who was strolling the beach at Winthrop, Massachusetts, one night in 1905, just before The Great Suitcase
Horror broke on New England? She was never apprehended
that I know of, nor even seen again. Did she have knowledge

of the contents of the suitcase? This was the first, or one of the
first "suitcase mysteries" in the United States, of more recent
years so common. (I have wondered if in earlier times some
murder was not known as The Great Carpet Bag Mystery. I
have seen a number of these old flowered bags in attics. Any
one of them had the necessary capacity.)

Who, now, killed Dave Merrill? Was it Harry Tracy, the
Oregon bad man, or was it that "man in a buggy" who fled
down the road near Napavine, Washington? Who called Starr
Faithful on the phone not long before that pretty girl was last
seen alive? Take the records of one hundred American crimes,
study them, and you will find—at least in those of any mystery
at all—that a Third Party, an Unknown, figures somehow
in half of them. This Unknown has figured in countless affairs,
both unsolved and at least officially solved. Have all of them
stemmed from the American love of mystery even when no
trace of mystery is present? I think not. I believe that many of
these Unknowns were actual persons, wholly innocent, who by
pure coincidence happened to be where they were when
glimpsed. But they are never seen again, so far as the records
show. Possibly they were never seen at all, although I cannot
believe that all were figments of imaginations made receptive
to suggestion by our lurid reporting of crime.

The record, such as it is, in the Hart–Meservey case almost
forces one to believe that some man other than Captain Hart
was walking the shore that night, and for no good.

Both the *Boston Globe* and the *Rockland Opinion* have good
summaries of this case. Professor Alvin R. Dunton's remarkable book, discussed in my text, is chaotic, but it does, by its
very detail and earnestness, make one feel that Captain Hart's
defense counsel did not exert itself to the utmost. In the admi-
rable study to be found in his *Five Murders* (New York, 1928)
Edmund Pearson seemed to think that though Hart was the
killer, not all the facts were brought out at the trial. I am
sure they were not.

My unscientific but fairly extensive research in the records of almost one hundred crimes from Oregon to Maine has led me to believe that the guilty party is almost but not quite always the one who is convicted. The guilty who go free, of course, are without doubt many indeed.

My research has also convinced me that the most interesting crimes in the United States have been committed by persons with rural and backwoods, or at least small-town, backgrounds. I don't think this proves anything in particular, or if it does that it is very important; but it does amuse me when I hear city people wonder, as I often do, what on earth the folks at the forks of the creek can find to talk about.

INDEX

A CATALOG OF SELECTED DOVER
BOOKS IN ALL FIELDS OF INTEREST

100 BEST-LOVED POEMS, Edited by Philip Smith. "The Passionate Shepherd to His Love," "Shall I compare thee to a summer's day?" "Death, be not proud," "The Raven," "The Road Not Taken," plus works by Blake, Wordsworth, Byron, Shelley, Keats, many others. Includes 13 selections from the Common Core State Standards Initiative. 112pp.   0-486-28553-7

ABC BOOK OF EARLY AMERICANA, Eric Sloane. Artist and historian Eric Sloane presents a wondrous A-to-Z collection of American innovations, including hex signs, ear trumpets, popcorn, and rocking chairs. Illustrated, hand-lettered pages feature brief captions explaining objects' origins and uses. 64pp.   0-486-49808-5

ADVENTURES OF HUCKLEBERRY FINN, Mark Twain. Join Huck and Jim as their boyhood adventures along the Mississippi River lead them into a world of excitement, danger, and self-discovery. Humorous narrative, lyrical descriptions of the Mississippi valley, and memorable characters. 224pp.   0-486-28061-6

ALICE STARMORE'S BOOK OF FAIR ISLE KNITTING, Alice Starmore. A noted designer from the region of Scotland's Fair Isle explores the history and techniques of this distinctive, stranded-color knitting style and provides copious illustrated instructions for 14 original knitwear designs. 208pp.   0-486-47218-3

ALICE'S ADVENTURES IN WONDERLAND, Lewis Carroll. Beloved classic about a little girl lost in a topsy-turvy land and her encounters with the White Rabbit, March Hare, Mad Hatter, Cheshire Cat, and other delightfully improbable characters. 42 illustrations by Sir John Tenniel. A selection of the Common Core State Standards Initiative. 96pp.   0-486-27543-4

THE ARTHUR RACKHAM TREASURY: 86 Full-Color Illustrations, Arthur Rackham. Selected and Edited by Jeff A. Menges. A stunning treasury of 86 full-page plates span the famed English artist's career, from *Rip Van Winkle* (1905) to masterworks such as *Undine*, *A Midsummer Night's Dream*, and *Wind in the Willows* (1939). 96pp.   0-486-44685-9

THE AWAKENING, Kate Chopin. First published in 1899, this controversial novel of a New Orleans wife's search for love outside a stifling marriage shocked readers. Today, it remains a first-rate narrative with superb characterization. New introductory note. 128pp.   0-486-27786-0

BASEBALL IS . . .: Defining the National Pastime, Edited by Paul Dickson. Wisecracking, philosophical, nostalgic, and entertaining, these hundreds of quips and observations by players, their wives, managers, authors, and others cover every aspect of our national pastime. It's a great any-occasion gift for fans! 256pp.   0-486-48209-X

THE CALL OF THE WILD, Jack London. A classic novel of adventure, drawn from London's own experiences as a Klondike adventurer, relating the story of a heroic dog caught in the brutal life of the Alaska Gold Rush. Note. 64pp.   0-486-26472-6

CANDIDE, Voltaire. Edited by Francois-Marie Arouet. One of the world's great satires since its first publication in 1759. Witty, caustic skewering of romance, science, philosophy, religion, government — nearly all human ideals and institutions. A selection of the Common Core State Standards Initiative. 112pp.   0-486-26689-3

THE CARTOON HISTORY OF TIME, Kate Charlesworth and John Gribbin. Cartoon characters explain cosmology, quantum physics, and other concepts covered by Stephen Hawking's *A Brief History of Time*. Humorous graphic novel–style treatment, perfect for young readers and curious folk of all ages. 64pp.   0-486-49097-1

CATALOG OF DOVER BOOKS

THE CHERRY ORCHARD, Anton Chekhov. Classic of world drama concerns passing of semifeudal order in turn-of-the-century Russia, symbolized in the sale of the cherry orchard owned by Madame Ranevskaya. Showcases Chekhov's rich sensitivities as an observer of human nature. 64pp. 0-486-26682-6

A CHRISTMAS CAROL, Charles Dickens. This engrossing tale relates Ebenezer Scrooge's ghostly journeys through Christmases past, present, and future and his ultimate transformation from a harsh and grasping old miser to a charitable and compassionate human being. 80pp. 0-486-26865-9

CRIME AND PUNISHMENT, Fyodor Dostoyevsky. Translated by Constance Garnett. Supreme masterpiece tells the story of Raskolnikov, a student tormented by his own thoughts after he murders an old woman. Overwhelmed by guilt and terror, he confesses and goes to prison. A selection of the Common Core State Standards Initiative. 448pp. 0-486-41587-2

CYRANO DE BERGERAC, Edmond Rostand. A quarrelsome, hot-tempered, and unattractive swordsman falls hopelessly in love with a beautiful woman and woos her for a handsome but slow-witted suitor. A witty and eloquent drama. 144pp. 0-486-41119-2

A DOLL'S HOUSE, Henrik Ibsen. Ibsen's best-known play displays his genius for realistic prose drama. An expression of women's rights, the play climaxes when the central character, Nora, rejects a smothering marriage and life in "a doll's house." A selection of the Common Core State Standards Initiative. 80pp. 0-486-27062-9

DOOMED SHIPS: Great Ocean Liner Disasters, William H. Miller, Jr. Nearly 200 photographs, many from private collections, highlight tales of some of the vessels whose pleasure cruises ended in catastrophe: the *Morro Castle, Normandie, Andrea Doria, Europa,* and many others. 128pp. 0-486-45366-9

DUBLINERS, James Joyce. A fine and accessible introduction to the work of one of the 20th century's most influential writers, this collection features 15 tales, including a masterpiece of the short-story genre, "The Dead." 160pp. 0-486-26870-5

THE EARLY SCIENCE FICTION OF PHILIP K. DICK, Philip K. Dick. This anthology presents short stories and novellas that originally appeared in pulp magazines of the early 1950s, including "The Variable Man," "Second Variety," "Beyond the Door," "The Defenders," and more. 272pp. 0-486-49733-X

THE EARLY SHORT STORIES OF F. SCOTT FITZGERALD, F. Scott Fitzgerald. These tales offer insights into many themes, characters, and techniques that emerged in Fitzgerald's later works. Selections include "The Curious Case of Benjamin Button," "Babes in the Woods," and a dozen others. 256pp. 0-486-79465-2

ETHAN FROME, Edith Wharton. Classic story of wasted lives, set against a bleak New England background. Superbly delineated characters in a hauntingly grim tale of thwarted love. Considered by many to be Wharton's masterpiece. 96pp. 0-486-26690-7

FLATLAND: A Romance of Many Dimensions, Edwin A. Abbott. Classic of science (and mathematical) fiction — charmingly illustrated by the author — describes the adventures of A. Square, a resident of Flatland, in Spaceland (three dimensions), Lineland (one dimension), and Pointland (no dimensions). 96pp. 0-486-27263-X

FRANKENSTEIN, Mary Shelley. The story of Victor Frankenstein's monstrous creation and the havoc it caused has enthralled generations of readers and inspired countless writers of horror and suspense. With the author's own 1831 introduction. 176pp. 0-486-28211-2

THE GARGOYLE BOOK: 572 Examples from Gothic Architecture, Lester Burbank Bridaham. Dispelling the conventional wisdom that French Gothic architectural flourishes were born of despair or gloom, Bridaham reveals the whimsical nature of these creations and the ingenious artisans who made them. 572 illustrations. 224pp. 0-486-44754-5

Browse over 10,000 books at www.doverpublications.com

THE GIFT OF THE MAGI AND OTHER SHORT STORIES, O. Henry. Sixteen captivating stories by one of America's most popular storytellers. Included are such classics as "The Gift of the Magi," "The Last Leaf," and "The Ransom of Red Chief." Publisher's Note. A selection of the Common Core State Standards Initiative. 96pp. 0-486-27061-0

THE GOETHE TREASURY: Selected Prose and Poetry, Johann Wolfgang von Goethe. Edited, Selected, and with an Introduction by Thomas Mann. In addition to his lyric poetry, Goethe wrote travel sketches, autobiographical studies, essays, letters, and proverbs in rhyme and prose. This collection presents outstanding examples from each genre. 368pp. 0-486-44780-4

GREAT ILLUSTRATIONS BY N. C. WYETH, N. C. Wyeth. Edited and with an Introduction by Jeff A. Menges. This full-color collection focuses on the artist's early and most popular illustrations, featuring more than 100 images from *The Mysterious Stranger, Robin Hood, Robinson Crusoe, The Boy's King Arthur,* and other classics. 128pp. 0-486-47295-7

HAMLET, William Shakespeare. The quintessential Shakespearean tragedy, whose highly charged confrontations and anguished soliloquies probe depths of human feeling rarely sounded in any art. Reprinted from an authoritative British edition complete with illuminating footnotes. A selection of the Common Core State Standards Initiative. 128pp. 0-486-27278-8

THE HAUNTED HOUSE, Charles Dickens. A Yuletide gathering in an eerie country retreat provides the backdrop for Dickens and his friends — including Elizabeth Gaskell and Wilkie Collins — who take turns spinning supernatural yarns. 144pp. 0-486-46309-5

HEART OF DARKNESS, Joseph Conrad. Dark allegory of a journey up the Congo River and the narrator's encounter with the mysterious Mr. Kurtz. Masterly blend of adventure, character study, psychological penetration. For many, Conrad's finest, most enigmatic story. 80pp. 0-486-26464-5

THE HOUND OF THE BASKERVILLES, Sir Arthur Conan Doyle. A deadly curse in the form of a legendary ferocious beast continues to claim its victims from the Baskerville family until Holmes and Watson intervene. Often called the best detective story ever written. 128pp. 0-486-28214-7

THE HOUSE BEHIND THE CEDARS, Charles W. Chesnutt. Originally published in 1900, this groundbreaking novel by a distinguished African-American author recounts the drama of a brother and sister who "pass for white" during the dangerous days of Reconstruction. 208pp. 0-486-46144-0

HOW TO DRAW NEARLY EVERYTHING, Victor Perard. Beginners of all ages can learn to draw figures, faces, landscapes, trees, flowers, and animals of all kinds. Well-illustrated guide offers suggestions for pencil, pen, and brush techniques plus composition, shading, and perspective. 160pp. 0-486-49848-4

HOW TO MAKE SUPER POP-UPS, Joan Irvine. Illustrated by Linda Hendry. Super pop-ups extend the element of surprise with three-dimensional designs that slide, turn, spring, and snap. More than 30 patterns and 475 illustrations include cards, stage props, and school projects. 96pp. 0-486-46589-6

THE IMITATION OF CHRIST, Thomas à Kempis. Translated by Aloysius Croft and Harold Bolton. This religious classic has brought understanding and comfort to millions for centuries. Written in a candid and conversational style, the topics include liberation from worldly inclinations, preparation and consolations of prayer, and eucharistic communion. 160pp. 0-486-43185-1

THE IMPORTANCE OF BEING EARNEST, Oscar Wilde. Wilde's witty and buoyant comedy of manners, filled with some of literature's most famous epigrams, reprinted from an authoritative British edition. Considered Wilde's most perfect work. A selection of the Common Core State Standards Initiative. 64pp. 0-486-26478-5

JANE EYRE, Charlotte Brontë. Written in 1847, *Jane Eyre* tells the tale of an orphan girl's progress from the custody of cruel relatives to an oppressive boarding school and its culmination in a troubled career as a governess. A selection of the Common Core State Standards Initiative. 448pp. 0-486-42449-9

JUST WHAT THE DOCTOR DISORDERED: Early Writings and Cartoons of Dr. Seuss, Dr. Seuss. Edited and with an Introduction by Rick Marschall. The Doctor's visual hilarity, nonsense language, and offbeat sense of humor illuminate this compilation of items from his early career, created for periodicals such as *Judge, Life, College Humor,* and *Liberty.* 144pp. 0-486-49846-8

KING LEAR, William Shakespeare. Powerful tragedy of an aging king, betrayed by his daughters, robbed of his kingdom, descending into madness. Perhaps the bleakest of Shakespeare's tragic dramas, complete with explanatory footnotes. 144pp. 0-486-28058-6

THE LADY OR THE TIGER?: and Other Logic Puzzles, Raymond M. Smullyan. Created by a renowned puzzle master, these whimsically themed challenges involve paradoxes about probability, time, and change; metapuzzles; and self-referentiality. Nineteen chapters advance in difficulty from relatively simple to highly complex. 1982 edition. 240pp.
0-486-47027-X

LEAVES OF GRASS: The Original 1855 Edition, Walt Whitman. Whitman's immortal collection includes some of the greatest poems of modern times, including his masterpiece, "Song of Myself." Shattering standard conventions, it stands as an unabashed celebration of body and nature. 128pp. 0-486-45676-5

LES MISÉRABLES, Victor Hugo. Translated by Charles E. Wilbour. Abridged by James K. Robinson. A convict's heroic struggle for justice and redemption plays out against a fiery backdrop of the Napoleonic wars. This edition features the excellent original translation and a sensitive abridgment. 304pp. 0-486-45789-3

LIGHT FOR THE ARTIST, Ted Seth Jacobs. Intermediate and advanced art students receive a broad vocabulary of effects with this in-depth study of light. Diagrams and paintings illustrate applications of principles to figure, still life, and landscape paintings. 144pp. 0-486-49304-0

LILITH: A Romance, George MacDonald. In this novel by the father of fantasy literature, a man travels through time to meet Adam and Eve and to explore humanity's fall from grace and ultimate redemption. 240pp. 0-486-46818-6

LINE: An Art Study, Edmund J. Sullivan. Written by a noted artist and teacher, this well-illustrated guide introduces the basics of line drawing. Topics include third and fourth dimensions, formal perspective, shade and shadow, figure drawing, and other essentials. 208pp. 0-486-79484-9

THE LODGER, Marie Belloc Lowndes. Acclaimed by *The New York Times* as "one of the best suspense novels ever written," this novel recounts an English couple's doubts about their boarder, whom they suspect of being a serial killer. 240pp. 0-486-78809-1

MACBETH, William Shakespeare. A Scottish nobleman murders the king in order to succeed to the throne. Tortured by his conscience and fearful of discovery, he becomes tangled in a web of treachery and deceit that ultimately spells his doom. A selection of the Common Core State Standards Initiative. 96pp. 0-486-27802-6

Browse over 10,000 books at www.doverpublications.com

CATALOG OF DOVER BOOKS

MANHATTAN IN MAPS 1527–2014, Paul E. Cohen and Robert T. Augustyn. This handsome volume features 65 full-color maps charting Manhattan's development from the first Dutch settlement to the present. Each map is placed in context by an accompanying essay. 176pp. 0-486-77991-2

MEDEA, Euripides. One of the most powerful and enduring of Greek tragedies, masterfully portraying the fierce motives driving Medea's pursuit of vengeance for her husband's insult and betrayal. Authoritative Rex Warner translation. 64pp. 0-486-27548-5

THE METAMORPHOSIS AND OTHER STORIES, Franz Kafka. Excellent new English translations of title story (considered by many critics Kafka's most perfect work), plus "The Judgment," "In the Penal Colony," "A Country Doctor," and "A Report to an Academy." A selection of the Common Core State Standards Initiative. 96pp. 0-486-29030-1

METROPOLIS, Thea von Harbou. This Weimar-era novel of a futuristic society, written by the screenwriter for the iconic 1927 film, was hailed by noted science-fiction authority Forrest J. Ackerman as "a work of genius." 224pp. 0-486-79567-5

THE MYSTERIOUS MICKEY FINN, Elliot Paul. A multimillionaire's disappearance incites a maelstrom of kidnapping, murder, and a plot to restore the French monarchy. "One of the funniest books we've read in a long time." — *The New York Times.* 256pp. 0-486-24751-1

NARRATIVE OF THE LIFE OF FREDERICK DOUGLASS, Frederick Douglass. The impassioned abolitionist and eloquent orator provides graphic descriptions of his childhood and horrifying experiences as a slave as well as a harrowing record of his dramatic escape to the North and eventual freedom. A selection of the Common Core State Standards Initiative. 96pp. 0-486-28499-9

OBELISTS FLY HIGH, C. Daly King. Masterpiece of detective fiction portrays murder aboard a 1935 transcontinental flight. Combining an intricate plot and "locked room" scenario, the mystery was praised by *The New York Times* as "a very thrilling story." 288pp. 0-486-25036-9

THE ODYSSEY, Homer. Excellent prose translation of ancient epic recounts adventures of the homeward-bound Odysseus. Fantastic cast of gods, giants, cannibals, sirens, other supernatural creatures — true classic of Western literature. A selection of the Common Core State Standards Initiative. 256pp. 0-486-40654-7

OEDIPUS REX, Sophocles. Landmark of Western drama concerns the catastrophe that ensues when King Oedipus discovers he has inadvertently killed his father and married his mother. Masterly construction, dramatic irony. A selection of the Common Core State Standards Initiative. 64pp. 0-486-26877-2

OTHELLO, William Shakespeare. Towering tragedy tells the story of a Moorish general who earns the enmity of his ensign Iago when he passes him over for a promotion. Masterly portrait of an archvillain. Explanatory footnotes. 112pp. 0-486-29097-2

THE PICTURE OF DORIAN GRAY, Oscar Wilde. Celebrated novel involves a handsome young Londoner who sinks into a life of depravity. His body retains perfect youth and vigor while his recent portrait reflects the ravages of his crime and sensuality. 176pp. 0-486-27807-7

A PLACE CALLED PECULIAR: Stories About Unusual American Place-Names, Frank K. Gallant. From Smut Eye, Alabama, to Tie Siding, Wyoming, this pop-culture history offers a well-written and highly entertaining survey of America's most unusual place-names and their often-humorous origins. 256pp. 0-486-48360-6

PRIDE AND PREJUDICE, Jane Austen. One of the most universally loved and admired English novels, an effervescent tale of rural romance transformed by Jane Austen's art into a witty, shrewdly observed satire of English country life. A selection of the Common Core State Standards Initiative. 272pp. 0-486-28473-5

Browse over 10,000 books at www.doverpublications.com